CHILDREN'S RIGHTS

CHILDREN'S RIGHTS

TOWARDS SOCIAL JUSTICE

ANNE B. SMITH

MOMENTUM PRESS
HEALTH

MOMENTUM PRESS, LLC, NEW YORK

Children's Rights: Towards Social Justice

Copyright © Momentum Press®, LLC, 2016.

First published by Momentum Press®, LLC
222 East 46th Street, New York, NY 10017
www.momentumpress.net

ISBN-13: 978-1-60650-777-3 (print)
ISBN-13: 978-1-60650-778-0 (e-book)

Momentum Press Psychology Collection

Cover and interior design by Exeter Premedia Services Private Ltd., Chennai, India

10 9 8 7 6 5 4 3 2 1

Printed in the United States of America

To past, present, and future Children's Issues Centre staff at the University of Otago (New Zealand)—in celebration of our past work together, and in the hope of many more years of the Centre's contribution to children's rights in the future.

ABSTRACT

A marked change in traditional thinking about children and childhood was promoted by the adoption by the United Nations (in 1989) of the Convention on the Rights of the Child. In the early 90s, sociologists in the United States and the UK developed Childhood Studies to promote a holistic view of children's lives, recognition of their competence and agency, and the impact and value of their everyday experiences. As a result of this impetus, different thinking has emerged about the role and recognition of children, the institutions of childhood, and the way we view and treat children in modern societies. This book focuses on research emerging from Children's Rights and Childhood Studies thinking, which has important implications for developing policies and practices to improve children's well-being and rights. The book looks at the implications of children's rights for six contexts of children's everyday lives: Families; Early Childhood Education; Schooling; Child Protection Services; Health Services; and Employment.

KEYWORDS

bullying, childhood studies, children's agency, children's citizenship, children's health, children's rights, children's well-being, discrimination, early childhood education, family law, racism, schooling

CONTENTS

FOREWORD

Certainly it would be difficult to deny that there has been a dramatic increase in the attention paid to children by national and international organizations. The activities responsible for this monumental change preceded the drafting of the United Nations Convention on the Rights of the Child (UNCRC), but this agreement, as was hoped by its advocates, has significantly increased the intensity and effectiveness of those efforts. The entire process of drafting, ratifying, and implementing a convention results from the acceptance of new societal values and practices. The codification of these values creates a formal acknowledgment of the need for change, and ratification reflects a commitment to working to achieve universal incorporation into national legal systems. Once the international community as a whole accedes to the treaty, a new regime emerges, making that which has been voluntary now compulsory, that which has been vague, more explicit, that which has been marginal, now central.

In light of the changes in our thinking about children, many articles and books have addressed specific and general topics relevant to the social, cultural, economic, and legal status of children and youth. Anne Smith's volume is a most valuable addition to this work on behalf of children. She has herself published widely on our need to respect and engage children, to enter their worlds, to explore through serious research and practice how best to interpret and implement the CRC and also the national and local laws and guidelines that are changing the way that we promote measures to ensure that all children are protected but also empowered. Her work brings new research and new insights to our understanding of what the CRC means in global, national, and local settings, explaining what the provisions may mean for those of us who are working to improve children's well-being.

When scholars and practitioners focus on the CRC, they understand that the agreement requires us to make fundamental assumptions about the lives of children. It is a mistake to assume that children's needs and desires are easily understood and to overlook the challenges and complexities of the socially constructed realities in which they function.

The CRC was preceded by a long history of national and international activity aimed at changing the conceptualization of children as objects and as precitizens, without rights and protections. Parents or guardians could view children as their property, and as such, assets to be treated as they saw fit. Normally children were viewed at best as minds needing molding, often through the use of verbal and physical punishment. Childhood, then was seen as a stage during which this shaping process would occur and the young would be transformed into proper adults. Scholars within the field of Childhood Studies have developed new ways of thinking about this period in a child's life and supported these insights through careful research and analysis. Childhood Studies has made significant progress in changing what it means to be a child, and therefore how children should be treated and respected.

A major reason that Smith's study is especially worthy of our attention is that she has set the CRC within the context of Childhood Studies, thus enhancing our understanding of both. Her work provides new avenues for designing policies and programs that respect the special nature of childhood and honor the rights of children and youth. The increasing awareness and acceptance of the conclusions of Childhood Studies meshes well with the development of children's rights. Considering childhood as socially constructed can help us to broaden our understanding of the social and cultural context with which we are most familiar, but also can help to sensitize us to the variety of childhoods, significantly those of children not from the dominant sociocultural milieu.

This book will provide political leaders, advocacy groups, governmental and nongovernmental agencies at the international and national level with tools to advance their work on behalf of children. Teachers, health workers, faith community leaders, and parents, among others, will find new and helpful ways to think about children's status and rights, and our shared mission to improve the everyday lives of all our children.

Natalie Hevener Kaufman
Distinguished Professor Emerita
University of South Carolina

ACKNOWLEDGMENTS

The contents of this book reflect the efforts of many past and present child advocates and activists, including people in child-related professions and parents, who have worked tirelessly to achieve social justice for children. Children themselves have been valuable partners and at times initiators of the promotion of their rights. Researchers from across the world have contributed to efforts to achieve evidence-based reforms. Some politicians have been brave enough to support new laws and policies to advance children's rights. I acknowledge all of these people's contribution to my thinking and to the writing of this book. I would also like to thank those colleagues who helped me by reading chapters of the book and offered suggestions, including Lisette Burrows, Michael Gaffney, Ruth Gasson, Natalie Kaufman, Iain Matheson, Helen May, Martin Ruck, John Smith, and Nicola Taylor. Thanks also to Paula Whitelock, librarian, who helped me with finding references.

CHAPTER 1

CHILDREN'S RIGHTS—HISTORY AND BACKGROUND

The CRC [Convention on the Rights of the Child] has, in the twenty years since it was adopted by so many states, exercised a deep and pervasive influence on the way in which we think about the status of children. Those who frame laws, design institutions, and seek to mold practices that have anything to do with the interests and well-being of children cannot avoid making reference to what the CRC insists must be done.

—(Archard, 2012, p. 324)

I have chosen to write about children's rights, as I believe that a rights lens for children's issues changes our way of understanding them, which can lead to improvements in children's lives and prospects. Human rights are "those moral-political claims that, by contemporary consensus, every human being has, or is deemed to have, on his society and on his government, and that are considered indispensable for the development of the individual" (Veerman, 1992, p. 24). Having rights means that the rights-holders should be accorded dignity and respect, while children's rights documents provide a resource for advocates to argue for reform to policies and practices that affect children (Freeman, 2011). Rights differ from needs and interests. "Needs and interests may be arbitrary, rights are principled and formally agreed entitlements and standards" (Alderson, Hawthorne, & Killen, 2005). During the course of the 20th century, there has been a global recognition that children are human beings with rights, which when realized, provide children with a better quality of life, opportunities for healthy development, and the fulfillment of their potential.

Under a rights based approach the place of children and their voice within the political economy can no longer be ignored, devalued or marginalised on the assumptions that decision makers whether they be parents, teachers, doctors, judges, institutions or government officials will automatically know what is in their best interests. (Tobin, 2011, p. 89)

According to Paula Fass (2011, p. 18), the articulation of children's rights on a universal scale emerged from "70 of the most tumultuous, violent and deadly years in human history." When the United Nations Convention on the Rights of the Child (UNCRC) was adopted in Geneva in 1989 following years of discussion and negotiation, it promoted a new vision of the child, and changed discourses and culture so that children's interests and concerns became more prominent on national and international agendas (Cantwell, 2011). The UNCRC has had a significant influence on governments in formulating laws and policies about children, but rights thinking can also change the perspectives of people who work and interact directly with children (including parents and professionals) in ways that affect how they treat children, and what they expect of them.

The very idea that children have rights is a transformative concept that reconceptualises the power relations between children, adults and the state. Instead of being seen as chattels of their parents or objects in need of benevolent guidance and protection, children become active subjects with individual entitlements which they are entitled to claim. (Tobin, 2011, p. 89)

While children's well-being is often considered to be a private matter for families to nurture, Stainton Rogers (2009) points out that while most parents do act in children's best interests most of the time, some do not. She sees one of the main arguments for children to have rights is "to acknowledge that adults do not always know best, and may not always act in the most honourable ways, and to recognise that there must be some limits on adult power over children" (p. 153). There are many other institutions besides families, who have power over children—such as schools, faith communities, courts and law enforcement and detention centers, and foster and other child welfare agencies. A rights discourse is not intended to undermine adults caring for children but to prevent the misuse of adult power.

It is a change in attitudes, perceptions, and ways of interacting with children that I hope to encourage by writing this book. I will argue that it really matters that we acknowledge that children have rights, and that an acceptance of children's rights makes a difference to the kind of lives that children lead. Children's rights thinking can be a dynamic agent in children's lives and a catalyst to support different relationships and interactions between children and adults (Jones & Welch, 2010).

I will start by outlining the history of the development of the UNCRC, explaining the different kinds of rights and the most fundamental principles and articles of the UNCRC, with attention to how children's rights frameworks have been critiqued, and discussing other theoretical frameworks for children's rights concepts. In this first chapter and throughout the rest of the book, I will discuss how children's rights frameworks position specific issues for children and show how research findings (mainly from the social sciences) are linked to the implementation of children's rights.

1.1 BRIEF HISTORY OF CHILDREN'S RIGHTS AND THE EMERGENCE OF THE UNCRC

When discussing the emergence of children's rights, the work of a Swedish feminist and humanist, Ellen Key, is often a starting point. Key had published a book in 1900 to mark the new millennium, entitled *The Century of the Child.* The book focused on psychological aspects of children's experiences, the positive rather than negative qualities of the child, and recognized that the child is a social human being whose spontaneous natural interests should be stimulated (Veerman, 1992). Key argued that children should have a rich home life with warm parent–child relationships, rather than harsh discipline, and was an early opponent of corporal punishment because of the harm it did (Lengborn, 2000). Key's work became the stimulus for the New Education Movement, which emphasized the intrinsic good of human beings and the importance of nurturing human development. The emphasis was on self-discipline rooted in children's own understanding rather than external constraint (Veerman, 1992). A new image of children and childhood was inherent in Key's influential writings.

A major impetus for the development of children's rights policies was the Great War of 1914 to 1918 in which women and children had suffered so much and were vulnerable to the many dangers associated with war, including violence, hunger, homelessness, deprivation, and displacement (Fass, 2011). Out of these influences, a new commitment to protecting children from adversity and injustice, and a right to full humanity, emerged.

An important pioneer of children's rights was a British woman, Eglantyne Jebb, who was deeply concerned with the effects of poverty and war on children. She was the only child of a wealthy family who was motivated by her Christian beliefs. She believed that the urban poor were created by society so it should be responsible for combatting poverty, and that this could not happen without structural changes and investment by community and state (Kerber-Ganse, 2015). She had wide networks in the UK and across Europe, and in 1919 established the Save the Children Fund in the UK to ameliorate the plight of children. Save the Children expanded to become a widely known international organization that has played a major role in relief efforts for children all over the world (Veerman, 1992). Jebb firmly advocated the important principle of universality that lasts to this day, that all children regardless of sex, nationality, religion, or race should be helped. Jebb was an influential figure in being the first to attempt to codify children's rights standards under the auspices of the League of Nations in 1924—the Geneva Declaration of the Rights of the Child. Although declarations are not legally binding, they are a statement of principles that help establish normative standards (Veerman, 1992). The Geneva declaration was a brief one-page statement stating that "mankind owes to the child the best that it has to give," and proclaiming the duty of nations to give relief to children in distress, provide material resources (food, health care) to them, protect them from exploitation, and give them the opportunity to earn a living (cited by Veerman, p. 444).

Sweden had a prominent role after the Second World War, and was at the center of various international organizations that were making efforts to define and promote the rights of children. Paula Fass (2011) suggests that Sweden was looking to increase its international esteem after the war in which it remained neutral, by providing support for children affected by the war. Sweden was closely identified with the development of the UN International Children's Emergency Fund (UNICEF), contributing both financially and administratively to children's welfare. Sweden along with other Nordic countries like Norway and Finland, introduced a much more proactive model of the rights of the child, initially within their own regions, and subsequently on the international arena. Radda Barna was a Swedish humanitarian organization, affiliated with the Save the Children Fund, which had a significant input into postwar efforts for children.

Another amazing contribution to the recognition of children's rights in the years before and between the wars (between 1912 and 1942) came from a Polish pediatrician, Henryk Goldszmit, who is generally known by his pen-name of Janusz Korczak. He was ahead of his time in proposing a principle of respect for children, later to become a key element of the

UNCRC. He said: "We are constantly at odds with the children .... We nag, admonish, scold and punish them, but we don't inform kindly" (Korczak, 1929, cited by Veerman, 1992, p. 94). He was also a forward-looking thinker in emphasizing the rights of the child of "being" rather as a "becoming." He said that the child had a "right to be himself" in the present day, rather than being thought of as an adult of tomorrow. "The child lives today. He has value as an individual today. Because we think of the child as 'a citizen in embryo' or 'a future man' valuable years are lost" (p. 95). Korczak put his ideas into practice by founding a Jewish Children's home, where he established a system of self-government in which children had a major role in making rules and enforcing them. He fought for a more independent and active role for children and a stronger position for children in social life and demanded their comprehensive participation in democratic processes (Liebel, 2012a). Korczak died a heroic death in 1942 when the Germans liquidated the orphanage, and he was transported with the children to Treblinka.

A concern for children's rights resurfaced following the Universal Declaration on Human Rights in 1948, with the Declaration of the Rights of the Child in 1958 (Earls, 2011). The 1959 Declaration was three pages long, and expanded on the brief 1924 Geneva Declaration. It declared a universal entitlement to rights but asserted the child's right to special protection, and to be among the first to receive help, to a name and nationality, to social security, to the care and love of parents, to free education, and to be protected from neglect and exploitation. Again the atrocities and deprivations of the Second World War had heightened concerns for children's rights, but the pre-UNCRC era of children's rights was "characterised by *ad hoc* charity to young children—who were seen as the most vulnerable and deserving members of society" (Cantwell, 2011, p. 38). Organizations concerned about children focused their efforts on welfare rather than autonomy or citizenship rights.

Another influence on children's rights in the 20th century was that "the middle classes, everywhere, turned their attention to elevating and universalizing standards for child welfare" (Fass, 2011, p. 20). The prevalent context for many children of poverty and abuse were accompanied by advances in public health, suggesting that better hygiene and nutrition could improve the well-being and survival of many children. There were aspirations for a continuing improvement in the lives of children and it was believed that nations would want to enhance children's lives and protect them from adversity (Fass, 2011).

In 1978, Poland presented a proposal for a convention on the rights of the child to the UN Commission on Human Rights. Following this, the UN declared an International Year of the Child (IYC) in 1979. Nigel Cantwell (2011) argues that the IYC had a remarkable role in clarifying and broadening the children's rights focus, so that issues that had previously been ignored like children in prison, sexual exploitation, child labor, and "street children" came to public attention. IYC was the precursor to Poland's initiative to draw up a convention on the rights of the child, and to the eventual adoption of the UNCRC in 1989. The lengthy drafting period took place under the auspices of the UN Commission on Human Rights bringing together human rights organizations (such as Amnesty International) with NGOs[1] working with children (such as Defence for Children International) as well as many representatives from across the membership of the UN. The collaboration between human rights and child welfare organizations led to the incorporation of general human rights issues, as well as specific child welfare issues into the UNCRC, which greatly broadened the children's rights framework (Cantwell, 2011). According to Philip Veerman (1992), there were East–West ideological differences during the drafting process, with Poland, for example, focusing on material rights, while the United States focused on citizenship rights like freedom of thought, conscience, and religion.

The UNCRC is the result of a negotiated consensus within the Open-Ended Working Group, "a group that is not wholly expert, does not speak the same language, and views the problem of creating a treaty through a myriad of jurisprudential lenses" (Fox, 1989, cited by Veerman, 1992, p. 183), which makes it all the more remarkable. On November 20th, 1989 the 54 article convention, the result of ten years of negotiation, was on the agenda of the General Assembly, and after only two minutes of discussion, it was approved by consensus from the 158 members.

1.2   THE NATURE AND PURPOSE OF THE UNCRC

Not only is the Convention a nearly universally adopted expression of respect for children as persons, but it is also unparalleled in its conceptual breadth. No other human-rights treaty directly touches on so many domains of life ... the Convention on the Rights of the Child (1989) offers an unparalleled framework to guide child research. (Melton, 2005a, p. 648)

---

[1] NGO is the abbreviation for Non Governmental Organization.

The UNCRC is a wide-ranging treaty that applies to children from birth to 18 years of age. Its 54 articles range across three main categories, provision, protection, and participation. Provision articles refer to the right of children to receive appropriate health care, social security, physical care, education, family life, recreation and play, and culture (Lansdown, 1994). Protection articles say that children must be safe from discrimination, abuse, exploitation, substance abuse, violence, injustice, and conflict. Participation articles refer to children's civil and political rights, to a name and identity, to be consulted on matters that affect them, to have access to information, to be able to express opinions, and to take part in decisions. The inclusion of participation rights in the UNCRC was a significant shift toward treating children as citizens and recognizing that they deserved human rights in the same way as adults did.

> The CRC thus reflects a hard-won consensus on the substance of the human rights of children, and it was indeed quickly heralded as the most widely ratified human rights instrument ever. (Cantwell, 2011, p. 42)

Conventions differ from declarations because they are treaties between states carrying specific obligations. They are considered "hard" law as opposed to the "soft" law of declarations, and require an active decision to ratify by individual states, a step which follows the signing of the convention (Veerman, 1992). Ratification entails a formal obligation for states to meet the requirements of conventions. Some states have requirements to incorporate international treaties into domestic law, sometimes as part of ratification, and sometimes a separate step requiring a court decision. In the case of the UNCRC, it is an essential tool to improve conditions for children because countries incorporate its articles into national plans, programs, and laws to secure the rights of children (Earls, 2011). Its portrayal of children as social actors and agents with a variety of entitlements, stimulated a sea change in the way children are treated in society.

The UN Committee on the Rights of the Child (CRC) monitors the progress being made by countries who have ratified the UNCRC. Each country makes a report, firstly two years after ratification, and subsequently at five yearly intervals. In addition to government reports, other information can be submitted by NGOs, often presenting an alternative perspective on the progress achieved. It is essentially a process of self-review (Doek, 2011), even though the CRC responds to each country's reports and submissions with a set of Concluding Observations. These are intended to provide input into the development of state agendas for the subsequent five years. The CRC's Concluding Observations are part of an up-to-date "virtuous cycle of 'monitoring-reporting-learning- recommending-applying-monitoring'," which reflect expanded knowledge, practices, and technologies. It is necessary to collect data and statistics in order to properly plan, monitor, and evaluate policies with the ultimate aim of ensuring "evidence-based public action for children's rights" (Maurás, 2011, p. 61).

States can ratify the convention but apply reservations to particular articles, which allow them to opt out of ratifying articles which conflict with current laws or policies. For example, New Zealand has a reservation about Article 37, which says that children in detention should be separated from adults. The government reserved the right to mix juvenile offenders with adults, on the grounds that they sometimes needed to be separated from peers (Ministry of Justice, 2011). The UK also had a similar reservation to Article 37 on the grounds of insufficient resources, but this reservation was dropped in 2007. The UK also has a reservation opting-out of rights for child migrants and asylum seekers, allowing them to be locked up for weeks and months before deportation (Jones & Welch, 2010). Saudi Arabia has lodged a blanket reservation about all articles that are incompatible with Islamic Sharia Law (Montgomery, 2010).

Currently, 195 countries have ratified the Convention, including all members of the United Nations except South Sudan and the United States. South Sudan is a very new country but has already passed legislation to facilitate ratification. President Bill Clinton did sign the Convention in 1995 on behalf of the United States but left office before it was ratified, although he signed two optional protocols concerning child prostitution and pornography and children in the armed forces, which were subsequently ratified. Young people in the United States cannot now enter the armed forces until they are 18 (previously it had been 17). President Obama is said to have expressed his embarrassment in 2008 that the United States found itself in the company of Somalia "a lawless land," in not ratifying the treaty (Attiah, 2014). Somalia has, however, recently ratified the convention, and South Sudan is on the verge of doing so. One commentator, Karen Attiah, asks if the U.S. nonratification is "hypocritical when the U.S. lectures other countries on children's rights," and she believes that the United States should join the rest of the world in ratifying. A chorus of other U.S. commentators expressed their support for ratification in a range of publications in 2010 and 2011, marking the 20th anniversary of the UNCRC.

There has been a legacy in the United States of opposition to the ratification of human rights treaties since the 1950s, when a group of conservative lawyers from the American Bar Association claimed that they were controversial, could threaten the American way of life, and make the United States vulnerable to world government and the expansion of communist influence (Kaufman, 1990). Kaufman's research with the Senate Foreign Relations committee in the 80s showed that foreign policy staff members believed there was little benefit to be gained by supporting human rights treaties, and that ratification would only stir up political controversy. This reluctance to support human rights treaties continues to this day.

Not ratifying the UNCRC limits the ability of the United States to promote children's rights both at home and in other countries (Bartholet, 2011). Since ratification requires a two-thirds majority in the Senate, the prospects for ratification are remote. The major current obstacle has been the fear that ratification would impede the rights of parents, and that international law would be able to supersede federal and state law (Earls, 2011). It would, however, have been possible for the United States to lodge reservations if there were conflicts between articles in the UNCRC and existing U.S. law, as was done by Saudi Arabia. As it is already a society where the ideal of human rights is deeply embedded in its Constitution (Cohen, 1995), it seems strange that children's rights are so controversial in the United States.

> The concept of rights is crucial to American political thought, predates the Revolution, and derives much of its content from the sixteenth-century philosophy of John Locke. Rights were so significant to those who drafted the American Constitution that the concept of rights was one of the main topics at the Constitutional Convention. Participants eventually agreed to the adoption of ten amendments to the Constitution which outlined those rights which the American government must guarantee its citizens. (Cohen, 1995, p. 166)

It therefore seems anomalous that human rights have not been extended to American children through U.S. ratification of the UNCRC. Although the UNCRC does not have official recognition in the United States, it can still be a helpful moral imperative and guide for professionals and parents, to ensure that their treatment of children incorporates the principles of social justice embedded in this influential international convention. It can be a guide for developing policies for children, and instructive for educators, health professionals, and others who work with children (Limber & Flekkøy, 1995). Natalie Kaufman (2015)[2] argues that the UNCRC is customary international law, and the fact that the United States has signed it, adds compelling arguments that the United States cannot do anything that contradicts or works against the spirit of the treaty.

It is heartening to see that an influential body of researchers and professionals, the American Psychological Association (APA), has endorsed the value of the UNCRC for its own work related to children (Melton, 2010a). Gary Melton has suggested that pediatric clinics and child guidance clinics, for instance, tend to act very differently if they have periodic conversations with children before they deliver services. Thus it is possible to translate the principles of the UNCRC into professional guidelines and standards, even without formal ratification.

> In the end, the question that should be of concern is whether people of good will are learning from the [UN]CRC. Meaningful implementation requires a learning community respectful of its youngest members and dedicated to their full integration into community life. (Melton, 2010a, p. 69)

The vision of the UNCRC expresses basic values about the treatment of children, which are to be found in four cardinal principles and major messages (Earls, 2011; Franklin, 1995). The first principle is universalism and nondiscrimination, that children regardless of race, sex, language, religion, disability, or class are entitled to rights (Article 2). In other words *all* children should enjoy their rights and should not be discriminated against. Secondly, there is the principle that "the best interests of the child" should be "a primary consideration" in actions or decisions concerning children (Article 3). In the past, children have often been invisible and voiceless in the development of policy, so this principle says that children's rights, not just those of adults, must be considered. Thirdly, there is the principle of the right to survival and development (Article 6), which is not just the right to live but to be protected from threats to life like disease. This has implications for the development of preventive measures such as immunization and other public health measures (Franklin, 1995).

The final very influential principle within the UNCRC is respect for the views of the child, and an obligation to take the views of the child seriously. It is to be found in Article 12, which I will quote the first part of

---

[2] N.H. Kaufman (personal communication, email April 3rd, 2015).

in full, because both theoretically and practically, this Article is pivotal to the messages in this book.

> State Parties shall assure to the child who is capable of forming his or her own views freely in matters affecting the child, the views of the child be given due weight, in accordance with the age and maturity of the child. (UNCRC, 1989, Article 12, 1)

Article 12 and other "participation" or "participatory rights" (such as Articles 13 and 14) assert that children should have a say in processes affecting their own lives. They have been the most controversial rights in the convention, and place the UNCRC well in advance of earlier international documents about children's rights.

> The articles specifying the participatory rights are arguably the most important in the pursuit of children's citizenship. These rights represent the more radical turn in our notion of children's interests and capacities and more generally in their status in society. (Earls, 2011, p. 9)

Participation rights have had a widespread impact in changing perceptions of children from the passive objects of adults' actions toward seeing them and treating them as social actors, and giving them space and support to take actions on their own behalf.

> Children develop a belief in themselves as actors who have the power to impact the adverse conditions that shape their lives. They develop confidence and learn attitudes and practical lessons about how they can improve the quality of their lives. (Rizzini & Thaplyial, 2005, p. 18)

Children's rights should be contextualized within their lives, rather than be matters only of state responsibilities and legal procedures according to several authors (Hanson & Niewenhuys, 2013; Liebel, 2012b). Hanson and Nieuwenhuys argue that children shape the meaning of rights through their own experiences. "Living rights" are those that are interpreted and enacted in children's daily lives. Abstract notions of rights are transformed through children's experiences of local contexts and relationships. Such living rights are an important focus of this book because they show how rights can actually make a difference for children, how research can access children's actual experiences, and how children can be empowered through their rights.

Within societies where adult power and authority is absolute, the concept of participation rights acknowledges children's role as citizens who can and do play an important part in democratic processes. Recognizing children's participation rights can therefore nurture children's sense of belonging and inclusion, and give them the opportunity to bring about change themselves (Smith, 2007). These qualities are essential both for individuals and for democratic societies.

1.3 CRITICISMS OF THE UNCRC

Almost everyone who is familiar with the UNCRC would argue that it is far from a perfect document, as like other international treaties, it is a result of compromises between a variety of countries, parties, and agencies, and within the context of a particular historical time. The UNCRC is also the result of a negotiated consensus involving the particular values, arguments and aspirations of many different countries and stakeholders. Nevertheless, the UN Committee on the Rights of the Child periodically elaborates, and adds detailed explanation and justification about particular themes within children's rights, by holding days of general discussion, and publishing General Comments (e.g., on Early Childhood Education and Corporal Punishment) and new Optional Protocols, so it does attempt to avoid stagnation and to keep people up-to-date with current thinking and events.

There have been, however, a variety of broader criticisms, and the most common one is that the UNCRC is culturally biased toward benefits for the individual child and an idealized Western vision of childhood (Boyden, 1997; Burman, 2008; Ennew, 1995).

> The Convention in drafting process, the resulting text and its implementation, takes as its starting point Western, modern childhood which has been "globalised", first through colonialism and then through the imperialism of international aid. (Ennew, 1995, p. 202)

Judith Ennew argues that the Convention was developed with a particular model of childhood in mind, in which children are confined to the domestic sphere within houses and nuclear families, and where children are dependent and powerless. She interprets this to mean that street children are "society's ultimate outlaws" (p. 202), because they are not only outside society but also outside childhood. Because of their marginalized status, these children are not accorded many of the rights of Western children and are regarded as criminals. While several UNCRC articles address the problems faced by street children (such as child labor and sexual exploitation), Ennew argues that these articles result in discrimination and stigmatization.

Similarly, Jo Boyden (1997) argues that contemporary conceptions of rights are intimately tied with cultural and societal values. She points how difficult it is to apply detailed rights prescriptions to varying social, cultural, and political contexts. For example, in some cultures children may be treated as dependents until well into their teens but in other cultures children are independent from an early age. In the UK and New Zealand, it is illegal for infants and small children to be cared for by other children under 14, whereas in Peru many 6- to 14-year-olds are the head of households and the main breadwinners for their families. When children are more independent and are absent from school or home, this makes them the legitimate targets for state intervention, while actually they have worked out ways of surviving in their particular cultural contexts. There are problems, for example, with Article 32, which says that children have the right to be protected from economic exploitation and work that interferes with their education.

> In some parts of the world, implementing this article is tantamount to disenfranchising children from participation in working lives on which their survival and often their family's survival depends. (Woodhead, 1997, p. 80)

The criticism of the cultural bias within the UNCRC is also related to its emphasis on individual freedom and autonomy, while some cultures give much more prominence to collective values and solidarity with others. Children in some countries are not viewed as self-sufficient individuals, but as part of a family or community, "embedded in a web of relationships, which come with duties, obligations, and sometimes expectations of sacrifice on behalf of the family" (Montgomery, 2010, p. 152). Children are accepted in such societies as integral members of the community, who are not rigidly separated from adults' activities and practices (Liebel & Saadi, 2012, p. 169). The type of family envisioned by the UNCRC is a group of biologically based relations between parents and children, while there are many other different family forms such as extended African-American kin networks, lesbian and gay families, and nonkinship-based households (Stephens, 1995).

Heather Montgomery (2010) cites Roger Goodman's description of the initial difficulty that Japanese people had in understanding the concepts of rights, because of its strong connotations in Japan of selfishness. Individual rights from such perspectives, undermine the structure and role of the family unit, and assume that individual interests can be isolated and separated from those of others (Burman, 2008).

John Tobin (2011) cautions against the risk that children's rights can be used to impose culturally-inappropriate agendas and points out that the UNCRC does not approve of such imposition. The preamble of the UNCRC emphasizes that it is important to take "due account of the importance of the traditions and cultural values of each people for the protection and harmonious development of the child" (Preamble, UNCRC, 1989), and Article 30 says that children should have the right to enjoy their own culture, so cultural sensitivity is inherent in the convention. Despite the universality of the UNCRC, Tobin points out that flexibility in its implementation is necessary because of cultural differences. Any children's rights policies and practices need to be considered within the social, political, economic, and cultural context in which they are to be implemented. Philip Alston argues that culture should allow for some flexibility and discretion in the interpretation of rights, but culture should not be allowed the status of "a metanorm that trumps rights" (Alston, 1994, cited by Freeman, 2009, p. 384). There is no cultural defense therefore for female infanticide, slavery, or genital mutilation.

While there are important regional and cultural differences in interpretation of children's rights, the influences of global modernity and global capitalism are apparent everywhere (Stephens, 1995). Sharon Stephens believes that it is not a choice between cultural relativism and universalism, and that legally binding international agreements do support children's and societies' best interests. She says, however, that children's rights discourses should be both more powerful and more flexible, and this involves using the UNCRC critically and strategically.

> It requires rethinking the nature of children's rights claims; disabusing them of their aura of timelessness, absoluteness, universality, and naturalness; and developing these claims as legal tools in the project of protecting and reconstructing spaces of childhood and adulthood in a time of far-reaching local and global change and uncertainty. (Stephens, 1995, p. 40)

The successful implementation of the UNCRC depends on its placement in a societal context of compatible meanings and social and economic infrastructures of support (Prout, 2005). Children are unlikely to be protected by the police, for example, when the police force is corrupt and contributes to children's oppression. That the principles of the convention are ambiguous, however, means that there is a great deal of space for local interpretation, and this can make it acceptable to countries with a wide range of cultural values and traditions (Lee, 1999, cited by Prout, 2005, p. 32).

The UNCRC has been described as "a beginning rather than the final word on children's rights" (Freeman, 2009, p. 388), because of its narrowness of scope, lack of attention to gender, sexuality or indigeneity, and its weak enforcement procedures. Philip Veerman (2010) believes that the convention needs to be reviewed and updated in the light of contemporary contexts for children, such as the advent of HIV/AIDS, the Internet, and a need to protect children against drug and alcohol addiction. Yet Michael Freeman, an eloquent advocate for children's rights, while acknowledging deficiencies in the UNCRC, believes that it is a convenient benchmark and a useful tool that continues to show that the world is failing children.

1.4 OTHER THEORETICAL LINKS

1.4.1 CHILDHOOD STUDIES

A reflective, internally coherent and sophisticated theoretical framework for children's rights, rather than a legalistic or pragmatic framework, helps to strengthen the conceptual foundations for rights-thinking (Tobin, 2011). Childhood Studies[3] provides a conceptual framework for children's rights, which is compatible with children's rights thinking and has developed alongside it. There are similar aspirations for children inherent in Children's Rights and Childhood Studies frameworks, such as the importance of constructing children as persons not property, supporting their citizenship and opportunities to participate, treating them as agents rather than passive recipients, and recognizing that children constitute

---

[3] Childhood Studies is also known as the Sociology of Childhood or the New Social Studies of Childhood. I prefer the term Childhood Studies as it emphasizes the interdisciplinary nature of the field.

multiple voices, and not one collective undifferentiated class (Freeman, 1998; McNaughton & Smith, 2009).

> Childhood Studies is about a more integrated approach to research and teaching about children's lives and well-being, a more "joined-up" view of the "child in context," which has also become a priority for policy and for professional training. For others, Childhood Studies is built around a rejection of the essentialism endemic in traditional theorizing, in favour of recognizing the multiple ways childhood is socially constructed and reconstructed in relation to time and place, age, gender, ethnicity etc. Childhood Studies also represents a critique of the ways children's lives are regulated in modern societies, an emphasis on recognizing children as social actors and empowering their participatory rights in all areas of social life, including child research. (Woodhead, 2004a, p. xi–xii)

One of the most significant contributions of Childhood Studies theory has been to highlight the social construction of childhood, and that it "is neither a natural nor a universal feature of human groups but appears as a structural and cultural component of many societies" (Prout & James, 1997, p. 8). The meaning of childhood, the expectations we have for children, and the structures that regulate childhood, have taken a variety of forms at different points in history and in different cultural contexts. Childhood therefore cannot be regarded as a singular universal concept applicable to all children, but is socially constructed within cultural discourses, which are sets of interconnected ideas that work together according to particular ideologies or world views (James, 2009; Stainton Rogers, 2009).

Childhood Studies has questioned the hegemonic power of the discourses of Western developmental psychology to shape our under-standings of childhood. These discourses have influenced generations of teachers, social workers, psychologists, and health professionals toward viewing children as on a stepwise pathway toward an end-point of ratio-nality and completeness as adults. The assumption that childhood is a universal experience for all children is encoded in our talk about children concerning milestones and developmental delay, and our institutional organizations like age-graded classrooms, segregation of disabled children into special facilities, and assessment policies of testing, streaming, and tracking according to ability (Smith, 2011). Alison James (2009) has described the dominant traditional framework for children and childhood as follows:

Although children are regarded as inadequate, incomplete and dependent, society must invest in their care, training and upbringing since it is children who represent the future of the social world. Within this conceptualization of "the child," therefore, there was little room for any notion of the agentic child—the radically different model of the child that was to become a key feature of the "emergent paradigm" within the new sociology of childhood. (James, 2009, p. 37)

The idea that children are "social actors" emerged from Childhood Studies because of the critique of developmental psychology, the dominance of the image of a universal child, and a large body of psychological research where children are treated as passive objects. Children in this new lens, are seen as "active in the construction of their own social lives, the lives of those around them and of the societies within which they live" (Prout & James, 1997, p. 4). They are not just objects of concern and in need of protecting and molding but competent social actors with voice and agency. The concept of "voice" acknowledges children's unique points of view and suggests that they are able to understand and act on the world (Pufall & Unsworth, 2004). Children are understood as people who can make a difference to relationships, decisions, and problem-solving. Such a perspective on children suggests that adults should be interested in and sensitive to children's opinions and feelings, make an effort to listen to them, ask for their views, and act in ways that provide a supportive context for their learning and development (Smith, 2013a).

Opposing the conception of children as "developing" or "unfinished" persons, recent childhood studies have perceived and valued children as "beings" and active social stakeholders. Instead of understanding children merely as future members of society who will start playing a decisive role when they come of age, they are considered self-determined members of society who readily act in their own interest. (Liebel, 2012b, p. 19)

That children, particular infants, have agency is often a difficult concept for adults to accept. But the assumption that agency and dependency are opposites has been challenged by Priscilla Alderson (2001). Alderson sees both agency and dependency as inherent in relationships between people. Acknowledging that children have agency does not mean that they are completely autonomous, or that the care and nurturance adults provide for them are unimportant. For example, adults can increase children's agency by providing interesting opportunities for them to explore and play, so in one sense the children are dependent on the adult's actions, but in another sense their opportunities for agency are increased.

> Evidence of agency and dependency fades when agents and dependents share numerous activities (proposing, persuading), and intentions (to control, influence, gain advantage) and when dependency is expressed through dependents' own agency (compliance, resistance). (Alderson, 2001, p. 25)

A final theme within Childhood Studies is the diversity of childhood and the wide range of perspectives, knowledge, and experience children bring to bear on issues and problems. What it is to be a child is understood within particular cultural contexts and historical times. It is therefore impossible to understand children's experiences without looking at the complexity of their lives in local contexts. Even children within the same family can have very different viewpoints on a specific issue, such as their parents' divorce (Smith, Taylor, & Tapp, 2003) or broader issues such as what it means to lead a good life, or how to treat your friends. This makes generalization of research findings very tricky, and suggests the value of ethnographic research studies of children within their natural contexts.

1.4.2 SOCIOCULTURAL THEORY

Because context is such an important influence on children's lives, a sociocultural approach helps us to understand how children in different cultures come to be able to formulate, understand, and implement their rights. Sociocultural theory originated with the work of Russian psychologist, Lev Vygotsky, who died at 38 in 1934. His writings were only discovered in the west in the 1970s, which at the time was dominated by the work of Jean Piaget. Piaget believed that children's development was dependent on their internal cognitive structures, and proceeded toward an endpoint of logical rationality. In contrast, Vygotsky (1978) thought that children grow into the intellectual life of those around them, through participation and with the guidance and support of others. Children, from a Vygotskian perspective, advance to more complex thinking through being challenged and extended at the outer limits of their skill by others. This means that the greater the richness of the activities and interactions in which children participate, the greater their understanding will be (Smith, 2013b). This is not just a one-way process from adult to child, but a reciprocal process in which adults engage with children to jointly construct understanding. Children initiate as well as respond to adults and peers, and their competence is enhanced when they engage with others who are sensitive to their current level of skill. Expectations of what children are capable of, clearly influence how adults engage with children, as explained by Holzman:

> Children—indeed people of all ages—learn developmentally by doing what they don't know how to do. Thus in schools, we must relate to children as readers, writers, physicists, geographers, historians, mathematicians, etc encouraging them to perform these activities whether or not they "know how." (Holzman, 1995, p. 204)

The implications of a sociocultural perspective for children's rights are that children's social environments are the source of their agency, because participation in sociocultural experiences provides a bridge from the known to the unknown (Rogoff, 1990). Families and communities are rich "funds of knowledge" that are passed through generations and adapted to suit contemporary society (González, Moll, & Amanti, 2005). Responsive and reciprocal relationships within families, communities, and schools can put children in authoritative roles, nurturing children's agency and helping them to stay engaged with difficult tasks even when there are setbacks (Carr et al., 2010). Instead of the traditional view that there is one pathway to development, sociocultural theory emphasizes that there are multiple possible pathways depending on other people, culture, and the tools of culture.

From a sociocultural perspective, if we want children to understand and "live" their rights and to be active participants in society, adults need to provide time, space, recognition, and support for them to gain self-understanding and develop identity. If children are to have views that should be listened to and taken into account, they need social contexts in which they are helped to formulate their views, evaluate alternatives, and find their own voices (Smith, 2002). If adults are to provide such supportive contexts, they need to expect participation from children and factor it in, and "to speak and understand the language of childhood" (Raynor, 1993, p. 75).

While this nurturing of agency might sound like a perspective suitable mainly for children in Western democratic countries, recent research suggests that young people "from a variety of non-Western cultural contexts have been found to endorse or support a number of participation or self-determination rights" (Ruck, Keating, Saewyc, Earls, & Ben-Arieh, 2014, p. 9). Research from Malaysia, China, South Africa, Israel, and the

Netherlands is cited by Ruck et al. to suggest that many young people, even in societies that do not emphasize children's rights in practice, value opportunities for such participation. The authors challenge the viewpoint that participation rights are less important in nondemocratic societies, and argue the special importance of civic, political, and economic participation for undocumented, asylum seeking and refugee youth, who may have the least opportunity to know about these rights.

1.5 SUMMARY

Thinking about children has changed in the 20th and 21st century toward recognizing children's rights, acknowledging children's previous lack of visibility and voice, and strengthening claims on governments to provide resources, institutions, and opportunities that support children's citizenship and quality of life. Perhaps more importantly children's rights frameworks have changed the ways that the adult world (or some parts of it) treats children, so that they are accorded dignity and respect, listened to, and allowed the space and opportunities for them to be active participants in society.

The move toward acknowledging children's rights emerged from 70 years of adversity, war, and deprivation for children and their families. Early 20th century pioneers, such as Ellen Key, Eglantyne Jebb, and Jan Korczak, promoted an alternative perspective about children and their lives, and heightened awareness of injustice in their lives. Nordic countries like Sweden, Norway, and Finland, took a proactive stance toward children's rights, and turned their attention to children all over the world rather than just in their own countries.

The brief Geneva Declaration in 1924 was the first encodement of children's rights, followed by an expanded version of it, the Declaration of the Rights of the Child in 1958. These declarations were nonbinding moral statements of normative standards, but they were useful preparation of principles that fed in to the development of the UNCRC. This binding convention was developed and negotiated by an international UN Working Group from 1979, and passed by the General Assembly in 1989. The combination of input from human rights organizations and child welfare NGOs means that the UNCRC includes a wide-ranging set of articles about children's provision, protection and participation rights, and incorporates four cardinal principles (nondiscrimination, best interests, survival and development, and participation). The UNCRC has been ratified by 195 countries, including all members of the UN except South Sudan and the United States. Ratification of the UNCRC brings obligations to reg-ularly report to the Committee on the Rights of the Child, and to receive feedback from it. Some critics of the UNCRC have said that it is based on an idealized Western view of childhood, which if used inappropriately can be harmful for children. Hence the UNCRC should not be used to promote culturally-inappropriate agendas, and should be implemented flexibly and strategically. It is a work in progress rather than the final word on children's rights, but provides a useful benchmark for our treatment of children.

Other theoretical contributions to children's rights frameworks come from Childhood Studies and Sociocultural Theory. Childhood Studies endorses the importance of children's agency, that children are persons now and not just adults in the making, the socially constructed nature of childhood, and the diversity of childhoods. Sociocultural theory suggests that children's agency and dependency is grounded in their experiences in social and cultural contexts, that children are not autonomous individuals but that rich responsive cultural contexts can promote their personhood and agency. Children are more likely to find a voice when their views are listened to and respected and adults and peers provide them with support.

CHAPTER 2

CHILDREN'S RIGHTS
WITHIN FAMILIES

Families, are ... inherently contradictory; they are a private space away from public life and the outside world yet they are also profoundly concerned with, and affected by, events outside themselves. While sometimes sentimentalized as a haven in a heartless world, the family is also a site of conflict and ideological strife between individual members and between itself and the state.

—(Montgomery, 2009, p. 77)

Families have a vital role to play in the realization of human rights as they determine whether children's dignity is either fostered or denied. While we tend to see families in idealistic terms, in reality they encompass a huge range of human experiences. Families span generations and geography, and encompass the full range of human goodness to human cruelty. They are both a source of continuity and agents of adaptation and change (Sokalski, 1994).

The UNCRC is unequivocal in its support of children's right to be cared for by their families, as is clear from several other articles and the following quotation from its Preamble:

Convinced that the family, as the fundamental group of society and the natural environment for the growth and well-being of all of its members and particularly children, should be afforded the necessary protection and assistance so that it can fully assume its responsibilities within the community.

Recognizing that the child, for the full and harmonious development of his or her personality, should grow up in a family environment, in an atmosphere of happiness, love and understanding. (Preamble, United Nations Convention on the Rights of the Child, UNCRC, 1989)

The issue of the influence of children's rights on families is sometimes a controversial one. A family is often constructed as a private domain that should not be interfered with by governments, and parents are believed to have the right to bring up their children the way they want to. Attempts to intervene in family life by government policies are often labeled as "nanny state" policies, and it is feared that promoting children's rights will decrease parental authority (Jones & Welch, 2010). Yet, the UNCRC urges governments to provide support for families, as political conditions relating to employment, economic conditions, and social welfare assistance have a big impact on families and how well they can carry out their role of caring for children. Also, children may experience harm within their families, and governments have a responsibility to protect children from such harm. Government policies directly, or indirectly, support and challenge harmonious family life, so it is important that they should be accountable for the effects of their policies on families and children.

Childhood studies scholars have been critical of the extent to which children's experiences are "hidden in the ideological apparatus of 'the family'" (Oakley, 1994, p. 18). A common assumption is that the interests of the child and the interests of the family are identical (Clark, 2010). Official statistics treat family as a unit, so the characteristics of children as individuals within families are obscured (Oakley, 1994). Children are assessed according to their parents' income and their fathers' occupation, dividing children up in ways that are "alien to their own life expressions" (Qvortrup, 1997, p. 90).

[W]ithin family sociology, children tended to be excluded, and where they were included, they were peripheral to marital relationships or construed as passive or as burdens. Children were interesting in so far as they became adults, not for what they were. (Morrow, 2009, p. 62)

While children used to be thought of as the property of their parents, it is now a more acceptable perspective that "parents are 'agents' or 'trustees' who exercise their parental rights on an implied license from the community, which entitles them to help and support, and also makes them subject to control" (Thomas, 2009, p. 9). Nigel Thomas argues that there is a complex, ambiguous relationship between the powers and responsibilities of the state, and that of parents. States want to support families but they don't want to undermine them, so there is often reluctance to interfere in family life, and if this takes place, responsibility is usually delegated to professionals. Moreover, it is often assumed that parents will represent children's wishes and interests.

A generational perspective on childhood highlights the interdependencies between generations, and the dynamic relationship between childhood and adulthood (Alanen, 2009; Mayall, 2009). Families are examples of generational structures: "What parenting is or becomes—that is action in the position of a parent in its defining relations—is dependent on the reciprocal action taken by the holder of the position of the child" (Alanen, 2009, p. 165). Instead of the actions of parents on children being understood as taking place in a one-way direction from adult to child (the socialization model), the generational relationship model suggests that parent–child relationships involve interdependency and reciprocity. How parents and children relate to each other within families (and adults and children in other social domains such as schools) is one of the basic principles of the social order (Alanen, 2009). The implications of this issue for children's rights can be seen in an emphasis on children as agents and social actors with comparable human rights to those of adults, but who are influenced by and, in turn, influence their families.

The UNCRC provides a really comprehensive list of rights for children within their families, including provision rights (to dignity, respect, nurturance, guidance, standard of living, education, health care), protection (from violence, removal and separation), and participation (to take children's views into account). Families play a mediating role in whether children's rights are realized.

There are many articles in the UNCRC that concern families. Article 5 asserts that governments should respect the rights and responsibilities of families to direct and guide their children. The UNCRC also states that children have a right to a name, an identity, and a nationality, and a right (as far as possible) to be cared for by their parents (Article 7); that governments should respect family ties (Article 8); that children should not be separated from parents against their will (Article 9); that children have a right to be reunified with their families when they live elsewhere or have moved countries (Article 10); that both parents (or legal guardians) have a responsibility for the upbringing and development of the child, and that states should support them in their child-rearing responsibilities (Article 18); that children deprived of their families are entitled to special protection and assistance from the state (Article 20); that the child has the right to a reasonable standard of living, and that this is the primary responsibility of parents (Article 27). There are many other children's rights that are directly under the control of families, such as respecting their best interests (Article 3), right to survival and development (Article 6), right to access education (Article 28) and health care (Article 24), right to be protected from abuse, violence, and neglect (Article 19), and right to express their views when decisions affecting them are being made within their family (Article 12).

A helpful way of examining the influence of children's rights thinking on children's well-being within families is to recall the four key principles of the UNCRC (see Chapter 1), and how these might play out in family life and also be evident in law and policy. The first is nondiscrimination, and this means that children in all types of family structures and arrangements (not just nuclear families) have rights, and that children should have their rights respected by their family members, regardless of their age, sex, temperament, disability, sexuality, or ethnicity. Second, the best interests of the child principle, suggests that families should be conscious of children's best interests and give primary consideration to them in family decisions and the activities of family life. Third, the principle of survival and development means that families have a responsibility to ensure that children are protected from harm and nurtured in a way that supports their well-being and ongoing development. Fourth, the principle of participation means that children's views should be sought, respected, and taken seriously by other family members. Most children spend the vast majority of their childhoods within their families, and families make a difference to children's lives, so they play a big role in implementing these principles.

Families sometimes find it difficult to support the different rights of their children, because there may be contradictions and tensions between the claims of competing rights. Jones and Welch (2010) point out that an especially difficult area is that of culture and religion. Article 14 says that children have the right to freedom of thought, conscience, and religion, but it is generally assumed that the child's religion will be that of their parents (which can become even more problematic when parents of different faiths separate and then disagree about which religion their children should follow). Yet, the authors point out that this may be in conflict with Article 12, the children's right to have a say in matters that affect them, and that families should give children the chance to develop their own views without pressure to follow the culture and religions of their families.

Since the influence of families is such an enormous topic, I will focus on some key issues. First, I will discuss the ecological context within which families lie, and, secondly, the diversity of families and the importance of affirming and supporting diversity for children's well-being. Third, I will explore the nature of family relationships and family discipline, and how families can ensure they respect and affirm children's dignity and rights in their relationships and interactions with them. Fourth, I will look at the issue of how states can support families to, for example, ensure that children have an adequate standard of living. Finally, I will look at how children and families can be supported in times of difficulty, such as parental separation and divorce.

2.1 THE CHILD WITHIN THE FAMILY WITHIN SOCIETY

An ecological and sociocultural perspective on families draws attention to how children's well-being is influenced directly by the social interactions and relationships within families, and indirectly by broader social and cultural settings that influence how families raise their children.

> Learning and development are facilitated by the participation of the developing person in progressively more complex patterns of reciprocal activity with someone with whom that person has developed a strong and enduring emotional attachment and when the balance of power gradually shifts in favor of the developing person. (Bronfenbrenner, 1979a, p. 60)

Research evidence strongly supports the long-term positive impact of sensitive, involved, cognitively stimulating family interactions, secure attachments, and warm relationships, in predicting outcomes for children (NICHD, 2005). Relationships are at the heart of identity, and family ties are one of the most important ingredients in the development of personality, but "rights have no meaning outside a social environment" (Melton, 2010a, p. 63). Melton argues that the right to personality (Article 29) implies that children should be able to grow up in a community and family environment.

Whether or not family members are able to interact sensitively and responsively with children in the family microsystem, and support children's rights to love, care, and agency is, however, dependent on other levels of the ecological system that do not include children. For example, parental employment conditions are included in the exosystem. Jobs that are "family-friendly" allowing parents flextime to accommodate family responsibilities (such as looking after sick children or attending parent–teacher interviews), are more likely to support children's rights to appropriate care by their families. The level of remuneration for employment is another key contributor to family functioning. If parents are earning below a living wage and are working long hours, they may be unable to resource the material rights of their children, let alone their rights to love and nurturance. The access parents have to quality child care for their children while they are working, is another key factor in supporting positive parenting (see Chapter 3).

The exosystem in turn is embedded in the next level of the ecological system, the macrosystem, referring to the consistencies in beliefs, values, and accepted practices in a society. These include political systems such as neoliberal policies that privilege the power of the market, and downplay the responsibilities of governments to support workers' rights or support family-friendly policies. The macro system also encompasses beliefs and laws about what children can do at different ages, such as driving a car, getting married, drinking alcohol publicly, or having an abortion. Similarly, the macrosystem includes pervasive ideas and policies about families, such as believing that it is fine for mothers in dual parent families to stay at home and not engage in paid work, but that single parents ought to work; or that the state has an obligation to provide paid parental leave for families with young children. Government policies, such as on poverty, education, employment, and the economy, therefore, have a major impact on children's rights and make a profound difference to the lives of children. Some of these policies will be discussed in this and other chapters.

2.2   FAMILY DIVERSITY

I wrote in Chapter 1 that a major criticism of the UNCRC is that it is based on a Western nuclear family model, and this can be seen in the way it discusses the relationship between parents and children, not readily bringing to mind the many forms of family that exist globally. It is important therefore to remind ourselves that family has a much wider meaning than a small group of biologically related parents and children.[1] Even within the developed world, there is a huge variety in types of family, and a danger that children from some families (such as gay families) who do not fit the

_____

[1] I do acknowledge that this book addresses more issues that affect children in the developed world than in the developing world. This is, in part, due to where most research has been carried out, but also to the likely audience of this book.

normative model could be marginalized. Such marginalization denies a fundamental principle in the UNCRC, that of nondiscrimination.

Family is a powerful structure for nurturing and sustaining human functioning, and has been defined as a group of people who are irrationally committed to each other's well-being (Bronfenbrenner, 1979b). The concept of family, however, may be viewed from different perspectives: for example, genetic or biologically based; psychological or emotion-based; legal or law-based; or ideological, based on a view of one type of family structure as ideal (Douglas, 2004, cited by Morrow, 2009, p. 61). Research suggests that, for children, it is the bonds of trust and affection, rather than legal structures, which are most important in their thinking about families, as I will discuss in the next section.

To ensure that children from all kinds of family backgrounds are included in thinking about children's rights, it is necessary to challenge the idea that the Western nuclear family is natural and universal, since families are formed in many different ways across the world (Montgomery, 2009). Diversity is now part of the social fabric of most societies, and ideas of the "normal family" have been destroyed because of the influence of broader global social and economic change. In New Zealand, for instance, in 1976, 89.6 percent of children lived in families with two parents, whereas in 2006 only 28 percent of them did. Other changes in New Zealand families involve later marriage, declining numbers of legal marriages, falling birth rates, increased participation of mothers in the workforce, and diversity in family structure (Smith, 2013b). Similarly, in the United States, there has been an increase in single parenthood, high levels of divorce and remarriage, lower fertility, increased acceptance of same sex parenting, and greater androgyny in gender roles (Qiu, Schvaneveldt, & Sahin, 2013). In 2011, around two thirds (63 percent) of American children lived with two married parents (much higher than New Zealand) and 28 percent lived in single parent households, so the majority of U.S. families do fit the nuclear pattern (Laughlin, 2014).

According to Heather Montgomery, however, there is no such thing as a universal family form:

> Families may be nuclear, extended, polygamous and even in very rare cases polyandrous (when a woman lives with several husbands). Husbands and wives may live separately and children may trace their descent from either their mother or their father or from both. Families may be recognized as such because there are blood or biological ties between their members or because there are social ties. (Montgomery, 2009, p. 78)

The care and upbringing of children, however, continues to be one of the central roles of families, and most children are brought up within families. (There are, however, in the Western world, increasing numbers of couples that choose not to have children.) Families give children a name and a status, and train and socialize them into adulthood, although the people who carry out these roles may not be biologically related, and in large parts of the world the functions are carried out by wider kinship networks.

Families are not only diverse at one point in time but also constantly evolving, depending on wider social contexts and government policies. For example, historically, in China the family has included extended families such as grandparents, siblings, aunts, uncles, nephews, and nieces, but as economic and business practices have changed they have shifted toward modernity and individualism (Qiu et al., 2013). The shift from collectivism to individualism in China has resulted in a greater "emphasis on egalitarianism, open-mindedness, independence, self-reliance, hedonism, and sexual equality" (p. 642), moving family members away from a sense of obligation to family and more on individual success. These shifts also led to changes in family structure, such as delaying marriage and childbearing to meet economic and educational goals, and having fewer children.

2.3 CHILDREN'S PERSPECTIVES ON THEIR FAMILIES

Families can be viewed through the perspectives of family members, and some interesting research studies have explored the views of children about families. Virginia Morrow (2009) found in the UK that the themes that emerged from interviews with children about families were: roles (what families do), the quality of relationships (love and affection), and the structure (the people who lived together). Children (especially the older ones) discussed the relationships and reciprocity within families and talked about "caring for each other," "sharing," and "looking after each other" (Morrow, 2009, pp. 65–66). Morrow's research showed that children were not only the recipients of care but also played an active role themselves in caring, as well as participating in domestic tasks. Hayley Davies (2012), in another UK study, found that face-to-face contact was an important aspect of family for children, including relationships, social interactions, and sharing activities, having an intimate knowledge of appearance, bodies and voices, and physical engagement such as hugging, laughing, or tickling.

U.S. children were interviewed to find out what they thought counted as families (Powell et al., 2010, cited by Qiu et al., 2013). The research showed that there were three main categories of child definitions of family: those who were narrow and traditional (exclusionists), those for whom love and commitment were most important (inclusionists), and those who were uncertain about their views (moderates). Exclusionists did not consider same-sex couples as family but tended to describe cohabiting couples as family if they had children.

New Zealand children seem to accept diverse family forms as "real families" (Anyan & Pryor, 2002; Rigg & Pryor, 2007). Most children and young people in this New Zealand research agreed that groupings of at least one adult and children, as well as extended family members constituted a family. Children and young people universally viewed married couples with children as families. The majority of young people's ideas about families, however, also included lone parents, cohabiting parents, and same-sex parents. Adolescents had increasingly complex and inclusive perspectives on families, compared to younger children (Pryor & Emery, 2004). Legal status, biological ties, or having two parents were not the defining features of families for these children, and they seemed to have inclusive and realistic views of New Zealand families today.

A comparative study of children from the United States, China, Ecuador, and Turkey, showed that five major themes arose from children's definitions of families—affection, procreation, protection, material support, and education (Qiu et al., 2013). The affective function was the most dominant in all countries except China (particularly in Ecuador and the United States), while in China children were more likely to see their families as suppliers of material goods (housing, furniture). A universal theme that appeared, regardless of cultural background, was that the family is an ultimate source of survival by providing shelter, nutrition, and protection. Children from Turkish and Chinese families tended to have more traditional views of the family than children from the United States and Ecuador, and this is assumed to be a result of their more collectivist cultures.

Children and young people from non-Western countries have broad kinship connections with their families, not always based on biological ties, and peers can become family for children separated from their birth families. A flavor of their different perspectives is given by interviews with children in Bangladesh and South Africa. A Bangladeshi 14-year-old, Moni, told the researchers:

I have so many relatives around me they all live around us and I really like it. I feel very close to them. If they go away I miss them so I really like that they are here .... My grandmother is right by us

... if something happens to the family she is always there. She takes care of us. When my mother can't do it, she always asks about things and she is always looking after us. (Monin in Maybin & Woodhead, 2003, p. 50)

Shane, a 15-year-old from Cape Town who lived on the streets, talked about his friend, Wilfred, a distant relative, as his family:

I saw him have a fight with big boys in Cape Town and then I help him—when he saw I have a fight then he help me ... so that's why we together. ... We can't go away from each other, we can't forget each other, cos ... three years we are together. (Shane, in Maybin & Woodhead, 2003, p. 50)

It is increasingly difficult to categorize the complex variety of family forms that have diversified the conditions in which children grow up (Prout, 2005). The complexity and changing nature of family forms, however, can provide children with opportunities for developing social and practical competence, which may not exist in traditional family settings. For example, children, who move between different households when their families are separated, manage multiple different contexts for their childhood (Simpson, 1998, cited by Prout, 2005, p. 25). Similarly, children in households where both parents work experience home as a place of comings and goings and engage with complex timetables, rather than a regular schedule where their mother is usually at home carrying out domestic responsibilities and childcare.

2.4   FAMILY DISCIPLINE AND ITS IMPACT ON CHILDREN'S RIGHTS

I have talked about diversity of family forms and structure, but there is another way that modern families have changed, and that is in the type of relationships and interactions that occur within families, including how families discipline their children. The move away from autocratic styles of parenting has been referred to as the "democratization" of the family (Giddens, 1998, cited by Clark, 2010, p. 38). Family democracy means that relationships are more equal and less authoritarian, and family decisions are more likely to be open to negotiation with input from different family members including children. Wives and children are less likely to be subservient to a patriarchal father figure (Clark, 2010).

The UNCRC is clear in its support of family relationships based on happiness, love, and understanding rather than power and authority, while acknowledging that families should provide appropriate direction and guidance for children (Article 7). Nevertheless, the Convention inherently acknowledges that children can be harmed within their families, and that children should be protected from "all forms of physical and mental violence, injury or abuse, neglect or negligent treatment, including sexual abuse, while in the care of parent(s)" (Article 19). Although there is no specific mention of corporal punishment within the UNCRC, in its country reports and in General Comments, the Committee on the Rights of the Child has made it clear that it regards corporal punishment as a violation of children's rights and that it disapproves of the continuing legal and social acceptance of its use (Newell, 2011). The Committee has made clear recommendations in its Concluding Comments to 140 countries, that they should take steps to prohibit corporal punishment, as well as to introduce education campaigns to encourage positive, nonviolent child-rearing.

> In the view of the Committee, corporal punishment is invariably degrading (para 11). The dignity of each and every individual is the fundamental guiding principle of human rights law (para 16). The practice directly conflicts with the equal and inalienable rights of children to respect for their human dignity and physical integrity. (United Nations Committee on the Rights of the Child, General Comment Number 8, 2006)

As I write in November 2015, there are now 47 states in the world that prohibit all corporal punishment including in the home, and another 51 are committed to law reform. In 1979, only one country, Sweden, had abolished corporal punishment and 20 years later, eight countries had banned it. In the past 16 years there has been a rapid acceleration of the number of countries recognizing children's right to be protected from violence and abuse to arrive at the current figure of 46 banning all forms of corporal punishment (Global Initiative to End all Corporal Punishment of Children, 2015). My own country, New Zealand, abolished corporal punishment in 2007, but unlike Sweden did not take steps to explain the law to the public or to promote positive parenting (Smith, 2015a). Nevertheless there are indications that attitudes are changing in New Zealand and that parents are becoming less likely to use physical punishment. Karl Bussman and his colleagues (Bussman, Erthal, & Schroth, 2011) showed that in countries with legal prohibition of physical punishment (Austria, Germany and Sweden) there was less violent parenting and more negative attitudes toward physical punishment, than in countries with no legal prohibition (Spain and France).

The decline in the use of physical punishment is a sign of increasing respect for democratic values and children's citizenship, and the importance of collective responsibility for children's well-being (Dahlberg, 2009; Lindahl, 2008). It is also an example of how intergenerational relationships provide opportunities for, or limitations on, children's agency (Mayall, 2009). While unquestioning obedience is a feature of the traditional family, with a move toward democratic families, children are being encouraged and expected to have a point of view, and to express it. But when physical punishment and other harmful disciplinary procedures are used, children feel powerless and disrespected, as illustrated by this child in an Australian study:

> Adults have more power. ... They can get really mad and swear ... and stuff ... Children can't do anything like that because they don't have enough power. We have to do what they say. Adults can ... hurt them. (Saunders & Goddard, 2010, p. 135)

There are now several studies that have sought children's perspectives on the issue of physical punishment (see Durrant, 2011; Smith, 2015a), and all of them reveal children's negative feelings about being physically punished. New Zealand children reported being hit with spatulas, tennis rackets, spoons, belts and canes, and having nasty tasting substances placed in their mouth (Dobbs, 2005, 2007; Dobbs, Smith, & Taylor, 2006). They were physically punished by parents, parents' girlfriends or boyfriends, siblings, step-parents, grandparents, uncles, cousins, and caregivers. They felt sad, unloved, scared, angry, and ashamed when they were physically punished, as illustrated by these quotations from the children in Dobbs' study.

> The thing that makes you cry is that if you don't see them and they go "whack." That's what makes you cry, even if it's a light one you can just get scared cause you never know when it's going to come. (10-year-old boy)

> It feels like they [parents] don't love you anymore. (nine-year-old girl)

You feel real upset because they are hurting you and you love them so much and then all of a sudden they hit you and hurt you and you feel like as though they don't care about you because they are hurting you. (13-year-old girl). (Dobbs, 2007, p. 154)

There is a considerable body of research on the effects of physical punishment on children's well-being and development, showing that physical punishment has harmful effects and unintended consequences (Durrant, 2011; Durrant & Ensom, 2012; Gershoff & Bitensky, 2007). I will not cover this research in detail here but, in summary, it shows that parental use of physical punishment is associated with the following outcomes for children: increased aggression and antisocial behavior; poorer academic achievement; poorer quality parent–child relationships (attachment); adverse mental health outcomes (depression, anxiety, low self-esteem); and diminished moral internalization (children's internalization of parental values and ability to control their own behavior). There is evidence that other methods of parental discipline are much more effective in bringing about favorable outcomes for children (Smith, 2005). Changes in parenting, however, are not a magic bullet that will solve all societies' problems; so external threats like poverty and inequality need also to be given attention (Ribbens McCarthy, Hooper, & Gillies, 2013).

2.5   CHILDREN'S RIGHTS TO AN ADEQUATE STANDARD OF LIVING

Article 27 in the UNCRC recognizes that children have the right to an adequate standard of living; that parents are primarily responsible for meeting this right; and that states should support parents in meeting this right. To a large extent families are dependent on their governments to maintain the conditions for them to provide for their children, but individual governments are influenced greatly by what is happening in the rest of the world. The insistence of the International Monetary Fund and the World Bank that developing countries adopt free market policies have contributed to inequality. Such policies involved cutting state expenditure on health, welfare and education, privatization, and deregulation (Prout, 2005). Globalization has also led to increased migration, and the mechanization of jobs, resulting in unemployment. These global trends of increasing inequality are also seen within richer countries. Children are often among the most vulnerable when local economies are opened to global market forces, without any protection (Desai, 2010).

The top 20 percent of the world's population enjoys more than 70 percent of the total income, while the bottom quintile only receives 2 percent of it (Ortiz & Cummins, 2011). A large number of the world's children live in the poorest families, with about half (48.5 percent) of the world's children confined to the bottom two income quintiles. The rate of change is very slow, with the bottom billion income-earners taking 17 years to improve their share of the world's income by 0.18 percent. There is a very strong relationship between income inequality and health and social problems. Sweden, Norway, and Finland, who have relative income equality, have the lowest number of health and social problems in the OECD, while the United States has a very high level of inequality and a large number of social and health problems (Figure 21, Ortiz & Cummins, 2011, p. 34). The UK, Australia, and New Zealand are also at the high end of the graph for inequality and social and health problems.

Children in low income families are more often exposed to negative psychosocial circumstances, such as family violence, punitive parenting, family disruption, poor housing quality, pollution, unsafe traffic, and lack of food security (Evans, 2004). Family income also has a major influence on child behavior, achievement, and health outcomes over time (Duncan, Ziol-Guest, & Kalil, 2010; Williams Shanks & Danziger, 2011). The earlier that low income occurs in children's lives, the stronger the negative effect it has on their outcomes.

It is not only material possessions that are limited by poverty but also cultural and social capital (Bourdieu, 1972, cited by Montgomery, 2009, p. 170). Low-income children may come from loving families, but their families may face intangible barriers from having different accents, being less knowledgeable about how to choose a good school, and lacking understanding of how schools operate, compared to children with parents who come from a similar background to the teachers:

> For socially marginalized children and young people, poverty is not simply that they lack education, go to poorer schools or do not have the books at home to help them, it is also the internal construction of self that makes certain choices unthinkable. (Montgomery, 2009, p. 169)

Coming from a low-income background can create different expectancies about what "disadvantaged" children can achieve. These lower expectations can be internalized by children, making them feel socially inferior and marginalized. Low-income children may therefore be doubly silenced by the low and dependent status of childhood and the marginalized social status of poverty (Ridge, 2009).

The realities of how poverty affects children's experiences are shown by studies that access the voices of children. The sense of difference that low-income children feel is revealed by these quotations from a British study (Ridge, 2003, p. 7):

> I would like to do more things with my friends, when they go down the town and that. But we can't always afford it. So I got to stay in and that, and just in here it's just boring. (Mike, 12 years)

> If you haven't got the right clothes and all your friends have got the nice clothes you feel left out like. Cos you think to yourself 'Oh they've got all the good clothes and they've got all the money to buy them' and that, and you feel left out ... I sometimes get really worried if, like I've got all these old-fashioned clothes and I don't like them and everyone else has fashionable ones. (Sue, 11 years)

Children are acutely conscious of the differences they experience because of social inequality, though they make informed choices within the constraints of their lives. Sometimes low-income children talk positively about being poor, for example, that they have everything they want and are close to their family and friends. Yet, Heather Montgomery (2009) points out that such thinking can also serve to cement social differences and maintain social divisions.

Some politicians are aware of and eager to ameliorate poverty, and one common response has been to argue that parents on welfare should be moved into work. Tony Blair, for example, said that their "best chance of a better future is for their parents to find routes into work" (cited by Ridge, 2009, p. 503), and the New Zealand Minister of Social Development has made many similar speeches. Many governments have attempted to reduce child poverty through welfare-to-work measures, including in Australia, Canada, New Zealand, the UK, and the United States. In New Zealand, welfare benefits for sole parents are now contingent on work obligations that require them to seek part-time work if they have younger children, and full-time work if their children are over 14 years (Ministry of Social Development, 2012). It seems that such neoliberal policies are increasingly common in wealthy countries. Unfortunately, the benefits of such policies are dubious when parents enter unstable, insecure, and poorly paid jobs (Ridge, 2009).

The impact of welfare-to-work policies on children are also not necessarily positive, as is shown by a UK study of children in low-income families where their mothers moved into employment (Ridge, 2009). Three main policy issues arose from the children's accounts. First, that the fear of unemployment and severe poverty encouraged children to negotiate and accommodate to the undesirable effects of their mother's employment, such as less family time and maternal stress. Second, that the unpaid caring work of mothers was unrewarded compared to paid employment, and that families were often in precarious employment situations. Third, that mothers being forced into unstable and insecure jobs ran the risk of alienating children from the value of employment. This quotation illustrates the stress involved for some mothers and children:

> When she's not working, I love it, it's great. It's absolutely great because I just love spending so much time with her. When she was at [work] she came in real late and rush cooking tea and stuff like that and then she'd get a bath and then it was time for bed already and then she'd do it the next day, and the next day and the next day and then she'd work about six days. (Karen, 15 years old, Ridge, 2009, p. 509)

Work for single mothers presents considerable challenges, and there is often a lack of support for the well-being of such families. Tess Ridge urges that enhanced in-work support, increased financial reward from work, as well as improved childcare options, are essential to enable such schemes to be effective in ameliorating poverty.

2.6 CHILDREN'S RIGHTS WHEN THEIR FAMILIES CHANGE

Article 9 of the UNCRC says that children should have the right to stay in contact with both parents if they separate, unless there has been neglect or abuse. In any legal proceedings, all interested parties including children, should be given the opportunity to participate and make their views known. The rights of children to have a say in decisions about where they live, and the nature of continuing contact with parents after separation, is also stated in Article 12, which stresses that children should have the opportunity to express their views and have these taken seriously. The article suggests that the views of the child should be "given due weight in accordance with the age and maturity of the child" (para 1). Unfortunately, this has sometimes been interpreted conservatively and it is often assumed that younger children are too young to form a view.

When change takes place within families, such as through parental separation, children have to adjust to many differences in their lives. Parental separation and divorce is not unusual in most Western countries.

For example, in the United States, Andrew Cherlin (2010) says that although divorce rates have declined from a peak in 1980, the lifetime probability of marital disruption is between 40 and 50 percent. The number of children not living with both parents has risen in the United States in the 2000s to more than 40 percent. Many children therefore experience living apart from one of their parents or their parents' multiple partnerships while they are growing up.

While change is an inevitable part of human experience, unexpected disruptions to family life can sometimes overwhelm children's capacity to manage them (Ribbens McCarthy et al., 2013). Transitions in children's lives are believed to be an important influence on learning and development, in ecological theory, because they result in changes to the roles, activities, and relationships in the microsystem of the family (Bronfenbrenner, 1979a). Parental separation is often accompanied by emotional upheaval for parents, impacting on their relationships with children, as well as sadness and distress for children. Other material changes, such as one parent moving away, loss of income, moving house or school, or their mother going to work, can all affect children's rights and well-being. Separation is not a single event but an unfolding process, often beginning before the actual separation, and continuing on beyond it as ongoing events are triggered, such as changes to living arrangements or schooling, parental repartnering, as well as psychological changes (e.g., parents becoming depressed).

Sarah's story shows how children may be caught up in events when parents separate. When she was 20 she looked back on her childhood and her parents' separation when she was 15: "We just saw our whole house and cats and dogs and pets and family members disappear—all just went 'bang'. Everybody was gone" (Smith & Taylor, 1996, p. 68). Sarah felt that people should have been more honest with her at the time to explain what was happening and why, but instead she felt that she had been told lies. The events took 10 years to unfold, and the problems started five years before the separation. After the separation, Sarah lived with her mother who was in a very disturbed state, and often angry with the children and punitive in her discipline, making Sarah feel that it was her fault. The hostile relationship in the family ("'I hate him'; 'I hate her' kind of thing … everybody just grumped at each other and grumped about each other", p. 68), made it especially difficult for Sarah. At the time that Sarah wrote her story, she said that everyone had started pulling themselves together and being honest (Sarah's story, Smith & Taylor, 1998).

There is a good deal of research on the immediate and long-term effects of divorce on outcomes for children, showing a range of moderate negative effects. Children with divorced parents, compared with children whose parents live together, score lower on a variety of emotional, behavioral, social, health, and academic outcome measures (Amato, 2010; Hetherington, 2006; Kelly, 2007). Overall, the research shows that parental divorce is associated with behavioral problems (withdrawal or acting out), lower achievement, and problems in parent–child relationships, achievement, and psychological well-being (low life satisfaction and depression).

Perhaps, the most important aspect of the research from a children's rights perspective is that it is not inevitable for divorce or separation to affect children adversely, and that many children survive this transition in an improved situation after the break-up (Hetherington, 2006). Children are most negatively affected when parental separation or divorce is accompanied by interparental conflict, hostility, and negative emotions. Good relationships between divorced parents are also associated with better family relationships (between parents, siblings, grandparents, and step-parents) many years later (Ahrons, 2007). Reducing isolation and increasing support for parents can help to improve the outcomes for children, as this makes it easier to provide a warm accepting family environment where children cope and do well. Supportive family and community networks are therefore valuable in helping children and parents in separated families. The extent to which government policies provide sufficient financial support for single parents, who are often the least well off, is another factor that influences the material resources available to children in separated families.

One of the problems with the bulk of research on children and divorce is that it arises out of a pathogenic model focusing on negative effects (Hetherington, 2006). From a childhood studies perspective, it is helpful to view children as active coping agents rather than as the passive vulnerable victims of their parents' actions. Finding out about children's perspectives provides an insight into the meaning of the experience from children's points of view, and helps to suggest ways to improve the situation for them. Every child, including within the same family, has different interpretations of their parents' separation, so it is valuable to talk with each child, as has been done now in a number of different studies (Cashmore & Parkinson, 2007; Neale & Flowerdew, 2007; Taylor, Tapp, & Henaghan, 2007).

In New Zealand, we asked children what parents needed to know about children when they separated, and they told us that they wanted to be listened to, to have a say, make choices, be given information about what was happening and why, to have an input into decisions and not to be forced into arrangements they did not want (Smith & Gollop, 2001).

They also wanted parents to be fair in postseparation arrangements, and to consider the children:

> The only thing I'd say would be to like listen to your kids and let them have their say because ... for the kids, it must be real hard ... They've got to really listen to the kids to let them know how they're feeling. Like say if they've split up and like parents wanted them, they'd have to like consult you and listen to you to who you wanted to go with. (Yvonne, 12 years, Smith & Gollop, 2001, p. 26)

Children's views in this and other similar studies, reaffirm the importance of implementing their rights to have a say in such important decisions (but not necessarily to decide themselves), to receive explanations about what has happened in the past and what will happen in the future, that efforts are made by parents to avoid conflict or hostility, and as far as possible to spend quality time with their children. Jamieson and Highet (2013) have suggested that managing troubling transitions can be achieved by:

> setting aside negative discourses framing loss as continuing trouble. This can only be confidently achieved with the help of effective interpersonal support and/or systems reaffirming belonging and self-worth by other means. ... Much depends on the capacity of this [interpersonal] network to offer support before and after loss. (p. 146)

When there is a family dispute about postseparation arrangements and the legal system becomes involved in decisions about children, it is important that children's rights to participate are respected in these legal processes. Children are not just objects of law but should be subjects and participants in decisions made on their behalf (Taylor & Gollop, 2015). The General Comment on Article 12 says that there is an obligation to allow children to participate in divorce proceedings, so that legislation on separation and divorce should include the right of the child to be heard by decision makers and in mediation processes (United Nations Committee on the Rights of the Child, 2009). The extent to which legislation permits or encourages children's participation varies in different parts of the world. Nicola Taylor and her colleagues (Taylor, Fitzgerald, Morag, Bajpai, & Graham, 2012) surveyed the extent to which children's participation rights were respected in private law in family law proceedings internationally. While they found that all responding countries (Australia,

Canada, Costa Rica, England, India, Israel, Japan, New Zealand, Nigeria, Northern Ireland, the Republic of Ireland, Scotland, and the United States) reported having laws regarding children's participation in adversarial family disputes, there was a gap between principle and practice with child participation being rare in half of the countries, and frequent in half of them. The primary means to promote child participation were through appointing lawyers for the child, or through children being interviewed by judges.

The attitudes of professionals and parents toward children and assumptions about their lack of competence, contributed to the lack of support for children's participation. That legal professionals can support children and scaffold their understanding when their parents are in dispute over their care, is illustrated by these quotations from a study of New Zealand children's perspectives about their lawyer:

> [Lawyer] gave me a number of options, sort of like a maths problem. 'Cos there's problems, and you get three or four answers, and you have to find the right answer. He'll round up a few possibilities and then I'll choose the best for me, the best possibilities that will suit me. (Craig, aged 13, Taylor, Gollop, & Smith, 2000, p. 121)

> Yeah, she's really good like at her job and stuff I reckon, 'cos like she explains it all. Like some people just quickly say it briefly, but she sits us down and tells us all about it really slowly and goes over it so we know what's going on. (Michelle, aged 10, Taylor et al., 2000, p. 126)

These children felt listened to, they had been given information and explanations, and they were also given support to formulate their views about what was important for them in their newly separated family. In contrast, other lawyers relied on listening to parents to find out what children's views and best interests were, and paid little attention to building up a relationship with children or talking to them.

2.7 SUMMARY

This chapter has discussed the importance of children's rights within the context of family life. The UN Convention strongly supports the role of families in children's lives, but the promotion of children's rights within families has often been interpreted as an attempt to interfere in family life and negate parents' rights. Yet, governments do have a responsibility toward supporting and protecting children within families, and their policies can have adverse effects on families. The subsuming of children within families has often ignored the fact that children have a point of view of their own, and that their interests aren't always identical to those of other family members. The relationships between generations is crucial to children's rights, so that within democratic families there are relationships of reciprocity and interdependency, rather than the traditional model of parental authority. The chapter has also discussed the relevant articles and principles within the UNCRC and focused on some issues that arise out of these rights including: the wider ecological influences on family life, the diversity of families, the nature of relationships and discipline within families, government responsibility for families' standard of living, and coping with family change.

CHAPTER 3

CHILDREN'S RIGHTS WITHIN EARLY CHILDHOOD EDUCATION AND CARE

Society's and individuals' views of children influence the ways in which they are cared for, provided for and educated in their early years. ... Do educators watch children's actions and listen to their voices with wide eyes and open minds, or are children seen as "adults-in-waiting" with no real rights, not yet real people, not yet able to think for themselves, no rightful place in the world? Do educators decide for children, working with their eyes closed and minds too narrow to accept the view that they are working with powerful and able people, however small and however young they may be?

—(Nutbrown, 1996, p. xvi)

"A right is like when you know in your heart it's okay to do it ... you can do it if you want and that's it." Another child added, "But only if it's okay, like you won't hurt somebody and it's not safe ... because the other person has a right to not be hurt too, right?"

—(Two 4-year-old children from Boulder Journey School talking about rights, Hall & Rudkin, 2011, p. 7)

Children usually have their first sustained experiences outside a family environment within early childhood education and care services, and these experiences can be a potent force in achieving social justice and rights for young children (Cannella, 1997). Attending an early childhood center is part of growing up for most children in the developed world, whether it be for a few mornings a week or for the equivalent of their parents' working day. The United Nations Committee on the Rights of the Child in its General Comment No. 7 (2005) suggested that early childhood should be defined as the period below the age of eight years. The committee acknowledged that definitions of early childhood differ in different countries according to the organization of preschool and elementary school systems. In the UK, this transition to school can take place as early as four years, in New Zealand it occurs at five years, though it is more common for this transition to take place (as in the United States and much of Europe) at six or seven years. This chapter refers primarily to the settings where children participate in education and care settings before they enter primary or elementary school.

I use the abbreviation ECE to refer to early childhood education and care services, in center or home-based settings. The term encompasses kindergartens, nursery schools, playgroups, crèches, childcare centers, Head Start programs, language immersion preschools, and family day care. ECE is conceptualized as including both education and care because, "the reality of any early childhood program is that it must provide a proper blend of education and care—*educare*" (Caldwell, 1989, p. 266). It is not possible to make a meaningful distinction between education and care in the early years, because spontaneous and reciprocal interactions within caring relationships are the ingredients that promote children's early learning. While education is often considered to suggest formal academic instruction, young children's learning emerges from their deep engagement in meaningful problems within the context of support and guidance from skilled adults, and in interaction with peers, in cognitively challenging tasks and activities. The idea that all ECE programs incorporate "educare" is, however, idealistic. In the United States, there tends to be a dichotomy between programs designed to enhance children's early education and development, and those that provide care for the children of working parents, and a seamless system that provides both is uncommon (Barnett & Ackerman, 2006).

The concept of evolving capacities helps to explain how children acquire competencies and understanding (General Comment, No. 7, 2006). The role of adults including teachers and parents (Article 5) is to offer appropriate guidance and direction, respecting children's interests and agency, and offering them opportunities to construct personal identity and acquire culturally valued skills and knowledge in the context of consistent secure relationships.

Although the original UNCRC (1989) makes no specific mention of preschool or ECE, there are many articles within it that have particular relevance for early childhood. This lack of mention of ECE was remedied when the Committee on the Rights of the Child in its General Comment

No. 7 (2005) expressed concern at the lack of attention to young children as rights holders, and pointed out that young children hold all of the rights in the Convention. The General Comment argued that governments should have a positive agenda for ECE and shift away from traditional beliefs viewing early childhood as "a period for the socialization of the immature human being towards mature adult status" (para 5). It urges recognition and respect for young children and viewing them "as social actors whose survival, well-being and development are dependent on and built around close relationships" (para 8).

This chapter asks how the four general principles of the UNCRC (see Chapter 1), to be found in Articles 2, 3, 6, and 12, can be implemented in policies and practices for ECE. The first principle of universalism (Article 2) suggests that all young children regardless of sex, race, language, religion, disability, or class should be able to participate in quality ECE, and to be protected from harm or discrimination within ECE. No child should be denied access to an ECE setting, because of disability or immigration status, for instance. The second principle is about "the best interests of the child" (Article 3), which suggests that individual children in ECE settings must be treated in accord with the best interests principle, and that children as a group must be catered for through policies that ensure their best interests. For example, ECE settings must be structured to support warm, nurturing, challenging, and responsive interactions between children and well-qualified staff. Without adequate structural conditions (ratios, group sizes, and staff qualifications), it is not possible to cater for children's best interests in ECE. The third principle of the right to survival and development (Article 6) is one which ECE settings are in a good position to implement, since the experiences of the early years have a lifelong impact. I shall show in this chapter how participation in ECE has an ongoing impact on children's development, can help promote other rights in a holistic manner (such as education and play), and support and enhance parents' ability to love, care for, and provide for their children.

The fourth principle in UNCRC of respect for the views and feelings of the child (Article 12) should be acted on in all ECE settings. There is a prevailing assumption that young children lack the knowledge, capability, and maturity to contribute actively in their ECE settings, and that they are the passive recipients of adults' actions and instruction. Yet, as the General Comment highlights, young children are sensitive to their surroundings, have a great deal of understanding of the people, places, and routines in their lives, make choices and communicate their feelings and wishes, well before they can talk. They also arrive at their early childhood settings having been able to draw on rich funds of knowledge from their families.

I will discuss the type of curriculum, processes, and assessment within ECE settings that are respectful of children's participation rights, and the harm that is done when these rights are not respected.

One article of the UNCRC that is of particular relevance to ECE settings, is Article 29, the first paragraph of which (29a) states that the education of the child should be directed to "the development of the child's personality, talents and mental and physical abilities to their fullest potential." Cathy Nutbrown (1996) links this first part of Article 29, to Article 13 asserting a child's right to freedom of expression, to seek, receive, or impart information in a variety of ways (through talking, writing, art, or any other ways). She asks ECE educators:

> How does early educare enable children to assert their right to express themselves, their love, their likes, their fears, their dislikes, their wants, their hates, their feelings? How often do adults try to make children smile, ask them for a kiss they do not want to give or limit their expression by either restricting their opportunities to "speak" or "be themselves"? (Nutbrown, 1996, p. 102)

The next paragraph in Article 29(b) concerns education being directed at respecting human rights, with the implication that educators have a responsibility to foster respect for human rights, and help children learn about their rights and the rights of others. Article 29(c) asserts the importance of parents' identity, culture, and language, suggesting that ECE programs should value and respect differences of appearance, skin color, language, culture, traditions, and celebrate diversity. Article 29(d) says that education should prepare children for a "life in a free society, in the spirit of understanding, peace, tolerance, equality of sexes and friendship." This paragraph highlights the importance of a climate of harmony, cooperation, mutual respect, and self-assertion in ECE settings. Adults should be able to provide help and support for children to resolve conflicts, tolerate difference, facilitate inclusion, and observe rules that are fair for everyone. The final paragraph in this article, 29(e) says that education should be directed at respect for the natural environment, an important issue in a time of major global environmental problems, such as climate change. It implies that children should be able to experience the natural environment in their ECE programs, that centers should have policies of sustainability (such as recycling), and that children should be encouraged to think about ways to cherish their natural environments.

This chapter looks at the following issues through a rights perspective: the lasting impact of ECE on children's development, curriculum models that support children's rights, components of quality ECE, children's perspectives on quality, and nondiscrimination.

3.1   THE LASTING INFLUENCE OF ECE

Family influences are clearly the most powerful in their effects on children's development (NICHD, 2005; Shonkoff & Phillips, 2000), but participation in ECE also makes a difference, depending on the quality of the programs. Since the early childhood years are the most formative in a child's life, participation in ECE programs can give children a good start in life, support their families in their parenting, and help children reach their full potential. Because the family is such a powerful predictor of outcomes for children, it is especially important that ECE programs focus not just on children but also on partnership and support for their families. Participation in ECE programs outside home, however, also offers risks, as children during these years are vulnerable to the influence of coercive, mediocre, and understimulating environments.

> A fundamental paradox exists and is unavoidable: development in the early years is both highly robust and highly vulnerable. Although there have been long-standing debates about how much the early years of life matter in the larger scheme of lifelong development, our conclusion is unequivocal: What happens during the first months and years of life matters a lot, not because this period of development provides an indelible blueprint for adult well-being, but because it sets either a sturdy or fragile stage for what follows. (Shonkoff & Phillips, 2000, p. 5)

While most families enroll their children in ECE programs because they want to give them challenging opportunities to learn social skills, to make friends, and to help prepare them for school, there are also parents who have no choice but to find alternative arrangements for their children, even when they are very young, because of having to work. "Parents of infants and toddlers deal silently and often alone with their anguish at having to return to work within weeks of the birth of their baby, with the worries about finding affordable and decent child care" (Phillips, 1995, p. 6). Such pressure to return to work is particularly strong for low-income families under welfare-to-work policies.

The NICHD study (2005) demonstrates that there is a large percentage of infants and toddlers participating in nonmaternal care in the United

States. They found that 80 percent of one-year-olds had received some form of regularly scheduled nonmaternal care, although only a minority (13 percent) of this group were in child care centers and 13 percent were in nanny or other home-based care. By the age of three, 92 percent of children had experienced nonmaternal care, and by then 44 percent were in child care centers and 25 percent in home-based care. Similar increasing participation of up to three-year-old children in ECE, and almost universal participation of three- and four-year-olds, is typical in developed countries.

There is therefore a strong obligation for governments to develop policies that fulfill all children's Article 29 rights to have access to high-quality affordable ECE programs that favorably influence outcomes, rather than mediocre ones with poor outcomes, especially when their families face other risks. I will explain in more detail the nature of high-quality ECE in the next section of this chapter.

There are several strands of research that come together to demonstrate the importance of the early years for later development: including neuroscience research on the developing brain (Fox, Levitt, & Nelson, 2010); econometric research on the contribution to healthy societies of investing in early childhood (Economist Intelligence Unit, 2012); and social science research on the influence of early childhood experiences on child development outcomes. It is the latter strand of research that I will focus on here.

The following quotation from Nobel laureate, James Heckman, explains why early experiences have such a lasting effect.

> Skills beget skills. All capabilities are built on a foundation of capacities that are developed earlier. This principle stems from two characteristics that are intrinsic to the nature of learning …. First, early learning confers value on acquired skills, which leads to self-reinforcing motivation to learn more. Early mastery of a range of cognitive, social, and emotional competencies makes learning at later ages more efficient and therefore easier and more likely to continue. (Heckman, 2011, p. 6)

There is a great deal of research on the effects of children's participation in ECE, so only highlights are provided here. Early studies in the 1960s in the United States were designed to break the cycle of poverty and disadvantage, and give poor children a better start at school. Examples of these early intervention programs, some of which followed up children's progress until adolescence, were the Syracuse Family Research Program (Lally, Mangione, & Honig, 1988), the Abecedarian project

(Campbell et al., 2012), and the Perry preschool project. Weikart's Perry Preschool Program (Berrueta-Clement, Schweinhart, Barnett, Epstein, & Weikart, 1984) is a famous and universally cited study, which studied 123 disadvantaged black children who were randomly assigned to a high-quality preschool program, based on Piagetian principles of active cognitively based learning or a control group, when they were between three and four years of age. Children in the treatment and control groups were followed up from the age of 3 to 19. The lasting beneficial effects included improved school achievement; lower rates of school failure, special education placement and school dropouts; higher rates of postsecondary training; decreased delinquency, crime and welfare dependency; lower rates of teenage pregnancy; and higher rates of functional competence.

Barnett (1995) reviewed the long-term effects of 36 early intervention studies that followed children through to school. The programs were either high-quality model programs (like the Perry Preschool Project) or everyday large-scale programs (mostly Head Start).

> The weight of the evidence establishes that ECCE [Early Childhood Center Experience] can produce large effects on IQ during the early childhood years and sizeable persistent effects on achievement, grade retention, special education, high school graduation and socialization .... Evidence for effects on high school graduation and delinquency is strong but based on a smaller number of studies. These effects are large enough and persistent enough to make a meaningful difference in the lives of many low-income children. (p. 43)

More recent reviews of model early intervention programs have shown that these early findings have been replicated (Barnett & Ackerman, 2006; Camilli, Vargas, Ryan, & Barnett, 2010; Karoly et al., 1998; Karoly, Kilburn, & Cannon, 2005). The findings of these reviews of research showed that better educational and social outcomes were associated with early intervention. The best outcomes were associated with programs that had more qualified staff, more favorable staff to child ratios and greater intensity.

According to Barnett & Ackerman (2006, p. 89) "In sum ECE can be a remarkable investment with high returns and important impacts on the educational, social and economic success of children growing up in disadvantaged circumstances." Although Barnett and Ackerman's review showed that there were higher returns for children in poverty, they also found that middle-income children had substantial gains from quality ECE, and they favor universal rather than targeted programs. The authors point out, that small scale model programs like the Abecedarian and Perry projects, had teachers with college degrees and reasonable salaries, and that they had teacher–child ratios of 1:7 and a group size no larger than 13. Having qualified staff with more years of education made an important difference to outcomes for children. Unfortunately these structural components of quality are not replicated in most regular ECE programs because they are usually provided at lower cost. These studies do, however, demonstrate that it is possible to substantially improve the life chances of children who participate in high-quality programs. Quality, however, carries a cost, which many governments are reluctant to pay, despite the evidence that investment in quality carries long-term benefits. Policies that allow low quality ECE programs to exist, and high quality to be unaffordable for families, are inimical to children's best interests, survival and development rights.

It is important to find out what the impact is, of everyday ECE programs that are delivered as part of a universal service. One such study is the Child Parent Center Project, based in Chicago. It provided preschool education in or near public primary schools in 24 centers in low-income areas to predominantly poor, three to five year-olds. There was a significant component of outreach family support to work with parents, and intensive and on-going work focusing on improving children's educational skills. Children who participated in the program had significantly higher rates of school completion, lower rates of grade retention and special education placement, and lower rates of juvenile arrests. The participants have been followed up until adulthood, and the effects have been lasting (Reynolds, 1994; Reynolds, Temple, White, Ou, & Robertson, 2011).

In the UK, the Effective Provision of Preschool Education (EPPE) project examined the impact of preschool education and care on the development of 3,000 three to seven year-old children (Sylva, Melhuish, Sammons, Siraj-Blatchford, & Taggart, 2004). Three year-old children who had attended a variety of types of preschool education were followed until age seven, and their developmental progress compared to a group of home children who had no or minimal preschool experience. Preschool experience enhanced the all-round development of children, including reading and mathematics scores and social or behavioral measures. Longer duration and higher quality preschool continued to impact on outcomes for children at age seven. The ECE settings with more qualified staff achieved better cognitive and social or behavioral outcomes. The effects were particularly powerful for children who came from more disadvantaged backgrounds.

The United States National Institute for Health and Development (NICHD) longitudinal study followed children from birth until adulthood, and followed children's naturally occurring participation in nonparental ECE, and the relationship between children's experiences in child care and their development over time (Shonkoff & Phillips, 2000). Quality of childcare was a consistent predictor of children's cognitive and language performance at aged three years. Later follow-ups at third grade (eight years of age) showed that experience in better quality child care centers continued to be associated with higher scores in maths, reading, and memory. More hours of care, however, were associated with poorer work habits and poorer social skills (NICHD, 2000, 2005). A recent follow-up at age 15 years (Vandell, Belsky, Burchinal, Steinberg, & Vandergrift, 2010) showed that both the quality and quantity of childcare were linked to measures of adolescent functioning more than 10 years after the children had left care. When young people had experienced high-quality ECE they were less likely to show externalizing behavior and (in centers with average or better quality care), to achieve greater gains in cognitive-academic outcomes. This study confirmed that developmental continuities "set the stage for and are then carried forward to later periods" (p. 751). Although there is some evidence that early entry and long hours of participation in childcare were associated with problem behaviors, these did not persist. Although the findings cited here are from the United States and the UK, other research in Australia and New Zealand show similar findings (Smith, 2013b, Chapter 5).

These findings demonstrate the big picture that participation in high-quality ECE programs supports children's education, best interests, survival, and development rights, since if they participate in such programs they do better. The evidence is particularly strong that children from high-risk backgrounds, such as poverty or other disadvantage, benefit from such programs. In addition children have a right to be protected from low quality harmful ECE experiences, particularly during infancy. One way to support children's rights is to ensure that their families have access to, and can afford to enroll them in high-quality ECE programs.

3.2   CURRICULUM MODELS THAT SUPPORT CHILDREN'S RIGHTS

So far my discussion has focused on demonstrating that children's participation in ECE programs has an influence on their development. Curriculum models provide guidelines for the pedagogical approach taken in ECE centers, and for the roles that adults and children should play.

They are a set of principles and a theoretical viewpoint to guide practice, although not all countries or centers have adopted ECE curriculum guidelines. Working with an effective curriculum model helps teachers to be intentional, plan, assess, and reflect on their programs, and this is a valuable component of quality ECE practice. In this section, I ask the question of what type of ECE programs and curricula, respect children's participation and education rights.

> A consistent feature of these models is that learning through play is not left to chance, but is channeled through complex reciprocal and responsive relationships, and is situated in activities that are socially constructed and mediated. (Wood, 2004)

One influential curriculum model that fits well with the principles of the UNCRC, is the Reggio Emilia approach, which was developed in Northern Italy after the Second World War. This curriculum exemplifies the concept of children as "active co-constructors of knowledge and culture, with their own identity as people and learners" (Anning, 2004, p. 59). The image of children within the Reggio Emilio approach is that: "the child is rich in potential, strong, powerful, competent, and most of all connected to adults and other children" (Malaguzzi, 1993, cited by Anning, 2004, p. 59). Reggio Emilia's construction of childhood is oriented to the present rather than to the future. While children are seen as individuals, they have an important place in their communities and neighborhoods. There are no centralized curriculum guidelines in the Reggio approach, and planning is based on recording and reflecting on what children are currently doing. Staff documentations of children's activities are the basis of weekly staff meetings to shape planning and resourcing of activities. Pedagogical work arises out of this construction of a rich child, and what staff think the child is (Dahlberg et al., 1999, cited by Fleer & Richardson, 2004).

Gillian Pugh and Dorothy Rouse Selleck describe their visit to a Reggio Emilia Centre in Northern Italy (1996). The authors found that the equipment and design of space was designed so that even the youngest children had a say in decisions about routine, pace, and control.

> For example cots, or "nests" as the staff called them, were made like baskets and were placed at floor level. As soon as babies can crawl they can choose the comfort of their personal nest without being reliant on adults to hoist them in and out of an inaccessible cage on stilts, which is the tradition in most nurseries. These babies could also collect their own clean nappy from low cupboards and

choose to climb on a little ramp up to changing mats where they were able to invited adults to change them. (Pugh & Selleck, 1996, p. 131)

The HighScope approach to curriculum was used in the Perry preschool project and has since been adapted for use not only in the United States but also in many parts of the world (over 20 countries in Europe, Asia, Africa, and Central and Southern America). Although originally Piagetian in orientation, it has been updated using the findings of ongoing research (Epstein, Johnson, & Lafferty, 2011). HighScope is also based on Vygotskian ideas, that children learn in the context of sociocultural contexts where adults engage with them in their "zone of proximal development"[1] to advance their thinking.

The role of adults in the HighScope approach is a proactive one. They work alongside children to plan and reflect on children's chosen activities, and to challenge children's reasoning, expand their critical thinking, and capture children's natural curiosity. "Scaffolding" involves adults supporting children's learning, while at the same time challenging them to extend their learning. Activities are both child-initiated to promote children's motivation to learn, and guided by adults, building on children's interests as well as directed toward eight curriculum content areas (such as language, literacy, social, and emotional development). HighScope is based on five principles (Epstein et al., 2011):

- Active participatory learning involving materials, choice, manipulation, child language and thought, encouraging children's initiative, independence, and self-confidence;
- "Plan-do-review" sequences where children make plans, carry out their intentions, and reflect on their learning;
- Curriculum content and key developmental indicators;
- Principles of active learning;
- Validated assessment tools (observational records).

Our curriculum in New Zealand is *Te Whāriki,* published in 1996 and compulsory for registered ECE centers in New Zealand. It, like Reggio Emilio and HighScope, is recognized in many countries throughout the world, such as the UK, Australia, Canada, Denmark, and Singapore.

---

[1] The zone of proximal development is the zone where children can perform a task with adult help, but they are moving toward being able to carry out the task independently.

It is based on sociocultural, bicultural, and holistic principles, and has a deliberate focus on incorporating children's and families' voices about children's learning (Smith, 2011). The name *Te Whāriki* is a Māori phrase meaning a "woven mat for all to stand on," a metaphor expressing the possibility of creating many patterns of ideas and philosophy, that can be used in a diverse array of types of early childhood centers, from sessional kindergartens, parent cooperative play centers, language immersion centers (such as *Kōhanga Reo*), to full day child care settings.

Te Whāriki deliberately avoids a subject and stage-based approach to ECE programs, as it is believed that there is no one path to learning, and that culturally rich settings provide different pathways for learning. Rather than focusing on the traditional domains of children's development (physical, cognitive, social, emotional), it takes a more holistic approach of providing a safe and trustworthy environment, opportunities for collaborative problem-solving, meaningful and interesting problems, avoidance of the risk of failure and competition, and the availability of assistance from teachers. The five strands and goals of *Te Whāriki* are well-being, belonging, contribution, communication, and exploration. It focuses on motivational aspects of learning rather than fragmented skills and knowledge, and encourages ongoing dispositions to learn and persevere with difficulties. Dispositions to learn are "habits of mind that dispose the learner to interpret, edit, and respond to experiences in characteristic ways" (Carr, 1997, p. 2). They are shaped by, and shape children's social interactions encouraging them to recognize, select, edit, respond to, resist, search for, construct, and modify learning opportunities (Carr, 2001). *Te Whāriki* encourages children's autonomy, exploration, commitment, and aspirations.

Such an open-ended curriculum provides challenges for assessment, but Margaret Carr and other colleagues (Carr, 1998; Carr, Hatherly, Lee, & Ramsey, 2005) have developed a narrative formative assessment process called "Learning Stories" to record significant learning moments in children's daily experiences. Children's voices, as well as those of their families, are included in learning stories allowing children to share meanings and ownership of their learning. Children's rights, to express and share their views (Articles 12 and 13), are embedded in *Te Whāriki,* and it provides an excellent model of a curriculum that incorporates children's participation rights.

> Children are valued as active learners, who choose, plan, and challenge. This stimulates a climate of reciprocity, "listening" to children (even if they cannot speak), observing how their

feelings of curiosity, interest, and knowledge are engaged in their early childhood environments, and encouraging them to make a contribution to their own learning. (Smith, 2007, p. 155)

3.3 STRUCTURAL AND PROCESS COMPONENTS OF QUALITY

I have mentioned that if ECE programs are to support children's learning, well-being, and respect children's rights, they must be of high quality, so it is important to explain what quality means. Quality is partly an empirical issue—what does research show about the nature of ECE programs that leads to positive outcomes? But it is also to some extent a culturally specific and subjective matter—what do we value in our societies and cultures as outcomes for children?

Quality is defined as the essential components of early childhood environments that are valued in our society, and which support the well-being, development and rights of children and support effective family functioning. (Smith, Grima, Gaffney, & Powell, 2000)

It is important to look at research on measurable aspects of quality as well as to acknowledge that there is not only one way of providing quality, because a vision of quality depends on negotiation and argument between stakeholders (parents, teachers, children, and the community). When quality is looked at in terms of measured outcomes, structural aspects of quality are usually outlined, including: adult–child ratios, group size, staff qualifications and experience, staff stability, staff wages and working conditions, and aspects of the physical environment (such as space and equipment). Decades of research have established that ECE centers that have smaller ratios of children to adults, smaller group size and trained teachers, result in more favorable outcomes for children (Barnett & Ackerman, 2006; Goelman et al., 2006; Lamb, 1998; Meade, Robinson, Smorti, Stuart, & Williamson, 2012; NICHD, 2005), and such research cannot be ignored in assessing the quality of ECE programs.

The main reason that these structural aspects of quality impact on children's learning lies, however, in how they impact on the processes that take place in ECE centers, how ECE staff interact with children and provide challenge for their learning. Process quality involves reciprocal, responsive, and warm adult–child relationships; adults who listen to children, engage with and share thinking with them, provide opportunities for them to explore, and affirm their culture, language, identity, and family.

Opportunity to engage with another person in shared experience (joint attention) is a valuable learning context for infants and young children (Meltzoff, Kuhl, Movellan, & Sejnowski, 2009; Schaffer, 1992; Smith, 1999; Tomasello, 1999). Episodes of joint attention take place when children and adults (or other children) are jointly focused on an activity, object, or idea. This happens in brief interactions during a day when a child turns to a teacher when she strikes a difficulty or an interesting situation, and a teacher responds with interest, support, information, a label, or a suggestion. These episodes might occur when helping a child to put shoes and socks on, building a tower of blocks, or looking out of the window at a fire engine going past. Bruner (1995) referred to such joint attention episodes as allowing a "meeting of minds," which allow children to learn that other people too are agents trying to achieve goals, and that there is a "standing for" relationship between arbitrary signs (such as language) and the worlds of experience. Familiarity and warm relationships between adult and child foster the mutual sensitivity that facilitates joint attention. When children are comfortable with adults, they are likely to initiate communications with them, and the teacher who knows the child well, is able to interpret the communications and respond in a way that they understand, which is a starting point for learning.

My research (Smith, 1999) on joint attention episodes in ECE centers for infants, showed that about a third of 200 under-two-year-olds were never observed in any joint attention episodes with adults, and that such episodes were less likely to occur with large group sizes and untrained teachers. In centers with unfavorable adult–child ratios, it is difficult for teachers to develop close relationships with children, and engage in the sensitive responsive interactions that promote learning. When there is a high turnover of ECE staff in centers (often the case where wages are low), children struggle to develop warm, stable relationships with adults. Having early childhood qualifications helps teachers understand how to implement a rich curriculum, and to plan, manage assess, and reflect on their practice. Staff without qualifications are more likely to provide mere custodial care. One of the reasons that model ECE programs like the Perry Preschool project were so successful is that they employed qualified staff had good ratios of adults to children, small group sizes, and paid their staff well.

Children in poverty are unlikely to participate in such high-quality programs, and it has been reported that in the United States the majority (86 percent) of childcare is of mediocre to low quality (Helburn, 1995), with staff turnover rates of between 30 and 37 percent. Low levels of quality in child care settings for many children in the United States were demonstrated in the NICHD study, which showed that only 12 percent of children in the 10 sites were experiencing high-quality care (Ramey, 2005). If these findings are extrapolated to the whole population of the United States, only 9 percent of children in child care centers experience positive care, while the rest are subjected to nonresponsive, nonstimulating, indifferent, or neglectful care. Sharon Ramey describes these findings as "shocking" and "intolerable" (p. 433). I would add that the human rights of the majority of American children in child care centers are being denied.

Researchers have shown, however, that it is possible to improve low-quality ECE programs, as is shown in a recent study (Landry et al., 2014). The study provided a professional development program for staff in 65 centers catering for low-income infants and toddlers, with random assignment of classes to treatment groups. The Responsive Early Childhood Curriculum (RECC) was employed in the treatment, which was designed to increase staff contingent responsiveness. Teachers were coached to respond promptly and sensitively to infants' signals, maintain and build on children's interests with rich language input, and provide age-appropriate cognitively stimulating activities. The findings showed that there was a positive impact of the RECC. The teachers in the intervention groups scored higher on the quality of their interactions with children including rich language input, classroom organization and planning, and use of engaging learning activities. Children in the intervention groups outperformed the control group on measures of social and emotional development. The study was important because it demonstrated that staff with relatively limited education, learned to become more responsive to children with a positive impact on their development, after coaching sessions over 37 weeks and a total of 92 hours of training.

3.4   QUALITY FROM CHILDREN'S PERSPECTIVES

Quality is deeply embedded in the engagement of adults and children together, but from a rights perspective, the core aspect of quality is listening to children's voice and perspectives and taking them seriously. The principle that arises from Article 12 is respect for the views and feelings of the child and the importance of taking the views of young children seriously. Harcourt & Hägglund (2013, p. 286) describe a "bottom-up perspective on children's rights," which is a commitment to inviting children's perspectives. This is "not an option which is the gift of adults, but a legal imperative which is the right of the child" (Lundy, 2007, cited by Harcourt & Hägglund, 2013, p. 289). ECE programs need a culture where young children are listened to and taken seriously, which is difficult to achieve, when societal attitudes are not particularly respectful of the views of children of any age. Sensitivity to the "views" of infants, who are not yet verbal, is even harder to achieve. Yet, it is still possible to be respectful and "listen" to how they are feeling as is shown in this quotation:

> "Listening" to very young children does not necessarily mean taking all of their utterances at face value, but it does mean observing the nuances of how they exhibit stress, or curiosity or anxiety, or pleasure in a manner which is congruent to their maturity. It does not imply that their views carry more weight than the powers of wise and loving adults over the outcome of any decision making process but it does require that their views are respected. (Pugh & Selleck, 1996, p. 121–22)

A context of close relationships makes it possible for mothers to understand the nuances of their infants' nonverbal communications, such as crying, vocalizations, or gestures. Teachers and caregivers can also develop close relationships with infants, but this is easier in ECE programs with primary caregiving arrangements, where one or two key people are responsible for the care of a particular infant.

Ellen Lynn Hall and Jennifer Kofkin Rudkin (2011) write about how listening to and respecting children's rights in ECE centers, requires patience. Teachers need to be willing to spend time while children master new skills (such as washing hands or eating), and to wait while children communicate with them. "Tuning adult ears to the voices of children," the title of a chapter in the authors' book, is a phrase that encapsulates the task of discovering children's perspectives, a task that requires adults to listen "with all of *their* creativity" (Hall & Rudkin, 2011, p. 10). They write that while adults tend to be future-oriented,

> Children, on the other hand, are sensitive to the wonders of the here and now, wonders for which they eagerly forego other agendas. ... They exist in the moment and focus on what they find before them. Children encounter numerous marvels on the way to the car or the store that merit examination—the intriguing shapes and splashes of puddles, the intricate pathways of bugs and worms, the irresistible

gleams of shining treasures lying on the street disguised as trash. (Hall & Rudkin, 2011, p. 13)

Being a good teacher involves sharing children's fascination for the here and now, and letting children know that their interests are shared. Teachers who understand children's rights, are likely to construct them as competent, capable, and creative people, rather than vulnerable, unformed, and untrustworthy. Overprotection and overemphasis on safety can limit children's opportunities to explore and learn. Instead adults can guide children by giving them space to find their voice, and inviting them to engage with challenging and meaningful tasks. Teachers also have a major role in providing the space, opportunity, and openings for children to formulate and express their points of view (Peters & Lacy, 2013).

When a teacher of one-year-olds at Boulder Journey School watched children play in an area where hobbyhorses were stored in tall buckets beyond the children's reach, she noticed that children were pointing, tugging at the toys, and vocalizing persistently and had no difficulty in interpreting the children's actions. The school worked hard at providing different ways of listening to children's perspectives, by adjusting their language toward concrete and away from abstract terms, providing numerous materials (e.g., drawing, painting, clay, photography) to facilitate children's communication, and providing a climate where conversations about play took place. Conversations with children, making links with familiar and shared experiences, allowing time for children to exercise their autonomy, and formulate their thoughts and wishes are all essential components of an ECE culture that respects children's views.

"Authoritative and accountable positioning" means crediting children with authorship and supporting their agency" (Carr et al., 2010; Greeno, 2006). The concept helps us to understand better how to facilitate children's voice and visibility.

When children were deemed to be authoring ... they were: initiating; enjoying; taking on identities as "grown-ups", expert readers, writers, soccer-players, drivers and artists; deeply engaged in activities often with a high level of affect (excitement, emotion); inclined to communicate their opinions; focused and persevering, "locking on" to learning; interested and enthusiastic, balancing desires and goals; taking responsibility and taking on the role of the teacher. (Carr et al., 2010)

Whether children are positioned as authoritative and accountable is very much influenced by teachers, and whether and how they facilitate children's agency and voice in the ECE classroom. The use of language can be very influential. When five year-old, David, who had previously been reluctant to engage with literacy activities, joined in a story-writing session at school, he said "I won't need help today; if I need a little bit of help I'll put my hand up" (Carr et al., 2010, p. 94). When David showed the teacher his "story," the teacher wrote on it: "You are a very clever writer." His mother recognized that something clicked that day about writing for David, and he subsequently recognized himself as a writer and enjoyed writing.

In Boulder Journey School four year-old children decided to construct "the largest rocket ship ever built," and called upon their parents to help with the project. They asked their parents to help "with the hard jobs like nailing the floors together," and said: "We want the shape of the rocket ship to be tall and pointy. We will make the engine and the rocket boosters" (Hall & Rudkin, 2011, p. 57). In this example of authoring, the children realized that they needed help and, with the teachers' support, wrote a letter to their parents to ask for this. Parents willingly responded to this call for help and helped build the frame for the rocket. This example shows how adults can provide input without taking over the project from children.

Another example cited by Clark (2010, p. 103) of authoritative positioning was when a group of children between three and eight years of age from a run-down housing estate, wrote a report for the council including photos, maps, and drawings and other children's views. The outcome was that the senior officials changed their plan to better meet the children's suggestions.

These examples all involve deliberate, intentional work by teachers to understand what children want to achieve, and to give children the chance to exercise autonomy and express themselves. Children gained skills and confidence, and used adult help where necessary in tune with their evolving capacity. The starting point for such meaningful episodes of children's agency is communication, establishing a relationship with children, listening to them and finding out about their interests and experiences, helping them to recall relevant information, responding to their initiatives, challenging them with the addition of new information, and providing them with the space and resources to reach their goals. Such a rich sociocultural climate is an important element in implementing children's participation rights, and starting children on a pathway "toward a lifelong love affair with learning and to be the beginning of their journey rather than the end" (Ransom, 2012, p. 396).

3.5 NONDISCRIMINATION IN ECE SETTINGS

This chapter has established that participation in high-quality ECE programs makes a difference for children and supports their survival, development, best interests, and participation rights. But before these rights can be implemented, it is necessary for *all* children to participate fully in such programs. The UNCRC principle of nondiscrimination (Article 2) states that *all* children should be entitled to rights, regardless of race, sex, language, religion, disability, or class. The importance of access to a place in an ECE program is illustrated by this recommendation to the Australian government from the Australian Human Rights Commission (2014): "Develop accessible, affordable, flexible, quality early childhood education and care services, including out-of-school-hours care services, and *ensure each child has an entitlement to attend*" (p. 3, italics added).

The Australian HRC report also draws attention to the fact that the UNCRC sets out a number of specific rights for vulnerable children. While all children benefit from participation, vulnerable children participation in quality ECE makes a critical difference to their life chances. Vulnerable children include those who are at risk of violence or abuse (Article 19), children temporarily or permanently deprived of their family environment (Article 21), children seeking refugee status or a refugee (Article 22), mentally or physically disabled children (Article 23), and children belonging to a linguistic, ethnic or religious minority, or of indigenous origin (Article 30). Some countries, such as Norway and Denmark, have established a legal right to ECE guaranteeing children a place, but many countries do not have such a legal right enshrined in their law (Australian Human Rights Commission, 2014).

Children with disability are one group that face significant barriers to engagement in ECE programs in many countries. Yet, early intervention for children with disability is much more cost effective than intervention later in life, and can reduce differential educational outcomes for children with and without disability. Historically, children with disabilities were placed in institutions separated from the mainstream and from other children. In most developed countries, there has been a move toward full inclusion of children with disabilities into mainstream education programs. Full inclusion in ECE is particularly important for disabled children as this gives them access to wider curriculum learning and social environments, opportunity to learn alongside nondisabled peers, and more stimulating social interactions (MacArthur, Kelly, & Higgins, 2005). There are many social and physical barriers to full inclusion of children with disabilities in ECE, including lack of funding for teacher training and professional development, and lack of additional resources (such as teacher aides, technological support, and ramps of wheelchair access). The chief barrier to inclusion, however, is adult attitudes and values that are unaccepting, rejecting, or ignoring of disabled students (Connors & Stalker, 2007). Disabled children are particularly likely to be viewed predominantly as passive and vulnerable victims of their impairment, but like other children they are active agents in interpreting their lives and negotiating their way through barriers and difficulties. Difference can be experienced negatively when disabled children are teased or bullied, and teachers do not provide sympathetic support, or mediate the attitudes and actions of other children, to defend disabled children from such treatment, and give them support in responding to it.

The exclusion and lack of full inclusion of children with disability from mainstream ECE programs is an important social justice and human rights issues that must be addressed. ECE providers may refuse to accept disabled children into programs (often on the grounds of lack of resources), which denies their human rights. If accepted into ECE programs, it is important that teachers have the knowledge, understanding, and resources to support these children's rights to an education that supports their development and helps them to achieve their potential.

There are many other groups of marginalized children whose rights to survival, development, best interests, and education rights are being denied by lack of access or full inclusion into quality ECE programs. When lack of public subsidies prevents poor families from accessing ECE for their children, this further accumulates risk and disadvantage for them. When refugee children in Australian detention centers are prevented from the opportunity to participate in regular ECE programs, their chances of surviving the trauma and losses they have experience are diminished (Garvis & Austin, 2007). The denial of access to ECE for particular ethnic groups, such as Roma children in Greece, is a violation of their rights (Karagianni, Mitakidou, & Tressou, 2013). When Māori children in Aotearoa New Zealand are denied the opportunity to learn in their own indigenous language in a culturally appropriate context, their rights are ignored (Ritchie & Rau, 2013). When children in foster care experience multiple placements and experience changes and disruptions to education, their rights and life chances are diminished (Ritchie, Morrison, & Patterson, 2003). While countries like Australia, New Zealand, Canada, the United States, and the UK may have high participation rates of children in ECE programs, the question needs to be asked about whether there is equal access to high-quality ECE for children from all segments of society.

3.6 SUMMARY

This chapter has focused on how children's best interests, survival, development, education, and participation rights can and should be catered for in ECE settings. Since the early childhood years are the most formative in a child's life, and most children's first experiences outside home are in ECE settings, these should be of high quality. There is evidence that ECE can make a difference for children and can help to ameliorate poverty and disadvantage. There is also evidence that poor quality settings can be harmful and increase children's disadvantage.

The evidence suggests that programs and curricula differ in their respect for children's rights and incorporation of quality. A core component of good programs is warm, sensitive, and responsive relationships between adults and children, intentional, theory-informed practice, and understanding of the sociocultural context of children's learning. The High-Scope curriculum in the United States and *Te Whāriki* in New Zealand are examples of programs that both build on children's interests and strengths, and provide challenge to encourage further learning.

ECE quality incorporates both subjective and objective aspects. The objective components are established by research showing relationships between measurable aspects of ECE settings and developmental outcomes. The subjective components are arrived at through negotiations between stakeholders about their desired cultural values and goals for children. Structural features of quality include staff--child ratios, staff qualifications , and group size, and when these are favorable, the ECE settings are more likely to encourage opportunities for reciprocal, responsive relationships, and shared thinking. Regrettably, there are some disturbing findings that the quality of many ECE settings for children in the United States are low or mediocre.

A bottom-up view of quality, which fits well with the participation rights enshrined in the UNCRC, attempts to access children's perspectives and strengthen their agency. This means providing opportunities for children to find their voice and express their views, requiring patient efforts by teachers to facilitate children's communication and expression of views, and to share children's meanings. Positioning children as agentic and authoritative learners helps build children's motivation and confidence, encourages them to engage enthusiastically with learning, and stimulates them to take responsibility for their own learning.

In order to benefit from quality ECE programs, it is necessary for children to be able to participate in them. The nondiscrimination principle of the UNCRC states that all children, regardless of their characteristics, have the right to access quality ECE programs, and that "vulnerable children" have additional rights to such participation. It is therefore important that ECE policies and practices ensure that affordable, accessible, and high-quality ECE programs for all children are available, and that mediocre or poor programs are prevented from operating. For this to take place, governments have the responsibility to provide funding that supports quality and ensure through regulation and accountability measures, that low quality is not permitted. One of the most important policies is to support measures to ensure that all early childhood teachers and caregivers have recognized degree level qualifications, that ECE programs have access to quality curricula, and that teachers are able to access professional development opportunities to support the implementation of the curriculum. In order to prevent unstable high turnover of staff in ECE centers, teachers should be paid a reasonable wage in keeping with the importance of their work in maintaining the rights and well-being of children.

CHAPTER 4

CHILDREN'S RIGHTS IN SCHOOL

Some children feel oppressed by their teachers use of their greater power, and the ways in which this impinges on their autonomy and well-being. Their experiences in their interactions with teachers indicate to them that they are not taken seriously at school and consequently they feel oppressed and detached from their schooling.

—(Osman, 2005, p. 190)

And the teachers will say NO!! ... And if you're busting what can you do!! Wee in your pants!! Be constipated!! You don't really have a choice!! ... and they think they have control that they can't let you go to the toilet 'cause your going to run off or something ... I don't know!!'

—(Drew, a Sydney primary school child, in Osman, p. 185)

I have as much respect, authority, and as many rights, as the other members. They treat me with respect as I have a right to. I am not a "junior" member.

—(Secondary school student representative on School Board of Trustees, in Smith, Nairn, Sligo, Gaffney, & McCormack, 2003, p. 29)

Children today spend most of their childhood in school, so how their rights are respected in school has a major impact on their lives in the present, and on their future rights and life chances. Yet, measures to safeguard children's rights at school are not very common, and the idea of children having rights in educational contexts is controversial. Children's rights are invisible in education law, and the UNCRC seems to have had little impact within education (Blair, 2005; Willow, 2015). In the United States, education is not a constitutional right but a matter for states, and there is no federal framework to ensure that children have a right to quality education (Baiyee, Hawkins, & Polakow, 2013). Education should respect children's other rights such as freedom of conscience (Article 14), privacy (Article 16), expression (Article 13), and to be protected from abuse, neglect, and cruel and inhumane treatment (Article 19) (Lundy, 2012). Teachers and schools therefore have a burden of responsibility to promote education and other rights in school settings.

UNCRC gives a high priority to education. The first General Comment by the Committee on the Rights of the Child (2001) was on the Aims of Education. Article 28 states that all children have the right to education; that elementary education should be free and compulsory to all; and that secondary education should also be available and accessible to each child. The principle of nondiscrimination (Article 2) says that children should not be denied access to school because of disability, ethnicity, language, religion, or any other characteristic. General Comment No. 1 (para 10) says that children with disabilities, with HIV/AIDS, or refugee or asylum seeker children, should be able to access a good quality education.

Article 29 says that education should develop "the child's personality, talents and mental and physical abilities to their fullest potential" (Article 29, 1a). Education should promote respect for human rights, cultural identity, and for the natural environment. Article 29 "insists upon the need for education to be child-centred, child-friendly and empowering" (General Comment, 2001, para 2). The aims of education are therefore quite broad-ranging and go beyond formal schooling and academic goals, "to empower the child by developing his or her skills, learning and other capacities, human dignity, self-esteem and self-confidence" (para 1). Article 29 recognizes the need for "a balanced approach to education and one that succeeds in reconciling diverse values through dialogue and respect for difference" (General Comment No. 1, para 4). The curriculum should therefore be holistic, relevant to children's social and cultural contexts, tailored to the individual needs of different children, and foster basic life skills (including, but not only, literacy and numeracy) (para 9).

Article 29 asserts the importance of human rights education, and children seeing human rights principles practiced at school (General Comment No. 1, para 15). Article 42 says that countries should make the provisions of the UNCRC widely known, so schools should ensure that staff and students know about the convention and promote human rights (General Comment, para 19). Schools should be inclusive and harmonious environments, which do not permit bullying, racism, or sexism. "A school which allows bullying or other violent and exclusionary practices to occur is not one which meets the requirements of article 29 (1)" (General Comment No. 1, para 19). Compliance with Articles 29 and 19 is compromised by the use of corporal punishment at school. Children should also be able to express their views and have them taken into account in school, according to Articles 12 and 13.

Laura Lundy (2012) carried out a documentary analysis of the published reports of the UN Committee in relation to educational policy. She found nine common themes in the criticisms of education policies in the CRC's responses to country reports, and these highlight areas where there is a particular need for scrutiny of children's rights at school. Areas of concern discussed in this chapter, include the following: access to school, corporal punishment, bullying, exclusion, discrimination, school discipline, and participation.

4.1   ACCESS TO SCHOOL

All children should be able to go to school, but that is not a reality for many children on a worldwide basis. UNICEF (2011) estimated that 101 million children were not in school. The Young Lives project coordinated by Oxford University (Woodhead, Dornan, & Murray, 2014) has studied children's educational access and progress in poor countries (Ethiopia, India, Peru, and Vietnam). Children's access and progression through school is greatly affected by poverty and ill health. Parental death or illness and child health problems (such as malaria or diarrhea) lead to frequent absences and children dropping out from school early. In Ethiopia, one in five children lose a parent by the age of 12, so that many children leave school to take up domestic or paid work. There are marked wealth-linked inequalities, with children in the lowest quintiles being much less likely to be at school than those in the highest. Children in rural areas and those of minority ethnicity are also less likely to be attending school, but surprisingly gender was not as important as expected. Most (90 percent) of Ethiopian 15-year-olds were enrolled in school, but only 18 percent had completed primary education. Poor countries differ, however, in whether attending school ensures access to quality education. Vietnam does particularly well in bringing disadvantaged children up to the required educational level, perhaps due to their concern with teacher qualifications and a centralized teacher training system (Woodhead et al., 2014).

NGOs such as UNICEF expend considerable efforts to ameliorate the situation where many of the world's children do not have access to school. For example, a decade-long partnership between UNICEF and

ING (a Dutch multinational bank) was recently renewed, and their work has resulted in access to education being improved for a million children due to the partnership (UN Children's Fund, 2015). Their projects include addressing the problem that 37,622 girls in India were not attending school because school was too far away or on a road too dangerous to travel. The partnership resulted in setting up 720 education centers and provision of resources and teacher training in 3,000 primary schools in remote areas. Similar projects in Ethiopia and Zambia successfully increased children's participation in school, so large-scale macropolicies are needed to get children into school in poor countries.

For schools in developed Western countries, the problem is not so much ability to access school, but to equity, social justice, and quality education within school. All children should experience a quality education that maximizes their opportunity to learn, but there is a large achievement gap for poor children compared to middle-class children. "The 'gap' is not restricted to one society (e.g. USA or New Zealand) or to one type of society (e.g. English-speaking); it occurs in every developed society. Students with good family resources out-perform those without" (Snook & O'Neill, 2010, p. 4). The ability and attitudes that students bring to school from their families and communities influence their educational progress. Schools, however, can make a difference to diminishing that gap, depending on how they allocate their resources and develop pedagogy that responds to individual and cultural differences.

The existence of achievement gaps is part of the wider problem of inequality identified by Wilkinson & Pickett (2010). The more unequal the society, the wider the gap, and the greater the demand and pressure on schools to reduce the gap. It is therefore unreasonable to expect teachers and schools on their own to eliminate unequal outcomes, which requires a more holistic focus on reducing poverty and social and economic inequalities. The United States has almost a quarter of children living in poverty, while in Finland only 5 percent are, and the United States has quadruple the rate of poverty of the Nordic countries (Ravitch, 2013). New Zealand also has a high (and increasing) rate of child poverty, two and a half times as high as the Nordic countries and higher than the UK (Boston & Chapple, 2014). The countries with the smallest achievement gaps, such as Finland and the Netherlands, do more to support early childhood education, health, and well-being of children and families, and to reduce inequalities in income.

Snook and O'Neill (2010) argue that schools can and do make a difference but that there are limitations to how much of a difference they can make. They argue that the answer to the achievement gap does not just lie with schools.

A focus on achievement and the use of progress data to target instruction are certainly needed but there also have to be deeper changes in the culture of the school: involvement of parents and community, professional development of teachers, improvements in the selection and training of teachers, the involvement of other professionals in the school (counselors, doctors, nurses, social workers) and education of parents as well as children. These together can make a difference to the learning achievement of students from relatively deprived backgrounds and such educational policies should be encouraged. (Snook & O'Neill, 2010, p. 15)

In a review of research on overcoming the socioeconomic achievement gap in schools in the United States, Barbarin & Aikens (2015) suggest that the poorest students frequently attend schools that lack resources, and are unable to provide learning environments that are likely to lift the academic achievement of poor children. Schools can to some extent compensate for family disadvantage, but unfortunately poor children are more likely to attend struggling schools catering for large numbers of low-income children, and being in these schools can compound rather than reduce the gap. According to Barbarin & Aikens, teacher beliefs and expectations about students' ability to learn are just as important as qualifications in increasing student achievement. Teachers in low-income U.S. schools were found to have less training and experience, and to hold less favorable beliefs and expectations about their students' abilities. They concluded that inequalities arose out of differential teaching loads, lack of teacher experience, and unfavorable expectations of students. Class size had a greater impact on the achievement of poor students than it did for middle-class students. The authors advocate creating professional learning communities where teachers problem solve and share strategies; team teaching is used; there is provision of teaching assistants; flexible instructional grouping is used; and individual and small group instruction is used, including community volunteers. They are critical of the blame and lack of support for teachers in these difficult schools, which often leads to teacher burnout and increased student problems.

The achievement gap is not just a socioeconomic gap, however, but an ethnic one, because differences in academic achievement between white American and African American and Latino children have existed for many years (Nelson, Palonsky, & McCarthy, 2007), just as in New Zealand there are long-standing achievement gaps between indigenous Māori and pakeha children (Bishop, Berryman, Cavanagh, & Teddy, 2009). Inequality of educational opportunity for different ethnic groups stems from a variety of racist policies some direct and overt, and others subtle and covert. Overt discrimination restricted African American children to attending segregated schools, and Māori children were punished for using their own language, in the nineteenth and early twentieth centuries. But covert monocultural and racist discourses of language and cultural deprivation still exist, blaming educational "deficits" on children's limited family backgrounds. The language deficit model is a victim-blaming approach, explaining lack of educational success as due to the inability of families to prepare children for school.

That it is possible for schools to change their monocultural and racist discourses about underachievement of minority cultural groups was demonstrated in the research of Russell Bishop and his colleagues in New Zealand (Bishop & Berryman, 2006; Bishop et al., 2009). Teachers in Bishop's study explained Māori students' lack of school success as due to family deficiencies, and teachers had lower expectations of Māori students, perceiving them as unmotivated and uninterested in learning, and teachers were not knowledgeable about or sympathetic to children's cultural backgrounds. For example, a teacher said:

Well they [Māori] lack good models at home—too much alcohol and weed, too many late nights—they lack the desire to come to school. You hear the parents talking about how much time and money is being wasted on their schooling. They talk about they should leave school and get a job .... They are disorganized. So are their families. They lack acceptable social skills. (Secondary school teacher, Bishop & Berryman, 2006, p. 218)

Students described how teachers' interactions with them made them feel, resulting in them internalizing the messages, and alienating them from school.

When you play up you get withdrawn from class. Yeah. You get sent out. Sometimes it's not your fault, but you don't get a chance to tell your side until you get to the deputy principal. So you tell your story and are allowed back, but you're shamed out. It's stink. (Student, p. 11)

People think Māori don't know how to behave. People think Māori are dumb. People think you're like your brother or sister, so if they were bad you will be bad; if they were good, you should always do better than you do. (Student, p. 11)

Bishop's research involved intervention through comprehensive professional development for teachers, using on-site school educational facilitators. The facilitators worked closely with teachers and engaged them in critical reflection based on the narratives of the students, teachers, and families, and introducing culturally sensitive pedagogies such as *manaakitanga* (reciprocal hospitality and respect) and *kotahitanga* (collaborative response to a community vision). There was a focus on engaging children in dialogue in a caring climate and a more collaborative approach to learning. The project resulted in marked changes in teacher practice, which were sustained over time, and improved student outcomes. A key aspect of the success of the program was the development of good relationships between students and teachers, which enhanced children's engagement with learning. The following is an example of a student's response to the program.

> I used to wag a lot of classes and stuff like that, but [now] I found that you come to school, and be yourself but learn at the same time too, and like I have achieved heaps, like I got my first merit in maths and my first excellence in cooking and I achieved a merit in science. (Bishop et al., 2009, p. 736)

Respecting children's cultural identity and values is a right asserted in Article 29(c) of the UNCRC, and research demonstrates that respecting it contributes to the wider goal of developing children's ability and talents to their fullest potential (Article 29a). Teachers, who understand the power of deficit discourses to undermine student motivation and achievement and make efforts to work from a culturally sensitive stance, are much better equipped to implement children's educational rights (Bishop, Berryman, Wearmouth, Peter, & Clapham, 2012).

4.2   PROTECTING CHILDREN FROM VIOLENCE AT SCHOOL

Article 19 of the UNCRC says that children should be protected from all forms of physical or mental violence, injury, abuse, or maltreatment, and this includes at school while children are under the care and authority of teachers. I will talk about two forms of violence at school in this section— corporal punishment used as a means of discipline, and bullying between peers.

Corporal punishment: As I have discussed in Chapter 2, corporal punishment is a grievous violation of children's rights, an assault on their dignity, and a direct invasion of their physical integrity (Newell, 2011). General Comment No. 1 (United Nations Committee on the Rights of the Child, 2001) says that corporal punishment is a direct violation of children's rights, and in many Concluding Comments on country reports the UN committee has been highly critical of legislation that permits corporal punishment either at home or at school.

Many countries have enacted legislation to abolish the use of corporal punishment, most often at first in schools, and then later in homes. In May 2015, 124 countries had prohibited the use of physical punishment in school, and 74 had no such legislation (47 countries now have *complete* prohibition of physical punishment including at home) (Global Initiative to End All Corporal Punishment of Children, 2015). The picture is somewhat complicated in countries with a federal or provincial structure. All states in Australia except Queensland and Western Australia have prohibited corporal punishment in schools. In Canada, a 2004 Supreme Court ruling instituted prohibition in schools. It is not clear whether these prohibitions apply to private as well as public schools, however. In the UK, abolition of corporal punishment was achieved in state schools in 1987 and extended to private schools in England and Wales in 1999, in Scotland in 2000, and in Northern Ireland in 2003 (Owen, 2011). In New Zealand, corporal punishment was abolished in all schools in 1989 (Taylor, Wood, & Smith, 2011).

A recent publication (Gershoff, Purtell, & Holas, 2015) gives a disturbing picture of the extent of corporal punishment in schools in the United States. In 19 U.S. states, corporal punishment in schools is still legal: Alabama, Arizona, Arkansas, Colorado, Florida, Georgia, Idaho, Indiana, Kansas, Kentucky, Louisiana, Mississippi, Missouri, North Carolina, South Carolina, Oklahoma, Tennessee, Texas, and Wyoming. Most of these states are in the South, where it is socially acceptable to use violence as a means of social control. While the overall rate of corporal punishment has dropped sharply in the United States between 1976 and 2006, it still seems quite high, considering that so many other countries have banned the practice in schools more than two decades ago. Gershoff et al. report that corporal punishment in U.S. schools is not a "last resort" practice for serious misbehavior but is commonly used for minor child misbehavior.

During the years from 2009 to 2010, a total of 218,466 American students were disciplined with corporal punishment, a rate of 5 out of every 1,000 students annually. Mississippi physically punished the highest proportion of students—8 in 1,000—and the lowest (0) was in Wyoming (this is within the states where corporal punishment is legal). The type of corporal punishment used in schools seems a lot harsher than that typically administered by parents. For example, in Alabama, the type of implement used to administer corporal punishment, is carefully defined, and it is also specified that it should consist of three licks to the buttocks:

> The instrument used in corporal punishment should be wisely selected. A wooden paddle approximately 24 inches in length, 2 inches wide and ½ inch thick is recommended. Paddles with holes, cracks, splinters, tape or other foreign material shall not be used for corporal punishment. (Pickens Board of Education 2014, p. 27, cited by Gershoff et al., 2015)

Other implements used in schools for corporal punishment include a belt, a shoe, a lacrosse stick, a baseball bat, an arrow, a rubber hose, a yardstick, a broomstick, a 10-foot board, a hammer, and a metal pipe! (Gershoff et al., 2015)

Schools which use corporal punishment are significantly more likely to be in states with large proportions of children living in poverty, large proportions of black children, in less educated populations, and where there are more single parent families. Boys were almost three and a half (3.43) times as likely to be corporally punished than girls in 2006, although this disparity has decreased markedly from 1976 (when the ratio was 5 to 1). On the other hand, the disparity by race has increased over time, with blacks being just over twice as likely (2.19) to be corporally punished than whites in 2006 (1.92 times more likely in 1976). Disabled students who constitute 14 percent of U.S. students received 19 percent of the physical punishment. There was an odds ratio of 1.37 disabled students receiving physical punishment to every disabled student in 2006 (Gershoff et al., 2015). Worryingly, the physical punishment was often given for behaving as a result of the symptoms of disabilities. One grandmother from Georgia described the injuries received by her five-year-old autistic granddaughter:

> You could see the bruising. Her whole arm was swollen by the time she got to the emergency room. Her right arm. The doctor said it looked like she's been hit by a baseball bat or been in a motorcycle accident. That's the only time he'd seen injuries like that ... To this day I have no idea what they hit her with ... The human hand doesn't have that kind of strength. (Human Rights Watch and ACLU, 2009, p. 19, cited by Gershoff et al., 2015, p. 33)

Many children in the United States are therefore having their rights to be protected from violence at school by teachers violated, and children with some characteristics are more likely to be singled out for punishment than others. Apart from the violation of rights entailed in these practices, the small amount of research on physical punishment in school and the large amount of research in the home suggests that there are some very undesirable consequences. An example of school research (Talwar et al., 2011 cited Gershoff et al., 2015, p. 38) carried out in West Africa compared two schools, one of which had a high incidence of corporal punishment (40 per day) with one that did not use it. Children in the school without corporal punishment had higher vocabulary and executive functioning scores and more intrinsically motivated behavior. Corporal punishment has in other research (see Durrant, 2011; Durrant & Ensom, 2012; Gershoff & Bitensky, 2008) been shown to be associated with many negative outcomes for children including poorer achievement, increased aggression, more mental health problems, and lower levels of moral internalization. Moreover, corporal punishment has been repeatedly shown to be ineffective, partly because it causes physical pain confusing and frightening children, models aggression as a way of dealing with problems, does not teach children why they behaved inappropriately or what they should do instead, and interferes with children's ability to internalize messages about discipline.

In reality, corporal punishment increases problem behaviors and the chances of violence in the wider community. Murray Straus (1996) found that the number of homicides is greater in countries that use corporal punishment. There is therefore no justification for its use at school, either from a rights or research perspective. Children already at risk from poverty and disability, or who come from minority ethnic groups, are more likely to be physically punished; this denies their human rights and discriminates against them. In countries where corporal punishment is still permitted, public and professional education about more effective forms of discipline and the negative impact that it has on outcomes for children are essential. Use of corporal punishment in schools is a sign of an abject failure in morality and justice and incompetence in educating young people.

Bullying at school: Another form of violence (not always physical) prevalent at school is bullying.

A student is being bullied or victimized when he or she is exposed, repeatedly and over time, to negative actions on the part of one or more other students .... It is a negative action, when someone intentionally inflicts, or attempts to inflict, injury or discomfort upon another .... Negative actions can be carried out by words (verbally), for instance, by threatening, taunting, teasing and calling names. It is a negative action when somebody hits, pushes, kicks, pinches or restrains another by physical contact. (Olweus, 1993, p. 9)

The difference between bullying and aggression is that bullying is carried out repeatedly and over time and involves a power imbalance between bully and victim. The perpetrators can be individuals or groups, and the victims can be one person or several. There are many kinds of bullying including physical—hitting, kicking, pinching, hair pulling; verbal—insults, name calling, derogatory judgments, or social—malicious gossip, exclusion, inviting others to torment an individual (Meadows, 2010). There has been very little research about children's perspectives on being bullied, but a Swedish researcher talked to young people about bullying. One student said:

School was hell too. Bullied, everything from words, to rumors, to beatings and knife threats. I have swapped schools several times, but they are closely located, and therefore the problems continue, when there are contacts between schools. In other words, the bullies knew people in the new schools, so it simply continued. (Anonymous child, Osvaldsson, 2011, p. 320)

Technology has now made bullying online or by mobile phone very easy to do, and much more difficult to monitor. Schools are a common (but not only) site of bullying, and a great deal of it can take place away from the gaze of the teacher, in playgrounds or through e-mails, chat rooms, texts, or the creation of websites targeted at particular students (Campbell, 2005). Schools that allow the misery that results from bullying to occur are violating a fundamental right for children to be safe at school, as well as their right to have a good quality education. Permitting this practice also lays the groundwork for future mental health problems such as suicide and depression. Research clearly shows that schools can make a difference in reducing the rates of bullying in school, and that the attitudes, routines, and behavior of the staff are a key influence:

Many adults have underestimated the significant social, emotional, and academic cost of bullying and overestimated the ability of victimized children to stop bullying without assistance from adults. It is common to find a handful of naysayers in any given school. Although the attitudes of some of these adults may be swayed by time and education, efforts to introduce and sustain a comprehensive bullying prevention programme may be doomed if the majority of school staff do not believe that bullying is a serious issue. (Olweus & Limber, 2010, p. 130)

Early estimates of bullying were carried out in Norway in 1983, where out of a sample of 130,000 students, 15 percent of students in elementary and lower secondary schools were regularly involved in bully or victim problems. By 2001, the percentage of victimized students in Norway had increased by 50 percent, and the most serious form of bullying had increased by 65 percent (Olweus & Limber, 2010). An international survey of 11- to 15-year-olds in 40 countries (Craig et al., 2009) showed that 26 percent of adolescents had been regularly involved in bullying, 10.7 percent as bullies only, 12.6 percent as victims only, and 3.6 percent as bullies and victims. The rates of bullying varied greatly between different countries, with the lowest being Sweden (8.6 percent of boys and 4.8 percent of girls), and the highest being Lithuania (45.2 percent of boys and 35.8 percent of girls). The English speaking countries of the United States, Canada, and England were in the middle, with the United States ranking 21st out of 40 for the rate of bullying for boys (22.2 percent reported it) and 17th for girls (16.6 percent reported it); Canada ranking 20th for boys and 15th for girls, and England ranking 28th for boys and 23rd for girls. Generally speaking, the Scandinavian countries had low bullying rates, and the Eastern European countries had high rates. Countries with low rates had national programs in place to address bullying, whereas countries with high prevalence had no national initiatives.

Cyber bullying through the Internet or mobile phones is a pervasive form of bullying which can preserve the anonymity of perpetrators and give more power to them (Cappadocia, Craig, & Pepler, 2013). While it is often associated with (or follows from) traditional forms of bullying, it can have a broader impact than other forms of bullying because hurtful messages can be sent to a large number of peers in seconds. Prevalence levels of cyber bullying are high, with some estimates suggesting that as many as one in four children are bullied through the Internet (Campbell, 2005; Williams & Guerra, 2007). Victimization rates ranged between 20 percent and 40 percent, and perpetration rates range widely from 5 percent to 35 percent across studies, while dual involvement in both cyber bullying and cyber victimization ranges from 3 percent to 14 percent (Tokunaga, 2010, cited by Cappadocia et al., 2013, p. 172). Cyber bullying is associated with many harmful effects on victims, such as hyperactivity, conduct problems, and physical symptoms. A Canadian longitudinal study showed that risk factors associated with cyber bullying, included higher levels of antisocial behavior such as excessive drinking, and fewer prosocial peer influences (Cappadocia et al., 2013). It is a particularly difficult form of bullying to prevent, since it can be largely invisible to teachers. Increasing the awareness and empathy for bullied students and fostering greater trust and cohesion among students can be used to combat cyber bullying (Williams & Guerra, 2007).

School-based antibullying programs in Norway have resulted in reduction in bullying rates of up to 50 percent, as a result of significant government funding to address this serious problem. Six large-scale studies in Norway have shown that more than 2,000 students have escaped from bullying due to intervention (Olweus & Limber, 2010). The Olweus Bullying Prevention Program (OBPP) was designed to reduce existing bullying, prevent future problems, and improve peer relationships. Adults were expected to show warmth and positive interest in students, set firm limits to nonacceptable behavior, use consistent nonhostile consequences for rule breaking, and be positive role models for children. The program includes school-level components (such as staff training and rule setting); classroom-level components such as rule dissemination and weekly class meetings; individual-level components such as staff supervision and intervention; and community-level components such as school–community partnerships and spreading of antibullying messages.

The program has been highly successful in Norway and has been implemented in about a quarter of schools. In the United States, however, there have been more difficulties in implementing the OBPP, where it is used in about 4 percent of schools. Dan Olweus and Susan Limber (2010) found that U.S. schools were often looking for a "quick fix," tending to cherry pick those aspects of the program that were thought to be easier to implement, because there were time and school organization constraints. Important elements, such as time for training and on-going professional development, were often not carried out. Despite many states having laws requiring bullying prevention policies, the ones used were frequently not research or evidence-based. The authors conclude that in order to achieve better implementation, schools need to understand the problem and its long-term consequences, be motivated to implement prevention programs, and have the resources to do so.

One method of preventing bullying that has been effective in New Zealand has been to seek out examples of good practice taking place in schools, and disseminate them to a wider audience of teachers and school principals. Case studies in two New Zealand elementary schools and one intermediate (middle) school (Gaffney & Taylor, 2004) looked for the ingredients of effective bullying prevention programs in schools. Leadership by the principal played a key role in success, because principals initiated change to the school culture about bullying. They established a "big picture" of the extent of bullying in the school, shared it with school staff, and encouraged them to join in, and implement a school-wide strategy for improvement. Children were also part of the team who opposed bullying. A variety of strategies were used in the schools, with a particular emphasis on clear expectations and immediate and known consequences for bullying. Developing warm relationships among staff, among students, and between staff and students was essential. The schools also recognized that change could not come about by adult action alone, and that it was necessary to obtain student support and use students as a resource to bring about change. In one school, all children were taught peer mediation skills and some children given extra training as peer mediators. In another school, safety audits were carried out three times a year to monitor the level of violence. Students and staff in these schools had a vision that school should be a safe and caring place. Children played their part and knew what to do if they saw a bullying incident—either actively intervening or looking for adult help.

4.3   EXCLUSION FROM SCHOOL

> From a rights-based perspective, children and youth who are excluded from school experience fundamental violations of their human rights … the dominant discourse of punishment and sanctions for non-compliant behavior ignores students' voices and the questions of rights, and maintains a silence about the toxic impact of educational exclusion. (Baiyee et al., 2013, pp. 41–42)

The process of excluding children from school as a disciplinary measure is problematic from a children's rights perspective. Exclusion policies violate all four of the UNCRC principles and are part of a punitive discourse about consequences for children. Children are seen as problems in need of discipline, rather than respected as developing human beings with rights to education, justice, and the affirmation of their dignity. According to Baiyee and her colleagues, there has since 1994 been an unprecedented era of educational exclusion for millions of American children, so that they are denied access to education, often for minor offences such as fighting, bringing Midol (for menstrual cramps) to school, or for demonstrating a grandfather's Swiss army knife at Show and Tell in kindergarten. Similarly, English children have no right to be notified that they are to be excluded from school, no right of appeal, no right to appear before a review panel (Willow, 2015). Even in Wales, where the UNCRC has been enshrined in national legislation, children can be excluded from school for engaging in disruptive behavior, and several reports there (from NGOs, the inspectorate and government) have expressed concerns about excessive use of punitive rather than preventative approaches to discipline (McCluskey, Riddell, & Weedon, 2015). In Australia there is no national policy relating to school suspension and exclusion or guidance about ways of reintegrating students back into school, and policies vary depending on state, region, and district. The principal usually makes decisions on exclusion, students have no voice, and their parents are not able to support them if they are treated unfairly (Hemphill & Schneider, 2013).

Exclusion policies do not support the best interests of the child because they have many long-term negative outcomes for children, and they are discriminatory because poor children, disabled children, and children from minority racial groups are more likely to be excluded. Children's survival and development rights are diminished by exclusion, as it can lead to a downward spiral of dropout from education, unemployment, antisocial behavior, and even imprisonment. Children who are suspended are 2.2 times more likely to be incarcerated than nonsuspended students (Hemphill & Schneider, 2013).

The UNCRC principle of children's right to participate, to have a say, and to have their views taken into account, are seriously violated by exclusion and suspension processes. There is little indication of fairness through hearing children's explanations, or other procedures to ensure due process in the educational policies of most countries. Young people who were excluded from school in Baiyee et al.'s U.S. study, complained about not being listened to, of others making decisions about them without hearing from them, and of unfairness. Melanie, said:

> I mean, no matter what, the teacher or adult is always right and we wrong. I mean some kids are bad and they deserve what they get, you know ... fightin' and stuff over dumb boys or whatever. But little stuff like talking or wearing certain clothes isn't something you should get in trouble for. (Baiyee et al., 2013, p. 46)

Another girl, Jenny, who had been excluded from school for a year for being around a group of other children smoking marijuana, said:

It was really hard 'cause they don't care what we have to say. They think that they already know the situation so they don't care. Like, its kind of sad that they can't hear from all of us ... I think I was treated unfairly by the school board ... and they already had their minds made up that they were going to expel all of us. (Baiyee et al., 2013, p. 48)

In many cases, children who are excluded or suspended, face major barriers in re-enrolling in school, as other schools will not accept them, they are often never able to return to school, and alternative educational provisions are not always available. Baiyee et al. report that hundreds of thousands of American youth are cast out into the street from school, as in many education districts there are few alternative education programs. Once excluded, these young people (usually from disadvantaged backgrounds) are at further risk for alienation, future antisocial behavior and alcohol or drug use (Hemphill & Schneider, 2013). This has been described as part of "the criminalization of children" (Baiyee et al., 2013, p. 40).

Another very concerning aspect of school exclusion policies is that they discriminate against children and young people with disabilities and of minority ethnic status. U.S. statistics (Rich, 2012, cited by Baiyee et al., p. 43) showed that students with disabilities are twice as likely to be suspended as nondisabled students, and that in 10 states 25 percent of African American students with disabilities were suspended in 2009 to 2010. Students from the United States and the UK who are excluded or suspended are also more likely to belong to an ethnic minority, be poor, and be male (Hemphill & Schneider, 2013).

When asked about possible solutions, students in Baiyee's study recommended that students be listened to at school, that conflict resolution processes be introduced, and that students should be encouraged to stay at school. Reducing class size, improving training for teachers to work with students at risk, additional support for students such as mentoring programs, building trusting relationships between schools and parents, moving away from a climate of competition between schools, and targeting policies to reduce school exclusion, are other suggested solutions (Hemphill & Schneider, 2013).

An innovative Australian project being applied in 36 Victorian schools entitled Hands on Learning (HOL), is a preventative approach providing enabling spaces for students at risk of leaving school, while they remain at school and as part of their regular schooling experience (O'Donovan, Berman, & Wierenga, 2015). HOL uses cross-age teams of two HOL artisan-teachers working with 10 students on creative construction projects at school and in the local community, for one day every week. In one project, teams built a hut and pizza oven at their high school. The teams work on building respectful relationships, fostering a sense of belonging in students, encouraging and developing self-efficacy, and helping students to develop a sense of purpose. Students and teachers work together on meaningful projects where they collaborate with others, solve problems, and can take control and initiative. The projects help children connect the learning they encounter in class with the real world, and maintain their connection with mainstream school. This is an example of a creative solution to the issue of disruptive or disengaged students, which respects their rights, recognizes and builds on their strengths, and avoids the negative consequences of exclusion from school.

4.4   DISCRIMINATION AT SCHOOL

School can be a context for all kinds of exclusionary or discriminatory practices that marginalize some children and prevent them from engaging in opportunities that are open to other children. Discrimination can be based on a variety of child characteristics—ethnicity, sexuality, religion, life style, or disability, for example. I will focus on discrimination based on disability in this section. Disability is the product of interactions between individual characteristics (including impairment) and the social and cultural context (Read, Blackburn, & Spencer, 2012). The UNCRC has many articles relevant to disabled children. Article 23 states that disabled children have the right to a decent life and to dignity and independence. The familiar Articles 2, 3, 6, 28, and 29, say that like all children, disabled children have a right not to be discriminated against, to survival and development, to have their best interests catered for, and to have access to a quality education that allows them to reach their full potential. Another UN treaty, the UN Convention on the Rights of Disabled People (United Nations Convention on the Rights of Persons with Disabilities, 2007) advocates inclusive education, the importance of voice and participation for disabled people, the availability of alternative communication techniques like sign language, and the removal of physical and social barriers.

Disabled children face barriers (both social and impairment-related) at school, and these have to be overcome before disabled children can be fully included in school communities. Disability can be overemphasized and children can become the objects of intervention and interactions based on "fixing" their disability, with often harmful effects (Kelly, 2005). Disabled children are constructed as vulnerable victims of their impairment, but they like other children, are active agents interpreting their lives at school and negotiating problems. The language of special education is based on medical and psychological deficit models, assuming that disability is an individual problem that requires separate and different teaching. Yet, the outcomes of such practices are stigmatization through labeling and segregation, leading to alienation and student disengagement. There is, however, a fine line between denying challenges faced by disabled children and not stigmatizing them, since it is important not to compromise their access to resources and teaching that can support their learning (MacArthur, Sharp, Kelly, & Gaffney, 2007). Disability is only one part of children's identity, however, and as Berni Kelly (2005) explains, disabled children are children first, not just a disability.

One Australian school principal described a class segregated because of behavior problems:

> They grouped together as a small group. They got aggressive— wouldn't mix. They were embarrassed. They were shy. They were angry. They weren't learning. They were kids who, when they started an argument, they wanted to fight because they didn't understand the arguments. (Graham & Harwood, 2011, p. 136)

As a result of his dissatisfaction with the outcome of segregation, this principal disbanded the special classes and spread the students around other classes. He used the teachers of the segregated classes to supplement the other teachers and to reduce class size. Such regular school placements increase the likelihood of better outcomes for disabled children because they have access to a wider curriculum, richer environments for learning, and benefit from interaction with nondisabled peers (MacArthur, Kelly, & Higgins, 2005). Students without disabilities benefit from learning about diversity, and help teachers to be more versatile and confident about teaching diverse students, in collaboration with professionals. In order for inclusive practices to work, it is essential though, that teachers have positive attitudes toward disabled students, understand inclusive pedagogical approaches, and have access to resources and support. nondisabled peers need support too, to understand how to respond to disabled children, to act in ways that do not undermine disabled children's sense of belonging, and to respect diverse ways for their disabled peers to be part of a group (Rietveld, 2005).

In order to facilitate inclusion, attention has to be given to encouraging communication with disabled children, to elicit their views and hear their voice. Physical communication difficulties may impede communication, but adults and peers can take the trouble to learn how to communicate with disabled children. Kelly (2005) found that adults tended to underestimate disabled children's understanding and communication skills. Other barriers to inclusion are overprotection by worried adults; "dumbing-down" of the curriculum; assumptions of student incompetence; social isolation; and bullying. There can be physical barriers for students in wheelchairs. Sanderson (2011) gives an example of how secondary school children placed all their schoolbags on a wheelchair ramp, so that disabled children could not get into the weekly school assembly. Disabled students often have difficulty accessing physical spaces and activities that are culturally valued by other children at school. Teacher aides can be barriers to inclusion because their constant presence with disabled children differentiates them from other students and excludes them from many aspects of school life, including developing relationships with other children. One student described her aide as overprotective and constantly "on her case" while she would have preferred to do something different and have a bit more space (Rutherford, 2012, p. 767).

Schools can be more inclusive by reducing the categorization and marginalization of diverse students, modifying and adjusting school processes to accommodate diversity, and resist dumbing down the curriculum or lowering expectations for disabled students. Schools can work on a variety of ways to enhance disabled students' engagement and success, including upskilling teachers, since "they are the only ones with the power to modify the conditions of access" (Graham & Harwood, 2011, p. 149). Teachers can support disabled students in resisting discriminatory practices, by identifying, understanding, and denouncing any discourses and practices that legitimize educational exclusion (MacArthur, 2013). Listening to and prioritizing students' perspectives can help teachers to understand why disabled students are not able to join in with peers or feel excluded, and this can inform teachers, help remove barriers to participation, and lead to more respectful and inclusive approaches.

4.5 PARTICIPATION RIGHTS AT SCHOOL

Articles 12 and 13 of the UNCRC are pivotal to children's participation rights. Article 12 recognizes children's personality and autonomy and their right to be listened to and have their views taken into account. It affirms that children are not just objects of concern, but social actors with a right to play a part in decisions that affect them. Article 12 does not give children the right to complete autonomy or suggest that they should make decisions on their own, but it does mean that they should have an input. Article 13 says that children have the right to give and receive information, so they deserve explanations for decisions that affect them, and should be able to express their views. In schools where adult authority and power is absolute, participation rights are often ignored. Realizing children's participation rights at school helps children understand democratic processes, supports their sense of belonging and inclusion, and teaches them how to bring about change. Children come to believe in themselves as social actors who can improve the quality of their lives and those of others. Democratic processes and structures in school have a role in strengthening children's agency, identity, self-control, and independence. On the other hand, denial of these participation rights can lead to alienation, disempowerment, apathy, or hostility (Smith, 2007).

> The more children participate, the more effective their contributions, and the greater the impact on their development. Children acquire competence in direct relation to the scope available to them to exercise agency over their own lives. (Lansdown, Jimerson, & Shahroozi, 2014)

Lack of recognition of participation rights seems to be pervasive in schools in many countries (John, 2003; Osman, 2005; Peters & Lacy, 2013; Willow, 2015).

> [There are] ... dominant policies and practices in the United States to reify or perpetuate children's position as passive or peripheral participants within the systems of schooling, and ... [these] challenge commonly held assumptions about the capacities of children to contribute to the decisions made for and about their educational experiences. (Peters & Lacy, 2013, p. 117)

Talking to young people about their rights usually shows that they would like to have more of a say. We found that the majority (96 percent) of 721 New Zealand 16-year-old secondary students wanted to be allowed to express their opinion about things that affected them (such as choosing subjects, school camps, school trips, dress codes), but very few (13 percent) strongly agreed that there were opportunities to express their views, or that these were taken into account (7 percent) (Taylor, Smith, & Nairn, 2001). An English case study of two primary and two secondary schools found that children had strong views about their lack of participation. Formal mechanisms for eliciting children's views were absent at all of the schools. One child talked about a teacher phoning his mother and talking to her in a "nice" voice, but then shouting and speaking in a harsh tone to him (Wyse, 2001). In Australia, Osman (2005) found that children felt powerless and denigrated by humiliating punishments at school. Children wanted more control, to be respected by teachers, and to have a part in school policy and decision making. In Scotland, focus group discussions with 200 9- to 16-year-old children, revealed a dominant theme and consensus that children wanted more of a say on such issues as the curriculum, examinations, conditions at school, leisure opportunities, transport, financial decisions about school priorities and school organization (Stafford, Laybourn, Hill, & Walker, 2003).

> Instead of asking the parents, ask the children .... They were having this big debate about Section 28 and whether it should be taught in schools, and they never asked the children whether they wanted it taught or not/they asked the parents and teachers. (p. 363)

Schools can have a positive role in supporting children's participation rights, through creating openings and opportunities to hear children's voices, providing a school climate of respect for children's opinions, taking children's concerns seriously, and taking them into account in decision-making processes. The way that teachers talk to children and whether they have positive relationships with them, is a powerful aspect of school climate and one to which children are particularly sensitive. Formal school structures like student councils are important democratic account-able policy forums. In New Zealand, Boards of Trustees, the governing bodies for secondary schools, must by law include an elected student representative, who is supposed to have equal rights to the adult members of boards. This policy is an example of young people being given a genuine opportunity to exercise power and decision making (Smith, 2007).

Formal structures, even if they exist, however, do not always work effectively. Stafford et al. (2003) found that when secondary students had experienced consultation, it was often unsatisfactory because the students consulted were unrepresentative, and because student views were not acted on. As one child said: "If they're not going to do something, don't ask" (p. 365). Children may be disappointed and become cynical when nothing happens as a result of consultation. Members of school councils may be picked by adults, and are often seen as controlled by adult power. In order for consultation to work, children need "good preparation and clear information about the purpose, constraints and limitations of the consultation process" (Stafford et al., 2003, p. 372). In an evaluation of student representatives on Boards of Trustees in New Zealand, children reported being intimidated and overwhelmed by the power of other board members, within the context of one lone student member on an adult board. There were examples, however, where adult board members developed supportive relationships with student representatives, helping explain procedures and giving children encouragement to voice their views (Smith, 2007). Adults in education thus have a lot of power to give young people space and motivation to articulate what is important to them, either formally or informally.

It is important for children and teachers to be aware of children's rights, because it is unrealistic to expect rights to be respected if people do not know about them. It is stipulated in Article 42 of the UNCRC that countries should make the provisions of the convention widely known, and Article 29 asserts that education should include learning about human rights education. As educational institutions, schools have a particular responsibility to educate both teachers and children about human rights. In Wyse's study (2001), only one teacher in four schools was even aware of the UNCRC. While many schools espouse rhetoric of teaching about citizenship and civics education, there is very little sign that children are taught about children's rights, or that respect for children's citizenship is inherent in school processes.

A UK school program for year seven, eight, and nine children, entitled Rights Respecting Schools, promotes children's rights and helps schools "to model and respect rights in all relationships, including those between teachers and students and those between students" (Lansdown et al., 2014, p. 7). An evaluation of the program in 30 schools showed that it was associated with improved social relationships, behavior, and achievement among students. Students in schools who participated in this program were more respectful and helpful to others, less aggressive and disruptive, and more careful with school property such as books, desks, and equipment. Their critical thinking skills, self-regulation, motivation, and achievement also improved. One of the most encouraging findings was that the program became self-perpetuating over time, because of its continuing positive outcomes for teachers and students (Sebba & Robinson, 2010, cited by Lansdown et al., 2014, p. 7).

4.6 SUMMARY

Children spend much of their childhood in school, so it is the site of the realization or denial of many of their rights. School should be free and accessible to all children, and education should be child-friendly and broad ranging, empowering children, and nurturing their dignity and self-esteem. Children at school should be treated equitably, not be subjected to violence, unfair discipline, or discrimination, and should have their citizenship enhanced through being active participants in school life.

Many majority world children cannot attend school for reasons like poverty or geographic isolation. Most children in the minority world do have access to school, but there are persistent achievement gaps between poor and minority group children and middle-class children. Children of minority ethnicity are also less likely to succeed in school than their white counterparts. Education can, however, make a difference for disadvantaged children, when cultural awareness, pedagogy, and resources are modified appropriately.

One gross violation of children's rights is corporal punishment, a surprisingly common event in the United States, where research has demonstrated that children from disadvantaged backgrounds, minority ethnic groups, and those with disabilities, are more likely to experience it. Bullying is another source of school violence and a source of unhappiness, disengagement, and long-term negative outcomes (such as suicide and depression) for many children. School-wide efforts and programs are necessary to eliminate bullying.

School exclusion policies mean that many children are treated unfairly especially if they are poor, minority, or disabled. Exclusion often leads to a downward spiral, with children being unable to access other education, lacking skills to gain employment, and being drawn into antisocial and criminal activities. Programs that promote engagement in school and provide schoolwork with meaning and dignity can reduce school exclusion. Children with disabilities are at particular risk of not being fully included in school, and schools need to be aware of barriers to inclusion such as lack of physical access and attitudes that construct disabled children as vulnerable and incompetent.

Many schools are disrespectful of children's participation rights, and children have no space or opportunity to formulate and express their views, or have them taken into account. The implementation of human rights education in schools can make a positive difference for both students and staff at school, promoting many positive outcomes.

CHAPTER 5

CHILDREN'S RIGHTS IN CHILD PROTECTION SYSTEMS

the current child protection system objectifies the children whom it seeks to protect and the parents whom it accuses. The ostensible mission of the system is lost as children are treated as evidence and 'treatments' are designed to provide verification of parents' failures. In effect, a culture of caring is replaced by a culture of surveillance.

—(Melton, 2009, p. xii)

I'll say it to her but she doesn't listen to it. So like how I feel when I first tell her. I still feel it a month later, 2 months later, 6 weeks later, like 6 months later. So she doesn't really help. I feel that she doesn't even listen to me.

—(Kate, a 14 year-old complaining that her social worker had not arranged contact with her family, Barnes, 2012, p. 1283)

I had this worker ... she was great. You know, she really cared. And she listened to what I had to say. She wanted to know what I thought and said stuff like we could do this or we could do that, what do you want. But she was the only one.

—(The views of a young person about a worker, in Bessell, 2011, p. 498)

The UNCRC defines child abuse in Article 19 as "all forms of physical or mental violence, injury or abuse, neglect or negligent treatment, maltreatment or exploitation, including sexual abuse." While child abuse is difficult to define precisely, because of a diversity of cultural values and beliefs about child rearing, it is usually categorized as consisting of four main types (Munro, 2008). *Physical abuse* involves physically harming a child through hitting, shaking, throwing, burning, or other violent acts which cause a child bodily pain. *Emotional abuse* involves rejection, humiliation, arousing fear, or giving children messages that they are unwanted, unloved, worthless, or inadequate. *Sexual abuse* is forcing or enticing a child to be involved in sexual activities (including penetration, nonpenetration, inappropriate touching, looking at pornography, or behaving in sexually inappropriate ways). *Neglect* is failure to supply the child with the necessities of life, including food, shelter, and clothing, and protecting the child from danger. More generally, child abuse has been defined as any acts or failures to act, which impede children's healthy development (Munro, 2008).

Although there are cultural differences in what counts as abuse, there is usually agreement on a definition at the more severe end of the continuum, but at the lower end (particularly in relation to physical abuse) there is very little consensus on what constitutes abuse and what constitutes discipline. The UNCRC is, however, unequivocal that any form of physical punishment violates Article 19, and that even mild corporal punishment should not be permitted. Preventing physical punishment is essential to addressing child abuse (Freeman & Saunders, 2014).

Abuse is associated with a range of adverse consequences for children in the present and the future. These include behavior problems (such as noncompliance or aggression), attachment disorders, post-traumatic stress disorder, psychiatric problems (such as depression and suicide), poor educational achievement, criminal behavior, obesity, substance abuse, and precocious sexual knowledge and behavior (Berger & Shook Slack, 2014; Miller-Perrin & Perrin, 2013). Child abuse and neglect also result in costly negative outcomes for society at large, so that effective intervention can greatly reduce these costs.

The second paragraph of Article 19 says that states should set up procedures for the "prevention, identification, referral, investigation, treatment and follow-up of child maltreatment" (Article 19 [para 2], UNCRC, 1989), in other words, establish child protection systems (CPS). "Child protection" is a term that has been used since the 19th century to describe actions taken to protect children from abuse and neglect (Masson, 2009). All developed societies have some form of legislated and institutionalized CPS, to protect children from the harm caused by child abuse, thereby recognizing that children do have rights to be safe and to be cared for adequately within their families. Such systems usually involve notifications (by professionals or community members) of suspected abuse, investigations, a decision-making process about future plans for the child, sometimes resulting in removal from the birth family and placement in another family, or of additional monitoring and support for the family. In many cases (about two-thirds in the United States, according to Melton [2005a]), allegations of abuse are unsubstantiated by further investigation and no action is taken. It is an ongoing challenge for CPS to decide on the point at which action should be taken, in response to concerns about the safety of children (Masson, 2009).

This chapter examines how CPS respect children's rights generally, not just their right to be protected from abuse. Supporting children's rights within CPS is a challenging task. Privacy within the family is sacrosanct within liberal democratic countries, so the state usually avoids intervening unless it is deemed to be absolutely necessary. The rights of parents to have control of children are often pitted against children's rights. Wendy Stainton Rogers (2009, p. 152–53) argues that the very idea that children have rights within the family can "touch a very raw nerve when it puts adult decisions and actions to the test." Yet children are vulnerable within families, especially when there is a context of isolation, poverty, single parenthood, or lack of support from wider family and community networks. Once intervention has occurred, if children are removed from home (or even if they remain), they are subjected to the actions and attitudes of a variety of stakeholders. These stakeholders include birth parents and extended family members, foster parents (or residential caregivers), social workers, and legal professionals, such as lawyers and judges (and the system and policies that control their roles). Teachers, health professionals, psychologists, police officers, social workers, judges, and lawyers are some of the varied professions that impact on how children's rights are respected within CPS. Another major resource or hindrance is the community within which children and their families live—either while within their birth families or while in state care. It is important that all of these individuals and systems are sensitive to and instrumental in realizing, children's rights to:

- be protected from physical and mental violence (Article 19);
- be provided with special protection if they have been deprived of a family environment (Article 20);
- have decisions made in their best interests (Article 3);
- not be discriminated against (Article 2);
- survival and development (Article 6);
- have an adequate standard of living which supports their development (Article 27);
- have the opportunity to have a say in decisions that affect them (Article 12);

- privacy (Article 16);
- be allowed to express their views and to receive and impart information (Article 13);
- the highest possible standards of health care (Article 24); and
- access education which results in the fullest development of their potential (Articles 28 and 29).

The responsibility for ensuring that these rights are balanced and implemented falls to the many stakeholders whose decisions and actions within CPS, impact on children. While decisions about children living at home are usually made by one or two adults that the child knows well and has a relationship with, decisions for children in CPS are often made by a larger number of adults including parents, caregivers, workers from one or more agencies, judges, magistrates, and lawyers, who do not know and may not even have met the child (Cashmore, 2002).

5.1 DISCOURSES OF RISK AND VULNERABILITY

A discourse is "a whole set of interconnected ideas that work together in a self-contained way; ideas that are held together by a particular ide-ology or view of the world" (Stainton-Rogers, 2009). Discourses of risk and vulnerability tend to predominate in the child protection field. This may have the effect of focusing on children's protection rights, to the detriment of concern for their other rights, particularly participation rights. A discourse of vulnerability is informed by psychological theories that stress children's lack of rationality, dependency, and need for protec-tion. Such discourses can have the effect of reducing children to being the objects of treatment or intervention, not recognizing their agency, de-skilling them as unable to contribute to their own safety, and restricting their privacy and freedom. It is important therefore that child protection professionals take a balanced view of the rights of children, and do not allow their concerns for safety to overwhelm other rights issues.

Most children and young people have no idea about the information that is stored on files about them and, because they are not considered to be citizens until they are 18 years old, they have no capacity to have any influence at this level [government activity and welfare health policy]. And, yet, it is interesting to contemplate the potential erosion of their rights when the state promotes a wholesale categorization of their lives from birth to adulthood—in the interests of their safety and well being! (Lonne, Parton, Thomson, & Harries, 2009, p. 10)

It is often unrecognized that children are not merely the dependent objects of abuse but are social actors in their lives and have some control over them. Judith Masson (2009) points out that growing up is about taking increasing responsibility for self, including learning about risks and how to avoid them. Being in a system where they have no power or voice in authoritarian families, institutions, or systems, militates against children acquiring coping strategies and learning to take care of themselves. Living in a climate of risk and vulnerability can create a moral panic leading to the impression of a breakdown in social order, and a climate of fear. When children's safety is always the focus of public attention, it is difficult to retain a sense of perspective, and recognize children's agency and self-efficacy (Boothby et al., 2012; Kennedy, 2010). Andrew Kennedy argues that the tendency to treat individuals as helpless victims results in:

a sense of powerlessness which is accentuated by societal changes which have led to a loss of social solidarity .... In these circumstances people become vulnerable to claims of every alleged new danger, and their belief in their own powerlessness leads them to demand that someone in "authority" do something to protect them. (Kennedy, 2010, p. 77)

Discourses of vulnerability and risk therefore tend to decrease children's resilience, by denying them the agency, support, and resources to challenge or resist abuse. I am not suggesting that they can do this alone, because a social context which recognizes children's competence, listens to children, and gives them space and encouragement to communicate about their experiences, is essential to empower them and realize their participation rights.

5.2   CHILD PROTECTION SYSTEMS

The social welfare and legal structures that characterize CPS are part of the macrosystem of ecological influences that indirectly impact on the rights and well-being of children. The laws, policies, and decision-making processes within CPS, influence the way that professionals fulfill their roles, develop relationships and interact with families and children, and how they approach families and children when abuse is alleged or suspected. CPS are set up in order to protect children from abuse, but many critics have argued that the typical Western model of child protection may actually be ineffective and diminish the safety of children (Featherstone, Morris, & White, 2014; Lonne et al., 2009; Melton, 2005b; O'Donnell, Scott, & Stanley, 2008; Scott, 2006).

What is considered to constitute abuse and neglect, and what laws and policies are in place to address these issues, differ considerably among countries. According to Berger and Shook Slack (2014), there are three primary processes that take place within CPS:

- Reporting
- Screening, assessment and investigation
- Service provision and disposition

State laws, regulations, and policies set out how a child abuse report should be made, and to which agency, and whether it is mandatory to report cases of child abuse or neglect. Following a report, there are processes which control screening procedures, the information that is collected, and what is considered to be the threshold to trigger further investigation of abuse or of family's needs. When severe maltreatment is detected at the investigation stage, police and law enforcement agencies may become involved, though this is not common (Berger & Shook Slack, 2014). After assessment and investigation decisions are made, authorities may take no further action, refer families for voluntary participation in services or offer support, or mandate intervention (most commonly through out-of-home placement). In some countries perpetrators of abuse are placed on child maltreatment registries.

As well as systems to detect and intervene in cases of child abuse, most developed countries have policies that take a preventative approach to abuse and neglect. Efforts to prevent abuse "include media campaigns, community-level interventions, school-based prevention programs, parenting skills and other services provided by local agencies, and home-visiting and other in-home services" (Berger & Shook Slack, 2014). CPS vary on a continuum from a narrow focus on protecting children from abuse and neglect, to a broader focus on promoting child and family well-being. Berger and Shook Slack point out that most governments have considerable coercive powers to intervene in cases of abuse or neglect, and compel family compliance. Moreover, they argue that, even in countries that focus more on family welfare, child protections systems have in recent years included more focus on child safety and protection, and have established formal, legalized processes to ensure it.

Countries fall into three categories along the continuum proposed by Berger and Shook: a relatively narrow focus on child safety and protection; a mixed or hybrid focus on both safety or protection and child and family well-being; and a relatively holistic focus on child and family well-being. The Anglo countries, including Australia, Canada, Ireland, Israel, United Kingdom, and the United States, fall into the first category with a narrow focus where most resources are put into investigation and protection. New Zealand falls into the hybrid category along with France, Germany, Japan, Italy, Poland, and Spain. Belgium, Denmark, Finland, the Netherlands, Norway, and Sweden are countries that take a more holistic approach putting the most emphasis on family support. Countries that take the more narrow approach, concentrate on identifying children and families who have abused their children or are at high risk of abusing them. They tend to be characterized by mandatory reporting followed by authoritarian, coercive, legalistic investigations, and are more likely to engage in involuntary removal of children from homes. On the child and family end of the continuum, a more holistic approach to child and family welfare is taken, with the emphasis on providing support for all children and families, and universal and widespread provision of benefits and services. The mixed approach in the middle of the continuum contains features of both the narrow and holistic approaches. Countries that have adopted a holistic approach generally have the lowest child poverty rates and score higher on most measures of child well-being (Berger & Shook Slack, 2014).

Child protection experts have become increasingly concerned about countries with high levels of bureaucracy and a narrow targeted approach, about the failure of these "managerialist" systems to achieve their mission. Such systems, according to Lonne et al. (2009), have become "toxic" environments for managers, staff, families, children and communities, and are unsustainable in their present form. Their failure is due to the gradual expansion of their "core business" of identifying abuse, pressures from a variety of stakeholders, and a "blame culture." The problems with the approach have included: unacceptably high levels of error in identifying abused children (false positive and negatives), lack of capability to provide necessary assistance to disadvantaged families, preoccupation with surveillance and investigation, negative life experiences and outcomes for children in care, huge personal costs for staff, and increasing financial costs of running the systems. Such managerialist approaches, based on business culture, have reshaped power and responsibility in CPS, so that managers are very powerful, and professional staff are relatively powerless with little chance to use judgment and personal skills, in the face of performance criteria and accountability measures.

We contend that across most Western nations, but not all, the contemporary dominance of neoconservative social attitudes and neoliberal values that steer social welfare (workfare) has led to a blaming, punitive and socially divisive ideology prevailing, leaving little room for notions of social care as opposed to social control .... The social mission for social welfare and, in particular, child protection has come to act as a surveillance system upon those sections of the community who are perceived as dangerous, troublesome or dependent—groups such as the poor, single-parents who are mainly women, people of color, and other minority racial groupings, indigenous people, and those with disabilities. (Lonne et al., 2009)

Gary Melton (2005b) has been particularly critical of one feature of narrowly targeted systems in the United States, the use of mandatory reporting, to identify abusive families. He has been dismissive of the notion that abusive families are "either very sick or very evil" (p. 11), and that they are somehow fundamentally different from normal families. He says that the factors that are related to child abuse are directly linked to the ability to cope with poverty. Maltreatment, he says, usually occurs in the context of multiple serious social, personal and economic problems. The deluge of reporting of suspected abuse by the community actually diminishes the safety of children, because families who need help, are instead subjected to evidence gathering and preparation for court cases. Concern for children's safety is diminished as "workers spend their time checking off boxes in regard to parental conduct" (p. 13–14). Rather than focusing on what they can do to help, workers are focused on finding out what happened. The majority of the cases investigated do not substantiate abuse, and even when abuse is substantiated, a considerable proportion of the families receive no service other than the investigation. In addition the threat of reporting and investigation actually discourages families from seeking help. Even when cases are substantiated, there are many cases when no further services are provided (Miller Perrin & Perrin, 2013). For example child protection services offered no further services to 40 percent of substantiated cares in the United States in 2003.

Similar problems have developed in Australia and New Zealand, where child protection services have been described by Dorothy Scott (2006, p. 1) as "demoralized, investigation-driven bureaucracies which trawl through escalating numbers of low-income families to find a small minority of cases in which statutory intervention is necessary and justifiable, leaving enormous damage in their wake." She argues that when the State becomes a parent, it is unable to perform the functions of a family, or draw on the diminishing resource of extended family or community to care for children. She describes CPS as being overwhelmed by a flood of notifications most of which (four out of five in Australia and six out of seven in New Zealand) are not substantiated. Overloaded systems are dangerous, according to Scott, because they are either too slow or too hasty and superficial, resulting in poor decision making and premature closure of cases. It becomes impossible to help families where children are at risk because the level of risk does not meet the threshold for state intervention. Families are denied the assistance that may prevent abuse or neglect. Overloaded systems are also harmful to those who work in them leading to low morale and high staff turnover and a stigmatized, de-professionalized field.

One consequence of managerialism in the UK has been that social workers have become bound up in a focus on performance management, standardization and e-technology, and a diminution of direct contact between social workers and families. Technology, performance measurement and risk-aversive practice came to replace professional judgment, according to Featherstone et al. (2014), with many adverse consequences for families. Hands-on practical support is less likely to be offered to family, and instead parents are told what to do, or children removed from families.

This discussion of the failure of managerialistic approaches to child protection is highly relevant to children's rights and well-being. Children, even when their families face difficult circumstances, usually have their primary attachments to family members, and want to remain with their parents, even if their parents are not able to care for them. But if CPS do nothing to help parents to deal with their stressful circumstances and cope better with caring for their children, because they are focused on monitoring and surveillance, children are likely to suffer and their feelings and wishes are likely to be ignored. Overwhelmed social workers do not have time to form relationships with families or children. When abuse is judged to have occurred and children are removed from their birth families, this is often traumatic for children, and foster families or alternative caregivers are unlikely to receive the additional support that they need. There is very little evidence to suggest that the traditional Western approach to child protection, is adequate in fulfilling the obligation of Article 19 to protect children from all forms of physical or mental violence.

5.3 CHILDREN IN STATE CARE

When CPS deem that it is not safe for children to be with their biological parents, they come into the system of state care—usually foster care, kinship (or relative) care, or residential care. In the United States, the most common placement is into foster care, with 48 percent being so placed in 2010, 26 percent in kinship care, 15 percent in residential group care, and 12 percent in other types of placement (such as adoptive homes) (Miller-Perrin & Perrin, 2013). These percentages vary in different countries, according to child protection policies. In New Zealand the number of children in foster care is relatively low because of a strong philosophy of placing children with families, and many are placed with extended family (Smith, 2015b). About half (48 percent) of the children in out-of-home placements were with family or whānau,[1] 30 percent were in foster care, while less than four percent were in residential (including group home) care in 2014.

The placement of children in foster care is associated with better child development outcomes than placement in residential institutional settings (Schoenmaker, Juffer, van Ijzendoorn, & Bakermans-Kranenburg, 2014). Barber and Delfabbro (2005) found that on the whole Australian children adjusted well to long-term foster care in terms of both standardized measures of psychological adjustment and the children's own views. Most children reported being happy in their placements and feeling safe and well looked after, though about one in five said that they needed more help and that they did not always get on with their foster parents. Children in the care system, however, are at considerable risk of further disadvantage and discrimination (Barnes, 2012).

Children have the right to safe, effective, and caring contexts when they are placed into care. It is a particular challenge to ensure that children within the care system have their rights respected, and are able to experience good-quality care, stable placements, personal and financial support, and access to health and education services (Barnes, 2012). Looked-after children are likely to have low self-esteem, show aggressive, noncompliant and disorganized behaviors, become wary or anxious, and have difficulty developing relationships (Cicchetti, Toth, & Hennessy, 1989). They may not have experienced a consistent, caring environment, causing them difficulties in developing secure feeling of trust in their caregivers. Their difficulties may be compounded by the grief and loss that they experience at being removed from their families, even when they

---

[1] *Whānau* is a Māori word meaning extended family.

were abusive (Shealy, 1995). This often makes it an extremely challenging task for a foster parent to be able to achieve an emotional connection with children placed in their care. The trauma for children at being removed from their parents, suggests that their removal from home should be avoided if possible, and that it is better for families to receive intensive services to help keep children safe (Miller-Perrin & Perrin, 2013). Unfortunately, in some authoritarian CPS such as the UK, a philosophy of early removal from parents has been employed, instead of supporting families to provide appropriate care (Featherstone et al., 2014).

When children are removed, states have an obligation to provide good, secure alternative care arrangements. Article 20 of the UNCRC says that children who have been removed from their families are entitled to special care and protection. Caregivers have the responsibility to help stabilize children's lives when children have feelings of resentment or mistrust, and have experienced insecure attachments. Children have to make many adjustments in the unfamiliar environment of a foster home, including the loss of family, different caregivers' and family rules, siblings, peers, home, neighborhood, and school. When caregivers establish warm and trusting relationship with children, children are better adjusted and have fewer problems at school (Marcus, 1991). The stability of foster care is an important factor in achieving positive outcomes for children, with multiple placements being associated with more problems (Barber & Delfabbro, 2004). One major problem is that the difficult behavior of children in state care can lead to more coercive, negative, and over-controlling reactions from caregivers and teachers, which can further exacerbate problems (Cicchetti et al., 1989). When children in care are scolded or punished, this can result in their view that the world is against them being confirmed.

> Substitute caregivers should be able to provide therapeutic parenting and skillful and knowledgeable intervention. The requirements of the task go beyond ordinary competent parenting. There needs to be empathy, acceptance, an open mind and self-control even when behavior is challenging. (Smith, 1997, p. 24)

Foster parents (in partnership with social workers) have a major responsibility to ensure that children's rights to a quality education are realized. Participation in stable and high-quality education has the potential to enhance life outcomes for children in care, while poor educational achievement reduces life opportunities, limits employment prospects, and can lead to social exclusion (Cameron & Maginn, 2009).

Schools can achieve better results with foster children when there is close cooperation with foster parents, and the school understands and supports their efforts with children. Instability of placement is a particular concern for looked-after children, as it means that their education is interrupted and changed, and often gaps develop that never get filled. Most research has shown that children in state care have lower educational attainment than the general population, that social workers do not pay sufficient attention to ensuring suitable continuity of education for children in care, and that low expectations are too frequently held for these children (Kassem, 2010; Matheson, 2015). Looked-after children are also likely to receive less schooling, sometimes because they are not enrolled in school, or their attendance is poor. They may have been excluded from school for poor behavior, or leave school at the earliest opportunity. Efforts to engage looked-after children with stable responsive schools are very important for their future and present well-being, and foster parents and teachers can help by celebrating children's achievements, rehearsing and extending basic skills, and working together to understand and resolve children's difficulties.

Although it is not necessarily true that all looked-after children have behavioral or educational problems, inconsistent parenting and parental rejection do tend to lead to impulsive and other antisocial behavior (Cameron & Maginn, 2009). This may cause management difficulties for caregivers and teachers, but children can be taught basic skills such as empathy, negotiation and compromise through use of an authoritative parenting style that combines sensitivity, responsiveness, demandingness or expectations, and positive psychological control. There is no easy way of managing challenging behavior, however, and foster parenting can be a hard job. It is therefore all the more essential that caregivers receive additional support, education, and training so that they are able to provide safe and effective environments for children.

CPS have the responsibility of ensuring that caregivers are selected carefully, avoiding those who are likely to abuse or mistreat children or are themselves stressed, providing caregivers with appropriate training, and supporting them so that they are not left alone to do this work. Families who are under stress are less likely to be able to cope with the greater demands (compared to ordinary parenting) made by foster care. Situations where foster parents are isolated and unsupported are the most conducive to abuse (Daly & Dowd, 1992). Social workers have an important role in helping foster parents, providing advice when difficult situations arise, and sharing pleasure at successes. A good relationship between social workers and foster care providers includes:

- Reasonable accessibility either in person or by telephone, particularly at difficult times;
- That the social worker listened to the foster parent's thoughts about what is said; and
- That the social worker gave thoughtful and appropriate advice. (Bradley & Aldgate, 1994, p. 67).

It is impossible to have a high quality service for children in care that does not rely on social workers, and they ever have widening responsibilities to an array of stakeholders including teachers, birth parents, children, foster parents, siblings, and other relatives (Gilligan, 2000). Robbie Gilligan points out that new layers of complexity have been added to the role of social workers because they need to monitor and facilitate many complex relationships. These increasing demands give rise to a gap between what can be done and what should be done. Increasing the quality of social worker training, and investment for training and support and delivery of social work services are essential. Not only are more social workers necessary but they have to be better equipped and resourced for their roles. The problems of looked-after children are rooted in social inequality, and lack of investment in CPS, particularly in the low pay, and lack of training and resources for social workers and foster parents (Kassem, 2010).

Good relationships are unlikely to exist when social workers have heavy caseloads, and work in a bureaucratic system. Vivienne Barnes (2012) says that while the UK Children and Young Person's Act aimed to achieve a better quality of care for looked-after children, this has been difficult or impossible in a time of major cuts to public services. Barnes suggests that an ethic of care should operate between caregivers and social workers, so that a relationship of openness, trust, and honesty exists. Yet, she acknowledges the difficulty in achieving this when:

Managerialist practices of auditing and target setting have meant that professional workers spend large parts of their working day demonstrating accountability through keeping extensive records on both paper and computer. (Barnes, 2012, p. 1279)

In Australia and New Zealand, Dorothy Scott (2006) is also critical of the overloading of CPS that lead to high staff turnover and low morale, and a stigmatized and deprofessionalized field. In these circumstances, the chances of social workers fulfilling the important role of monitoring and support of foster parents, is greatly reduced. The impact of the nature of the CPS, on the rights of foster children to a loving, caring family environment and access to good education, is powerful although indirect.

5.4   BIRTH FAMILIES

The preamble to the UNCRC says that the family is "the natural environment for the growth and well-being of all of its members and particularly children" (UNCRC, 1989), so continuing involvement of children's biological families is to be encouraged when children come into contact with CPS. Extended family members from children's biological families have been increasingly involved in decisions about the placement and living arrangements of children. In New Zealand and the UK, these are called Family Group Conferences (FGCs) and in the U.S. Family Team Meetings (FTMs).

FGCs were a New Zealand innovation but they have been widely adopted in other parts of the world. They were designed to prevent the state having too much power in relation to children, and supporting families to care for their children (Tapp & Taylor, 2002). FGCs provide a forum for the family to come together with professionals to work out solutions to protect the child's safety and care. While there are many positive aspects to FGCs that can empower families, there is little or no research to show that they are associated with better outcomes for children. Critics have seen FGCs as a reflection of New Right fiscally driven policies to put the responsibility for child welfare back to families and communities, instead of the government taking responsibility, and as a way of reducing costs (Atwool, 1999). Because biological families are often of low socioeconomic status and low in social capital, they may lack the resources to cater adequately for children. Had the government invested more in supporting families and FGCs in New Zealand, it is likely that the policy would have been more successful. Nevertheless family decision-making policies are a well-meaning attempt to engage families in the well-being of children.

In many countries CPS aim eventually to return children to the care of their birth families and to maintain contact with birth families during separation, whenever practicable. In New Zealand a family empowerment model prevails, where children are expected to retain links with their families while in foster care, and these links are supposed to be maintained and strengthened (Smith, 2015b). In the UK too, it is a fundamental tenet of policy that foster children should remain in contact with birth family and be reunited with family if possible. In the United States, recent federal legislation (the Fostering Connections to Success and Adoptions Act of

2008) was introduced to foster the well-being of children in foster care, by strengthening connections to relatives through intensive family finding and engagement policies (Landsman & Boel-Studt, 2011).

It is generally believed, according to Barber and Delfabbro (2004), that contact with birth families helps maintain attachments between children and their families, increases the likelihood of reunification with family and enhances children's psychological well-being. However, the authors point out that these assumptions are controversial, and that there is no evidence of a causal link between family reunification and family contact. They suggest that children, who get along well with their families and are in care because of less serious problems, tend to have more regular contact with birth families, and go home sooner. Their research in Australia showed that while family contact was positively related to children's well-being in the first few years of care, it could become distressing for children who had been in care for more than two years. Clearly, there is a complex relationship between children's adjustment and contact, and it is unwise to adopt a blanket policy of maintaining contact, reunification, or both. Each case should be considered individually in the light of the particular family (and foster family) circumstances, children's attachments and children's wishes.

Even if it is not safe or practicable for children to have ongoing visits with birth family, they need to know about their family history, as this information is crucial to identity development and feelings about culture and heritage. If contact is not possible, different methods such as visits to old neighborhoods, photographs and historical information can be helpful. Social workers should support children in finding out this information, but with the other demands upon social workers' time, and high social worker turnover, such efforts are less likely to be made.

5.5   THE PERSPECTIVES OF CHILDREN IN CARE

The rights of children to have a say in decisions about their lives (Article 12) and to express their views and receive information (Article 13), are particularly important for children in state care. Looked-after children tend to be invisible and voiceless within bureaucratic CPS, where they become the passive objects of other people's decisions. Constructions of children in state care as vulnerable and in need of protection, often override any concern for their rights to participate. Adults' views of children's 'best interests' are often constructed without consulting the wishes and feelings of children. Legislation in some countries includes an obligation to take the views of the child into account, but in practice social workers often have reservations about the role that children should play in decision making. Even when families participate in decision-making processes through FGCs, children may not be present or have any input into those processes.

> Foster children are in an invidious position: most of them have a home somewhere but for a variety of reasons they must move out of it and live with strangers until some other adult works out what to do next. The dependence and powerlessness of children in this predicament are obvious, and the obstacles to their development seem formidable. (Barber & Delfabbro, 2004, p. 102)

There are obvious advantages to children's involvement in placement decisions, such as making better decisions, helping children feel connected and committed to the decisions that are made, and increasing feelings of mastery, control, and self-esteem (van Bijleveld, Dedding, & Bunders-Aelen, 2015). About half of a sample of children in kinship and foster care told us that they did not know why they were in care, and did not understand the role that agencies and professionals played in their lives (Smith, Gollop, & Taylor, 2000). Few children had been asked what they wanted and most said that other people had made the decisions for them. If explanations had been given to children it was usually by caregivers, but caregivers often lacked information about the child's history, because this was held by the agency.

Nicola Atwool (2010) also talked to children in care and reported that they wanted to be treated like members of the family, to be trusted and given freedom. Some children reported difficult relationships with siblings or peers, and compulsion to participate in activities they did not like. One child told the researcher that he wondered why he was included in an FGC, when others spoke for him and about him, and he did not get the chance to speak. Most children in the study wanted to be provided with information and to be listened to by adults who were prepared to act on what they were told. Most children found that adults did not listen; even though they wanted adults they trusted to be the ones with the most say about day-to-day decisions.

van Bijleveld et al. (2015) carried out a literature review of the barriers and supports to child participation within child protection and child welfare systems. The research showed that most children had limited opportunities to participate in decision-making processes about their lives, and were not well informed about what was happening, why they were in care, or what was likely to happen to them. Even if they were consulted, most children did not feel that their views were valued or acted on. They often wanted more contact with parents and relatives, and to be able to choose their social worker or what help to access, but this was not allowed. If they were listened to, children felt valued, even if they did not achieve what they wanted. Children complained about social workers' poor communication, being hard to reach, not keeping appointments and high turnover.

> Lack of consultation led to feelings of guilt, sadness, anger and worry. Moreover, young people felt that if they had the opportunity to have a say, there would be greater chance of a successful placement, a supportive relationship with their social worker and a more positive experience at school. (van Bijleveld et al., 2015, p. 133)

The most important facilitator of children's participation is the relationship between social workers and children. If there is a good relationship, children are more likely to say what they mean, and social workers are better able to judge the children's views in the context of their lives. Social workers are often uncomfortable talking to children and may not have any training for this. They can be over-ready to doubt the authenticity of children's views, and be overwhelmed by other work demands in a risk-averse environment. Adults think that they know what is best for the child, and they often view children as vulnerable and lacking the competence to have an input into decisions (van Bijleveld et al., 2015). Archard and Skivenes (2009) were surprised at the almost total lack of concern that social workers showed for how children arrived at their views, and their ready assumption that children are loyal to their parents or ignorant about other ways of living, leading them to discount or ignore the views of children.

All of the research suggests that many professionals in CPS lack skills or inclination to hear children's views in serious and respectful ways. This not only leads to problems with decision making but also adversely affects children's feelings about themselves and acceptance of decisions. Social workers need training and experience in talking to children, as well as a thorough understanding of human rights, and the legislation that underpins them. The quotations at the beginning of this chapter illustrate the difference that having a sympathetic adult to talk to makes to the feelings of children, but too many CPS are not fertile ground for social workers to be sensitive and responsive to children.

the key ingredients [to encourage children's participation] are skilled and resourceful staff prepared to listen to and encourage the participation of children and young people, proper resourcing, supportive policy and legislation, and some means of evaluating their performance. In addition, feedback from children and young people is required to indicate whether it is happening. (Cashmore, 2002, p. 845)

In some jurisdictions children are given access to an advocate to ensure that their views are taken seriously and taken into account. Research has shown that children's advocates in the UK had the time and space to talk to children, helped them to document their views, and were able to elicit information that their social workers or parents did not know about (Lagaay & Courtney, 2013). Another study (Barnes, 2012) showed that children had a very positive view of children's rights workers, and felt respected, valued and listened to by them, in contrast to how they felt about social workers. The children found the rights workers easy to contact and responsive, while social workers were unreliable and hard to contact. Rights workers had different attitudes to children seeing them as competent beings, while social workers saw them as immature and dependent. This study suggests that employing professionals whose main responsibility is to look after the rights of children, helps CPS to do a better job of looking after their interests.

5.6   PREVENTATIVE APPROACHES

This chapter has outlined the failure of child protections systems to protect or promote children's rights. Poverty and fragile networks put families at risk for child abuse. Prevention approaches support children and families before they reach the point of being abused. U.S. statistics estimate that children in poverty are 44 times more likely to suffer from neglect and 14 times more likely to suffer some other form of child abuse (Every Child Counts, 2010). A more effective way of preventing abuse is to address the underlying factors that cause it.

A public policy commitment to preventing child maltreatment should also emphasize various social ills directly associated with such violence. Poverty, unemployment, inadequate housing, births out of wedlock, and single-parent households are all statistically correlated with child maltreatment, and a societal commitment to eliminating these problems would be, at least indirectly, a commitment to eliminating child maltreatment. (Miller-Perrin & Perrin, 2013, p. 338)

Government neoliberal policies promoting competition, the free market, the control of inflation, restructuring, privatization, and cutting and bureaucratization of public services, also contribute to the conditions that cause child abuse and limit effective responses to it. If investigation focuses on identifying the most extreme and verifiable types of abuse, many stressed families do not meet the threshold for statutory intervention. About a fifth of children in the United States live in homes where the quality of parenting puts them at risk of poor outcomes, yet only about a third of these families come into CPS (Wald, 2014).

Public health approaches to prevention are scientifically based and coordinated efforts to determine the magnitude and causes of child abuse, and develop and implement primary prevention and intervention strategies (Miller-Perrin & Perrin, 2013). They encompass primary, secondary and tertiary prevention, focus on underlying causes and early treatment, and are part of broader strategies aimed at addressing social disadvantage (Scott, 2006). Public-health strategies include home visiting programs; wrap-around community support hubs (based in schools or early childhood centers); campaigns to eliminate corporal punishment of children and help parents use other methods of discipline; affordable and accessible universal high quality early childhood services; income support or conditional cash transfer programs; and infant and maternal health nursing support.

An example of a successful public health initiative is the Victorian maternal and child health services, which reaches 98 percent of infants in Victoria, Australia. Parent groups of about eight sessions are facilitated by nurses and offered to all first-time parents in the state. Initially they were focused on weighing, immunizing, and screening for developmental problems, but now focus on broader psychosocial interventions aimed at strengthening families and communities. After two years, 80 percent of the groups are still operating and self-sustainable, and they often result in lifelong friendships. "This service has also become a de-stigmatized platform for reaching out to those vulnerable families who might otherwise have been referred to child protection" (Scott, 2006, p. 13).

One means of preventing abuse is to bolster the resources that already exist in communities and neighborhoods. Gary Melton (2010a, 2010b, 2014) points out that in the United States there has been a dramatic societal trend toward greater isolation and alienation of families, leading to diminished involvement in civic, political, and religious life. Parents face the challenge of bringing up children alone, and experience difficulties, not due to negligence or ineptitude, but to loneliness and lack of support (and I would add poverty). Based on his concern that current CPS blame families, rather than help them, Melton and his colleagues developed a community-based approach to keeping children safe in South Carolina, called Strong Communities.

This multidisciplinary project mobilizes networks of friends and neighbors, through the initiatives of community outreach workers, to make sure that people notice and care about what is happening to others in the community, with the goal that "Every child and every parent should know that if they have reason to celebrate, worry or grieve, someone will notice, and someone will care" (Melton, 2010b, p. 451). Efforts were made to change the norms of communities by mobilizing community resources, such as schools, businesses, churches, and family health clinics. The outcomes of the project were transformative for the families, children, and community volunteers. Neighborhood surveys reported less parental stress, greater social support, more frequent help from others, more positive parental behavior, and greater community and personal efficacy (Melton, 2014). Substantiated cases of child maltreatment declined by 11 percent in the service areas but increased 85 percent in the comparison areas. The results showed that a small group of outreach workers were successful in making a difference, demonstrating that a universal approach to primary prevention can be effective.

As discussed earlier, approaches that support families are more effective than narrowly focused services, though they may be more costly in the short term (Berger & Shook Slack, 2014). The evidence that universal programs are more beneficial than targeted approaches has been recognized by the European Commission (2011), who point out the benefits of universalism, the difficulties in identifying target groups, and the dangers of stigmatization. The Nordic countries have been very successful in reducing the intergenerational transfer of poverty and poor education, by investing in high-quality early childhood education, parental leave policies and other policies to support parents (Esping-Andersen, 2008). Universal prevention activities not only prevent child abuse and neglect but enhance child health and well-being and improve school readiness (O'Donnell et al., 2008). Such approaches are cost-effective in terms of preventing costly harm, but also support children's rights to be protected from abuse, not to be discriminated against, to survival and development and to having their best interests catered for.

5.7 SUMMARY

Children who have experienced maltreatment or neglect within their biological families, are likely to come into the orbit of CPS. Removing children from their families is usually a last resort to maintain children's safety. Children in CPS become the subject of the actions of many stakeholders, including their birth families, caregivers, social workers, and legal professionals. Discourses of vulnerability amongst professionals tend to view children as the vulnerable objects of intervention, and this may have the effect of reducing children's resilience and agency. Children's participation rights to have an input into decisions and to receive explanations are often unrealized because professionals underestimate their competency, and there are structural failures within CPS.

CPS varies along a continuum from a narrow targeted approach involving a high level of monitoring and surveillance, to a more preventative approach focused on preventing abuse and providing assistance to families. Bureaucratic, managerialist systems have been criticized because they disempower both the recipients of child protection, and the staff who are directly responsible for children's safety. Such systems also blame families and focus on establishing the facts of abuse, rather than helping. In addition many families who do not reach the threshold for child protection intervention, receive no additional services. Such systems can become toxic for overloaded social workers making it difficult for them to establish warm and trusting relationships with children and families.

Child abuse and neglect is usually linked to conditions of poverty, isolation, unemployment, ill health, single parenthood, or other stressful family situations. Community-based and public health initiatives address the underlying cause of child abuse, and can be effective in preventing it.

When children come into state care, CPS usually places them into foster, kinship or residential care. While many children do well in foster care, looking after traumatized children can be a difficult task, and caregivers need training and financial and social support if they are to provide good quality care and enable children to develop a trusting relationship with them. Backup from social workers is essential though often lacking. The UNCRC says that children who cannot live with their families require special protection, yet this chapter has shown that CPS often fails to meet this obligation.

CHAPTER 6

CHILDREN'S RIGHTS TO HEALTH

Teaching on children's rights should be core to child health teaching for all disciplines at undergraduate level, so that doctors, nurses and allied health professional are used to the concepts and incorporate them into their core professional values, just as they do human rights.

—(Webb, Horrocks, Crowley, & Lessof, 2009, p. 431)

There is only one doctor who talks to me on my own without my mum and dad. But if I go anywhere else the doctor will just talk to mum and dad.

—(Rose, aged 13, in Kilkelly & Donnelly, 2011, p. 113)

Basic to all other children's rights is the right to survival and development, which is enshrined in Article 3 of the UNCRC. In order for children to live a normal life span and develop appropriately, they need to be healthy. Article 24 is the only article in the convention totally devoted to health. It says that children have "the right to enjoy the highest attainable standard of health and to facilities for the treatment of health and rehabilitation of health" (Article 24 (1)). This right is not only important in itself "but also the realization of the right to health is indispensable for the enjoyment of all the other rights in the Convention," according to the Committee on the Rights of the Child (General Comment No. 15, 2013, IIA). The committee points out that most child mortality, morbidity, and disabilities would be preventable if there was appropriate political commitment and allocation of resources. The committee also warns of states' obligations to ensure that there is no discrimination in access to health services, because of race, color, sex, language, religion, social origin, or disability.

The phrase in Article 24 concerning "the highest attainable standard of health" indicates some limitations on this health right, depending on the available resources, recognizing that lack of resources can hamper full realization of this right, and that it should be progressively realized. This is a necessary and realistic limitation, which was introduced to allow poorer nations flexibility and time to fulfill the mandate. It has, however, been criticized because it is a loophole and an overused excuse for governments' failure to act (Reinbold, 2014; Todres, 2010). State parties are expected to do as much as they can with the resources they have.

The World Health Organization states that: "Health is a state of complete physical, mental and social well-being and not merely the absence of disease or infirmity" (1948).

> Child health can be seen as the bedrock of well-being—without a basic level of physical health, then children's development is compromised, and their ability to develop the functional capabilities to participate reduced. On the other hand, well-being can be seen as synonymous with health in its broadest sense. Thus, health and well-being can be understood as complementary concepts. (Moore & Oberklaid, 2014, p. 2263)

Models of well-being tend to focus on child strengths rather than deficits. Well-being consists of four components—Agency, Belonging and Boundaries, Communication, and Physical Well-being, according to Roberts (2014, cited by Moore & Oberklaid, 2014, p. 2262). Physical well-being has two major components—individual health and development (eating and sleeping, motor development, health routines, managing illness) and environmental health (family income, housing, and local environment). Well-being is linked to the "functional capabilities" approach devised by Amartya Sen, who argues that, "a life worthy of human dignity requires at least a minimum threshold level of certain central capabilities" (Dixon & Nussbaum, 2012, p. 558). The Capabilities Approach is a human rights approach, asserting that all human beings have certain entitlements to what they can do and what opportunities are open to them. The first three items on Sen's list of central capabilities are: Life, Bodily Health, and Bodily Integrity.[1]

That health is greatly influenced by wider ecological contexts and social and cultural settings, is illustrated by the change in public health

---

[1] Other central capabilities are: Senses, Imagination, and thought; Emotions; Practical Reason; Affiliation; Other species (concern for); Play; Control over one's environment (Political and Material) (Dixon & Nussbaum, 2012, p. 558).

problems during the past century: from acute to chronic conditions; from a high level of pediatric morbidity, caused mainly by infectious diseases, toward a growing prevalence of conditions such as heart disease, diabetes, asthma, cancer, depression, and physical disabilities (Moore & Oberklaid, 2014). There are also new health problems such as HIV/AIDS, pandemic influenza, mental health issues, and noncommunicable diseases (UN Committee on the Rights of the Child, 2013). Because of improved health care, more children with such severe chronic health problems survive, but such conditions pose challenges to them and their families. Social factors during childhood have a profound effect on health throughout life, but their effect is particularly powerful in the first few years of life:

> Life course models view health as a developmental process, the product of multiple gene and environment interactions. Adverse early social exposures become programmed into biological systems, setting off chains of risk that can result in chronic illness in mid-life and beyond. Positive health-promoting influences can set in motion a more virtuous and health-affirming cycle, leading to more optimal health trajectories. (Halfon, Larson, & Russ, 2010, cited by Moore & Oberklaid, 2014, p. 2266)

There is an overlap between health rights and rights discussed in some of the earlier chapters in this book, since family (Chapter 2), early childhood experiences (Chapter 3), and freedom from abuse (Chapter 5), are particularly pertinent to health rights. The issue of children's right to bodily integrity and not to be exposed to violence in the form of physical punishment is very much a health issue, but I will not return to it in this chapter as it has been discussed in several other chapters. This chapter will address the following issues: infant and maternal health; inequalities in health provisions; children's participation rights in health services; and children's understandings of health.

6.1 INFANT AND MATERNAL HEALTH

The under-five mortality rate is the single most important indicator of child health and well-being (Reinbold, 2014). Since there are a significant number of deaths during the neonatal period related to the poor health of the mother during pregnancy, it is impossible to separate the health of the mother and the health of the newborn. According to UNICEF (2014), the first 28 days of life are the most vulnerable time for a child's survival, so a focus on neonatal health is essential. 44 percent of all under-five deaths are due to neonatal deaths. Promoting optimal health during pregnancy and immediately after birth is a key issue in ensuring children's survival and development (UN Committee on the Rights of the Child, 2013, Section D). States are obligated to diminish infant and child mortality with particular attention to neonatal mortality (Article 24, para 2a), "to provide appropriate pre-natal and post-natal health care for mothers" (para 2d), and to promote exclusive breastfeeding of infants up to the age of six months (para 2b). The UN Millennium Development Goal (MDG) four promised to reduce under-five mortality by two thirds between 1990 and 2015, while MDG five involved accelerating maternal survival. There has been good progress toward these goals, with the neonatal mortality rate declining by 40 percent between 1990 and 2013, but MDG four will only be reached (11 years late) in 2026 at the current rate of improvement (UNICEF, 2014).

Despite some progress in reducing infant mortality, 2.8 million babies worldwide died within the first month of life in 2013, mostly from preventable causes. Sixty percent of neonatal deaths were caused by preterm birth complications or complications during labor and delivery. Yet, only a third of women in the world deliver their babies with the support of a doctor, nurse, or midwife, and only about a half of mothers receive the recommended amount of antenatal care. Support for and education of mothers is essential to reduce neonatal mortality, as rates are much higher when mothers have no education. Neonatal survival is dependent on income, maternal education and place of birth, with most neonatal deaths in the world occurring in sub-Saharan Africa and South Asia (UNICEF, 2014).

There is a considerable range of neonatal mortality within rich countries. In the United States, for example, African American women are more likely to have low birth weight infants, and the infant mortality for them is more than twice that for white women (OECD, 2011). The differences in infant mortality rates between the majority[2] and minority[3] world are stark, with neonatal mortality rates[4] of 47 in Angola, 46 in

[2] Majority world refers to the poorer developing areas of the globe (in Africa, Asia and Latin America) where the majority of the world's population lives. The majority world is also referred to as the developing world.
[3] Minority world refers to the comparatively wealthy developed nations of the globe (Europe, Australia, New Zealand, Japan, U.S., and Canada), where a minority of the world's population lives. The minority world is also referred to as the developed world.
[4] The neonatal mortality rate is defined as probability of dying within the first month of life per 1,000 live births.

Somalia and 44 in Lesotho; and only 1 in Iceland, Finland, and Singapore (UNICEF, 2014). The rates for the English-speaking nations were four for the United States; three for the UK, New Zealand, and Canada; and two for Australia and Ireland (UNICEF, 2014).

The lives of many babies are influenced by breastfeeding, since if it is initiated within an hour of birth, the risk of neonatal death is reduced by 44 percent. Yet, only 43 percent of newborn babies worldwide receive the benefits of immediate breastfeeding. Breastfeeding strengthens infants' immune systems and protects them from diarrhea and pneumonia early in life, and from obesity and diabetes later on. For the first six months of life, breast milk is the only nutrition needed by infants (UNICEF, 2014). Breast milk contains nutrients that stimulate brain development, and the close physical and psychological contact associated with breastfeeding supports secure attachment (Bartle, 2002; Parnell, 2002). The promotion of breastfeeding is therefore an important component of supporting children's rights to survival and healthy development. Hospitals have been encouraged to take a variety of initiatives to improve their implementation of UNCRC, including the promotion, encouragement, and support of breastfeeding, such as through providing appropriate spaces for mothers to breastfeed (Southall et al., 2000). It is also important to encourage and support breastfeeding for infants when their mothers leave hospital and return to work. In New Zealand, the Ministry of Health has provided a set of guidelines for early childhood education services to support breastfeeding, by providing comfortable places to breastfeed, ensuring routines that accommodate children's individual breastfeeding schedules, and having clear policies that encourage breastfeeding (Bartle & Duncan, 2010).

6.2 INEQUALITIES IN HEALTH

There is overwhelming evidence that poverty during childhood (particularly early childhood) is a risk with a lifelong health impact. Poverty sets off a developmental trajectory that is cumulative, affecting every conceivable health outcome from perinatal and neonatal mortality, birth weight, height, dental health, respiratory illnesses, to accidents, and other educational and life outcomes (Bradley & Corwyn, 2002; Duncan, Ziol-Guest, & Kalil, 2010; Evans, 2004; Hertzman & Wiens, 1996; Hill & Tisdall, 1997; Williams Shanks & Danziger, 2011). The number of risks that children face have a cumulative effect over time, and the more adverse conditions children experience the more likely it is that their health and development will be compromised (Moore & Oberklaid, 2014). One pediatrician describes the way that health is impacted by poverty:

As a pediatrician, every day I see how New Zealand children in poverty have their health and education compromised for much of their formative years. Families living with the stress of insufficient money have to delay, cut back or eliminate essential items like food and doctors' visits. When a child grows up in an impoverished environment, the lived experience of material hardship impacts upon their health and wellbeing both now, and in the future. This in turn affects their ability to ever escape poverty. (Asher, 2015, pp. 1–2)

Dr. Asher (2015) says that she frequently sees children in poverty in hospital, despite the fact that New Zealand is a comparatively wealthy nation. When parents are on social benefits or earning very low incomes, children tend to get sick. A typical case seen by Dr. Asher, is an undernourished baby with a chest infection struggling to breathe, arriving in hospital. Her condition comes from living in an overcrowded, damp home with inadequate heating. Gaining medical attention is delayed because of difficulties getting the baby to a doctor because the car broke down. The baby will recover after several days in hospital but may have permanent damage to her lungs (bronchiectasis), which will cause her to lack energy, have a frequent cough, and miss a lot of school. This will affect her chances of completing a good education and getting access to a reasonable job, so an intergenerational cycle of poverty is perpetuated.

In poor countries the health issues are different, and the likelihood of access to health services or recovery in hospital are not so great, but income is still a powerful influence on health. *Young Lives* is a study that has explored the impact of poverty and inequality on children in poor countries—Ethiopia, Andhra Pradesh (India), Peru, and Vietnam (Woodhead, Dornan, & Murray, 2014). Malnutrition in poor countries has a very damaging long-term effect particularly through early stunting.[5] Within each country the lowest income groups have the most negative outcomes. For example, in a sample of 15-year-olds in Peru, the lowest income quintile was twice as likely to be in the group with the poorest health outcomes and they were exposed to a wider range of adverse events and risks than the least poor quintile. Shocks included crop failures (due to pests, disease or climactic events) and the death or illness of family members, meant that families ate less, accumulated debt, and had fewer household assets. Children who were assessed as "stunted" because of

---

[5] Stunting is defined as being 2 standard deviations below the average height according to age and gender.

early malnutrition were also at a disadvantage educationally. In Ethiopia stunted children were one grade behind nonstunted children by the age of ten. In Peru half of the children in the poorest quintile were stunted, compared to 10 percent in the wealthiest quintile. Children in poor countries were greatly affected by parental illness or death. In Ethiopia one in five children in the study had lost at least one parent by the age of 12. When children suffered common illnesses, like malaria, worms, or diarrhea, health care was difficult and expensive to access, and they were often absent or dropped out of school.

Article 24 (para 2f) of UNCRC says that states should develop preventive health care measures to support children's health. As has been argued in Chapter 5, public health approaches are necessary to prevent the conditions that cause ill-health such as inadequate nutrition, poor housing, low income, and lack of social support. *All* children in *all* families should have the opportunity to get a good start in life (O'Brien, 2015). The use of targeting to identify children and families at risk, reinforces stigmatization of children, while ignoring the harmful circumstances that have created the risks. It is also difficult to ensure that targeting reaches the most needy. Disadvantaged children, according to Esping-Andersen (2008), benefit from a universal program, but universalism should be supplemented by additional targeted support for the most disadvantaged children.

To ensure that all children have access to health services, a system of universal health care is necessary, so that families can access health and preventive care from a health care professional or agency. Universal health care supports the implementation of Article 2 of the UNCRC, stating that *all* children regardless of income, race, or other characteristics are entitled to rights. The United States is the only industrialized country without some form of universal health care and performs below many other countries in respect to health, such as infant mortality and premature and preventable deaths (Todres, 2010). Because there is no national health care system, individuals rely primarily on health insurance programs for coverage, but 11 percent of children in the United States have no health insurance coverage at all. Uninsured children are six times more likely than insured children to be unable to access health care when they need it. Moreover, there are greater obstacles to accessing high quality health care among low-income children. African American and Native American children have much higher infant mortality rates and lower immunization rates than white children. Recent reforms to health care in the United States should go some way to addressing these inequities.

In the UK, the National Health Service (NHS) was set up in 1948 and was based on four tenets: universality, free and funded through taxes, a secretary of state responsible and accountable to parliament, and that it should be an integrated whole (Alderson, 2015). Priscilla Alderson explains how successive governments in the UK have eroded the original vision. The four standards for the NHS were removed by Parliament in 2012, and it has become increasingly privatized. There have been many NHS shortcomings, such as the closing of local hospitals, so that large hospitals become increasingly overwhelmed with new patients. Alderson believes that the problems are largely due to underfunding and lack of staff time, training, and support, and that the problems are likely to increase with more privatization.

Access to a system of free universal health care for children is only part of the solution to the problems produced by inequality, as illustrated by New Zealand, where health care is free for children under 13 years. The New Zealand recent record for child health is not great, since it has moved from being in the top third for most child well-being indicators in the 70s, to the bottom third in the early 21st century. The country is doing very poorly in terms of injuries to children, rates of pneumonia, meningococcal disease, whooping cough, rheumatic fever, and hospitalization (Asher, 2008; Public Health Advisory Committee [PHAC] Report, 2010). Child poverty in the mid-80s was at half of its current level, because cuts to welfare services and other market-led policies (such as increased rents for state houses, deregulation of employment, and increased consumption taxes[6]) since the late eighties have had an effect, leading to New Zealand having the seventh highest rate of child poverty in the OECD (Expert Advisory Group on Solutions to Child Poverty, 2012). New Zealand's child poverty rate at about 24 percent, is about two and a half times higher than the Nordic average in countries like Sweden, Norway, Finland, and Iceland (Boston & Chapple, 2014).

Preventive primary health care programs are needed to combat poverty and associated ill-health, such as antenatal and postnatal health care for mothers and infants, immunizations, family planning services, income and housing assistance, injury prevention, and food security initiatives (such as through free school meals). Strategies to ensure that these preventive programs reach those in most at risk are necessary, through community health initiatives and community service hubs (such as in schools or early childhood centers), and increased funding for prevention.

Health care professionals have an important role in advocating for implementation of the UNCRC in health care systems (Webb et al., 2009).

---

[6] The consumption tax in New Zealand is known as the Goods and Services Tax (GST).

Pediatricians, because of their clinical and analytical experience, can play a role "to represent the plight of children affected by these problems [poverty, discrimination and lack of resources] and lobbying for change, a role best described as the pediatrician as advocate" (Webb et al., 2009, p. 433). Advocacy is a central role for pediatricians, both as individuals and groups, to draw attention to health inequalities and develop health priorities based on a rights-based approach. Inequalities in health are a major concern in the UK and other countries, and in order to bring about change, robust research is needed so that resources are not wasted on interventions that are driven by politics rather than evidence. Professional training is essential to ensure that children's rights are incorporated into health professionals' value systems and professional practice. In the UK, an organization of pediatricians established an advocacy committee to produce advice and information for pediatricians on how to advocate or children, and highlight health inequalities for children (Webb et al., 2009). Pediatricians can use the UNCRC as a powerful tool to improve health for children and young people, but so can other health professionals such as nurses, psychologists, physiotherapists, and play leaders.

6.3   CHILDREN'S PARTICIPATION RIGHTS IN HEALTH SERVICES

In considering children's rights to be healthy, there is often a heavy focus on protecting children from ill health, and ensuring that they have access to health care, but this often results in their citizenship or participation rights being ignored. Yet, if children are to be able to take control of their own bodies and health status, they need to understand what makes them healthy or ill and what their treatment is. When children are involved in healthcare decisions, their "adherence, adaptation, sense of competence and understanding of their illness" is greater (Kilkelly & Donnelly, 2011). Children have a right to be heard within health care settings, to have their views respected, to give informed consent for their treatment, and to have an input into decisions about their treatment. All too often it is assumed that children lack the capacity to understand their health and their parents are the people that health professionals consult, as illustrated by the quotation at the beginning of the chapter, where a child explains that the doctor hardly ever talks to her but talks to her parents. The views of health professionals about the capacity and rights of children are important determinants of how children's participation rights are respected within health systems.

Children are active learners from an early age, but their competence to understand their health and provide a rational input into health care decisions is often underestimated (Alderson, 2002). There are four levels of children's involvement in decision making (Alderson & Montgomery, 1996). First the right to be informed, second the right to express views freely, third that their views are given "due weight" by adults (depending on age and maturity) in any decisions about treatment. At the fourth level, the child is competent enough to be the main decider about treatment. Children who have had a lot of contact with health care systems are often very knowledgeable about their health.

> Young children's capacity to understand distressing and complex knowledge is shown especially when they have serious illness or disability. Children as young as two years can name their cancer drugs, and have the moral and intellectual understanding to co-operate with harrowing treatment .... It is vital that the children understand the nature and purpose of the treatment as soon as possible, to avoid misunderstandings which could induce grief and terror. (Alderson, 2002, p. 158)

In her research about consent to surgery with 8- to 16-year-old children and young people, Alderson found that children with long experience of severe illness had an exceptionally good understanding of their illness and treatment, and were able to explain the nature and purpose of their planned surgery. Alderson gives the example of a four-year-old girl with diabetes, who could detect when her blood sugar was too low or too high by how well she was feeling, was able to carry out her own blood tests and insulin injections, and understood that insulin helped turn sugar into energy. She also learned to refuse sweets while watching other children enjoy them, and explained to her friends why she could not eat sweet things. If young children are capable of understanding their illness in this way, there is no justification for not providing them with explanations or making them a part of health decisions. Few children will want to be the main decision maker about their health care, but most do want to be involved in some way, so parents and health care providers need to be sensitive to children's wishes about the level of their involvement.

It is important for health professionals to find out whether children are experiencing pain when they arrive at and leave hospital. A study of 7- to 17-year-old Canadian children found that three-quarters of children attending the emergency department of a hospital experienced severe pain, and that many were still experiencing pain when they left the hospital

(Weingarten, Kircher, Drendel, Newton, & Ali, 2014). About 40 percent of the children were discharged home with moderate to severe pain, and many of them did not recall receiving opiate analgesia, although this was recommended practice. Children were asked about their satisfaction with their treatment, and their satisfaction was linked to the ease of communication with their health care provider. Children said that active listening was important, and being asked questions about the level of their pain and their medication preference. The study highlighted the importance of health care providers having good communication skills.

One of the most common chronic childhood health problems is asthma, a condition that can be alleviated considerably when children take appropriate medications. A study of 296 families with an asthmatic child between 8 and 16 years, investigated the level at which children were involved in their treatment by health care providers (Carpenter et al., 2014). The study provides some excellent examples of providers involving children meaningfully in discussion, and giving and sharing information. The following is a brief extract from a long discussion between a provider and child:

PROVIDER: And are you having any problems using it? ["It" refers to medication]
CHILD: No, not really.
PROVIDER: You remember how we talked about using it?
CHILD: Yeah.
PROVIDER: You blow out ((blowing)) hold it up, press, pull in, hold it for ten seconds, do two puffs …
CHILD: We did two of them.
PROVIDER: Right, ten to fifteen minutes before you exercise.
CHILD: And we've tried it two times. (Carpenter et al., p. 269)

Although most of the children (96.6 percent) wanted to engage in discussions about their asthma treatment with their health provider, the study found that a third of providers did not ask the children any treatment-related questions. Older children were more likely to be asked questions than younger children, probably because the providers thought that younger children were less competent to answer questions. The authors argued that while it might require more effort to engage younger children, it was worth making the extra effort because such participation would empower children to manage their health condition better. Surprisingly, physicians who were older and had been practicing for longer were less likely to engage in discussion with children. Additional training and professional development is necessary, because respecting children's participation rights is a significant shift from traditional practice.

Article 13 emphasizes children's right to express, seek, and receive information in any medium they wish, and this is particularly important for young children and children with communication difficulties (Franklin & Soper, 2005). Irish research showed that when children between 5 and 14 talked about their experiences of participation within the healthcare system, a common theme was that the doctor spoke first to their parents and then to them, while they would have preferred to be spoken to directly and have their opinion sought (Kilkelly & Donnelly, 2011). Children said that there was no point in asking their parents, because parents didn't know how they (the children) felt. When Brenda (aged 13) had hay fever, they asked her mother instead of her what the symptoms were. She said "they could have just asked me to know more" (p. 116). Children distinguished between different kinds of health professionals, and nurses were often spoken of favorably. A 12-year-old, Trevor, said that the nurses are:

The ones that make you feel comfortable, more than the doctors. Doctors are trying to get organised and the nurse is just there to help them and to sort of speak to the children about what's going to happen. (Kilkelly & Donnelly, 2011, p. 114)

Children's experiences in different health institutions were different. One group of children who had spent time in a specialized children's hospital reported that they were asked for their consent before their blood was taken, prepared for procedures, and provided with better follow-up afterwards. In another hospital, children were not offered explanations before or after procedures. Children thought that doctors should get to know and build up rapport with their child patients because otherwise the children might be scared of them. They also wanted doctors to talk in words they understood, and to feel that they could ask questions if they did not understand. Making healthcare environments more child-friendly was mentioned by several children, for example, providing activities for children (including teenagers) to do while waiting (Kilkelly & Donnelly, 2011).

Young people with chronic conditions in another study, indicated that they wanted information on such issues as their condition, treatment, tests, investigation, and lifestyle factors, as well as how to live with physical symptoms, deal with negative emotions, and manage at school (Beresford & Sloper, 1999 cited by Franklin & Soper, 2005, p. 16). The young people said that parents too needed information, as they often were the ones who talked to children, and that professionals should inform parents too. Franklin and Sloper identify some ways to facilitate children's participation:

- Clarity and shared understanding about the purpose of participation and what it is intended to achieve;
- Staff training and development to enable staff to promote children's participation including changes in attitudes to consent and competence, and developing communication skills;
- Using flexible and appropriate methods to involve children, such as using multimedia resources, using advocates or mentors, making participation fun and rewarding;
- Organizational culture, systems and structures so that organizations change attitudes, procedures and styles of working across all levels to develop a shared vision.

The UNCRC has many implications for the practice of health care professionals who work with children, including the value of listening to children, providing them with information, encouraging questions and discussion, helping parents to involve children, and providing opportunities for children to have an input into decisions. Interviewing is not always the best way to access children's understanding. Other approaches such as play, art, and the use of props and other equipment can be more effective ways of communicating with children (Kilkelly & Donnelly, 2011). While these issues all relate to children's participation rights in health systems, attending to them will also promote children's chances of recovery from illness and having some control of their health, especially when they suffer from chronic conditions.

What is clear from the research is children's need to be understood, and to be treated with empathy, kindness and good humor during illness. Their views reflect a consistent understanding of the importance of being heard by their health professional and being provided with age appropriate explanations and information to help them cope with the consultation and treatment process. Many children expressed the instinctive view that a "good" health professional was one who listened to them, explained things to them in a language they understood and preferably, was good humored and kind. (Kilkelly & Donnelly, 2011, p. 122)

6.4 CHILDREN'S UNDERSTANDING OF HEALTH AND WELL-BEING IN CONTEXT

One important consideration in promoting children's right to the highest attainable standard of health, and their capacity to think critically and make good decisions about their health, is what good health means to children. Article 17 of the UNCRC says that children have the right to access to information aimed at promoting their physical and mental health, which implies knowledge about what health is and what makes people healthy. It is therefore useful to find out how children conceptualize their health, and what they believe makes a healthy person. A wider perspective on health is that it is not just of the absence of illness but includes well-being and capabilities, encompassing not only survival and bodily health but also imagination, emotions (being able to love and be loved), critical reflection, affiliation, play, and control over the environment (Dixon & Nussbaum, 2012).

Children's perspectives on health were explored in a study of primary school children's views of "what makes a healthy person" (Burrows & Wright, 2004). The most common way that children referred to health was as a bodily matter—strong muscles, working limbs, healthy lungs, glowing eyes, for example. Children also included eating the right food, drinking water, being physically active and cleanliness, as healthy attributes. Older children were more likely to mention appearance when describing a healthy person—someone who looks good or well, or has an appropriate (not fat) bodily shape. Children's understandings, however, extended beyond the body, to include psychological attributes, such as a healthy attitudes and thoughts, and being healthy in mind. Social aspects of health mentioned by children were connections with friends, family, and neighborhood, enjoying friendships, being loving and kind, being fair, and being courageous and respecting others. Children referred to identity concepts in their definitions, such as being yourself, not showing off, being self-aware, knowing who you are and not trying to be like other people. One 12-year-old said "Try and have a high self-esteem—if you have a low self-esteem you won't care about your body" (p. 200). Children's descriptions of healthy practices included sleeping, relaxing, exercising, eating moderately, drinking water, being clean and safe, laughing and smiling, being around friends, feeling good about oneself, being kind, helping others, and setting goals. The avoidance of risk was also a prevalent theme—being careful, keeping yourself occupied, and not doing things you wouldn't normally do. While the children in the study emphasized the bodily aspects of health, some of their understandings extended to other mental, spiritual, social, and environmental aspects of health.

Another study of children's conceptions of health used ethnographic methods involving digital cameras and notebooks, and participant observation in different everyday settings of children's lives (Reeve & Bell, 2009). Nine- to eleven-year-old children noted things they thought were healthy or unhealthy, and researchers talked to children about their observations. The two most important sources of their knowledge, according to children, were their parents and school, though some mentioned personal experience and television. Similarly, to Burrows & Wright's research, children had a broad concept of health. Their predominant meanings were associated with things that cured or caused injury or illness (e.g., drinking apple juice), losing or gaining weight (aerobic exercise), the food pyramid, vitamins, and minerals. But children also discussed other aspects: environmental health issues (cars that pollute the atmosphere and cause global warming); germs and bacteria (spoiled food); energy (tiredness); emotional and mental health (reading keeps your mind alert); sustaining human life (plants provide oxygen); and drugs or stimulants (caffeine).

Even preschoolers are able to articulate how they understand health and healthy behavior (McEvilly, Verheul, & Atencio, 2013). Many three- to five-year-old children in this study, talked about health in corporeal terms, such as through healthy eating practices (eating fruit), exercise, and fitness. For example, two boys discussed the importance of having healthy bones and doing vigorous exercise to boost their energy. Other children mentioned the importance of getting sleep, washing hands, cleaning teeth, not getting sunburnt, and being careful when crossing the road. One imaginative response to what children did at nursery to keep themselves healthy included "the most important thing is to never touch a crocodile" because "it will bite your thumb" (p. 13)! Only one child talked about avoiding overweight and obesity, and that it was important to run around "'cause if you don't run around …' cause run arounding is sporting and if you don't do sporting, your tummy will get fat" (p. 14). The authors say that it is important for researchers, policy-makers, and practitioners to evaluate and reflect on privileged and taken-for-granted discourses, and to encourage children to engage more critically with notions of health, physical activity, and exercise, for example, by emphasizing the importance of accepting a diversity of body shapes and sizes, and:

> Speaking with less certainty about connections between physical
> activity, food and health may help children learn that these issues

are not simply about "good" and "bad" practices and therefore "good" and "bad" people. (McEvilly et al., 2013, pp. 17–18)

A number of other writers criticize the pervasive dominant discourses about health through schooling and popular culture, relating to the "obesity epidemic" (Burrows, 2011; Burrows, Wright, & McCormack, 2009; Gard, 2008; McEvilly et al., 2013). They describe the myriad ways that a neoliberal discourse of healthy, self-managing, autonomous individuals who are responsible for what they do to themselves, is promulgated "by what at first glance seems an unending cacophony of messages telling them to shape up, get off the couch, eat better, exercise better and shed those youthful fat rolls" (Burrows, 2011, p. 350). These discourses about the dangers of obesity and lack of exercise and the promotion of a normative notion of what is healthy, result in blaming the victims, surveillance and classification of children's bodies, and internalization of messages about being morally lacking and irresponsible. Although well-intentioned, these messages often result in the stigmatization of people from low socioeconomic groups or cultural minorities, and to feelings of guilt, fear, anxiety, and unhappiness which may actually damage children's health. Burrows (2011) found clashes between children's culture and the health discourses of the school. Indigenous and low-income children were teased for being fat at school in New Zealand, but in Samoan culture being thin was ridiculed. Burrows also argues that there can be a mismatch between a school curriculum that embraces holistic notions of health, and children's emphasis on physical elements of health.

Contextual and structural issues affect children's experience, interpretation and enactment of health messages. Health promotion research in the UK has tended to focus on individual risk behaviors, and not enough attention has been paid to the broader social contexts of children's everyday lives, especially their neighborhood social contexts, according to Morrow (2004). She researched 12- to 15-year-olds subjective experiences of their neighborhoods in a low income area near London, including children's social networks, their activities, and where they felt they belonged. Being close to their friends was a central feature of children's activities in their neighborhoods, and their sense of belonging stemmed from people and relationships (with friends and family). Rock (15) said, "I think I belong in a community where I am treated right and a place that is warm and friendly" (Morrow, p. 216). There had been riots in the area several years ago, and many children described feeling scared and unsafe. Negative experiences of neighborhoods included noise, unfriendly neighbors, racial harassment, not being allowed to play, and dangerous traffic. Some children, however, mentioned kind and friendly neighbors. Morrow said that young people lacked self-efficacy and ability to participate in their neighborhoods, and did not feel that they shared in community life. She warns against focusing purely on social relationships in relation to children's health and well-being, and points to environmental and economic restraints such as not having safe places to play, danger from traffic, having nowhere to go except shopping centers, and having no money.

Environmental influences on children's eating and physical activities were explored in a deprived area of North London (Pearce et al., 2009). Children (10- to 11-year-olds) were given disposable cameras, took photos of places in their local environments where they were involved in physical activity or obtained food, and participated in focus groups discussions. The home was the most common place where food was photographed, followed by school dinners and packed lunches at school. Photographs of takeaway shops, small convenience stores, and large supermarkets depicted places in the neighborhood offering food. Physical activity was associated more with school than home and usually involved informal activities in the playground, though facilities like swimming pools, leisure centers, skate parks, and playgrounds in the community, also featured. Proximity was a recurring theme with children going to nearby places to get food and be physically active. The photographs of places for physical activities show rather bleak environments of concrete walled schoolyards, and empty playgrounds with minimal equipment, suggesting that their neighborhoods were not very enticing. The children clearly did not participate in much physical activity in their neighborhoods because of worries about "stranger danger," parental restrictions, and lack of safe and interesting places in the environment for them to go.

Another ethnographic study with six-year-old children in a low-income inner-city area, documented what children said about their health, and their activities in their everyday environments (Irwin, Johnson, Henderson, Dahinten, Hertzman, 2006). Although children believed that physical activity was important to their health, opportunities for them to spend time outdoors was limited, because they lived in apartments, and were not allowed out on their own. Lack of friends and fears about safety limited children's ability to explore their local neighborhoods. Children mentioned emotional health, being happy, and caring for themselves and others, as related to health, but safety was a prominent concern for them. Their parents did not think that they lived in a safe neighborhood or that others would look out for their children's safety, and these fears were communicated to children:

> Like—if there's a stranger ... you shouldn't go too close to them. Like—if they're trying to give you candy ... don't you shouldn't take it because it—like—when you got closer and closer to them they could grab you. (Sabrina, in Irwin et al., 2006, p. 356)

Children, therefore, had a very restricted range of play opportunities. What they thought was essential for their health, and what they experienced, were disconnected. They had little opportunity to learn about and negotiate identity through play with peers, or to explore their neighborhoods. The study suggests the importance of being aware of the broader context of children's lives, when discussing health, since living with adversity is not conducive to the implementation of health messages.

Research suggests that children have a broad range of meanings for what it is to be healthy, which are influenced by their parents and what they learn at school, as well as through the media and their everyday experiences.

> ... children treat the concept of 'health' as a multidimensional network of ideas, composed of multiple related knowledge elements. Instruction that focuses on simple, unitary definitions of health is not likely to coordinate well with the rich understandings these children have associated with multiple contexts and meanings .... Perhaps more important and necessary, however, for the overall goal of promoting children's health is connecting this knowledge of children's conceptions to an understanding of what motivates their actual behaviors and practices, and to what extent beliefs such as those cited here are relevant in health decision-making. (Reeve & Bell, 2009, p. 1966)

6.5 SUMMARY

To realize children's right to survival and development, and to the highest attainable standard of health, requires attention to a variety of levels of the ecological systems, to populations and individuals, and to the global and local. Health is a fundamental human right that underlies the attainment of many other rights. It has a much broader meaning than freedom from illness but extends to capabilities and well-being. Public policy has a huge impact on health and well-being in the majority and minority worlds, including social and economic policies that affect income and employment, pro- vision of housing, investment in universal health services, preventative public health care measures (such as immunization), and health education. The availability of resources to support antenatal and postnatal care of mothers and infants is essential to ensure survival and development from birth. Inequality has a profound affect throughout the world, and as the amount of deprivation and risk increase, so do negative health outcomes. In the developed world, children may be more likely to be able to access health care services in hospital, but if they are discharged to unhealthy houses and lack of good nutrition, their health will continue to suffer. At the individual level, health care professionals have an important role to play in advocating for the health rights of children, and supporting evidence-based interventions.

Children's right to be heard, and to have an input into decisions about their health is an important consequence of their participation rights. Children are active learners and participate in self-care from an early age, so they are entitled to have explanations about their health, and to be communicated with by health care professionals. Chronically ill children have been shown to be knowledgeable about their illness, and this knowledge helps make them resilient, and capable of actively participating in their own health care. Health care professionals need training and professional development opportunities so that they know about and promote children's rights, respect children's dignity and competence, and know how to communicate effectively with children.

Children's understanding of the nature of health and well-being, and the factors that contribute to it is important if they are to be agents in maintaining and improving their own health. Children articulate the meanings of health from an early age, and while nutrition and exercise are dominant in children's constructions of health, physical health is not usually seen in isolation from other psychological, spiritual, and environmental aspects of health. Investigations of children's everyday experiences in social and neighborhood contexts show that there is sometimes a disconnect between the major health promotion messages promoted at school and in popular culture and children's own experiences. Children may not have opportunities to play and socialize with peers, to explore, to have access to nutritious foods, or to have a sense of belonging in friendly communities. It is important for health educators to be aware of the wider context of children's lives when working with children. Normative constructions of children's health and moral panics about obesity and lack of exercise may be more harmful than helpful to children's health.

CHAPTER 7

CHILDREN'S RIGHTS IN THE WORKPLACE

The personal and cultural meanings and values children ascribe to their work experiences are one of the factors that will moderate its impact. When children feel their work is a normal thing to do, that they are doing something valued by their families, and are treated fairly, these feelings can serve as a coping mechanism that helps their resilience. When they feel stigmatized or ashamed, or unjustly treated this can add to their vulnerability and distress.

—(Woodhead, 2004b, p. 367)

After my dinner I go out with my dad to where I work at my brother's butchers shop. I usually help my brother and my dad for about two hours most evenings.

—(15-year-old UK boy, Morrow, 1994, p. 133)

It is poorly paid and very hard work [as a brick-chipper] .... I would have to sit and work under the sun the whole day .... Even if my head is spinning due to working under the sun, malik [employer] will insist that I continue to break bricks. And when it comes to paying he will pay me less since I was unable to break a lot.

—(Bangladeshi boy from 10- to 14-year-old sample, Woodhead, 1999, p. 34)

In Western cultures, employment is still not considered to be the normal context for childhood, which is more likely to be seen as a time for play, education, and socialization. Children's work has been an invisible and largely unresearched aspect of childhood. Yet, both in minority and majority countries, children commonly work both inside and outside home, both for pay and without pay, and under an enormous variety of conditions. Rather than being potential adults or citizens to be molded into adult roles, children are already active participants in society, and their role as workers demonstrates this (Bourdillon, 2006). When I refer to children's work in this chapter, I include both paid and unpaid work, unless paid work is being focused on.

Historically, children have always worked and taken care of adults (Tucker, 1974). In Roman times, boys and girls served their parents at table, and in the Middle Ages, children in all classes except royalty acted as servants either in their own homes or those of others. Work was regarded as a virtue akin to worship, and children were not excluded from work until the 19th century. Even children from aristocratic families in medieval times were sent away to reside with other households in order to learn manners. Children from seven to nine years of age were commonly apprenticed to trade. The natural condition of childhood was assumed to be working, though children got the jobs no one else wanted (Hendrick, 2009). It wasn't until the late 18th century that reformers became concerned with the negative effects of child labor. With industrialization in the 19th century, work moved away from families, and learning took place in schools where the state could instill its political values. Since then, the trend has been ever more schooling for more children (Zeiher, 2009).

Morrow (2010) shows how attitudes to children's work are influenced by historical context. During the Second World War in the UK, children (as well as women) were called on to do their bit for the war by taking part in a variety of work, such as recycling and salvage schemes, knitting socks, growing vegetables and in larger scale agricultural production. Labor laws were relaxed so that children less than age 12 could work on farms, and children were taken out of school during term time to work on farms. Children's work was recognized and valued, and it was acknowledged that planting and harvesting of potatoes would not have taken place without children's help.

Children today are still engaged in a multitude of work tasks, from helping with housework, childcare, or in family businesses, to working for employers outside home. The most prevalent form of child work outside home today and throughout history is within agriculture. Both in developed and developing countries, children's work outside school hours is seen as way of helping their families, gaining respect, and being responsible (Nieuwenhuys, 2009). Children's work, however, is seldom recognized as real work regardless of how time-consuming or onerous it is (Heesterman, 2005).

An estimated 250 million children aged between 5 and 14 years of age are working, with the largest proportion of these being in Asia and the Pacific, followed by sub-Saharan Africa (Castro, 2010; Woodhead, 2004b). Children's work is often associated with exploitation and ill treatment and the pejorative term child labor is used to identify it. With the onset of globalization, work from developed countries came to be outsourced to countries like China, Brazil, and India, and there it was often children who provided the cheap labor. The meaning of child labor is imbued with negative images of physical hard work, exploitation, and activities that are bad for children's health (Heesterman, 2005). "The prohibition of child labor became a major project of modern childhood" (Nieuwenhuys, 2009, p. 289). For many children in the developing world, however, work is viewed as a normal part of childhood and everyday life, a means of learning skills, and supporting family survival (Woodhead, 2004b).

The history of childhood in developed countries has been described as a roadmap for converting children from earners to learners, and this has entailed an increasingly sharp division between school and work (Morrow, 2010, p. 437). In European countries however, children also do paid and unpaid work but most often part-time and while still attending school. For example, 80 percent of German children and two-thirds of British children have had paid work experience by the time they leave school, while 80 percent of U.S. children have paying part-time jobs while still at high school (Liebel, 2004). Similarly, 80 percent of New Zealand children do paid work before leaving school, after school, or in the school holidays (O'Neill, 2010), and 77 percent of a concurrent sample of New Zealand 11- to 15-year-olds were working (Gasson & Linsell, 2010). Work in Western contexts tends to be seen as benign but peripheral, and as a way of children learning about the world, making a contribution, and taking responsibility. The construction of children's work, however, is highly contested and influenced by beliefs about children's development and cultural norms about the roles, responsibilities, and activities normal for children (Morrow & Boyden, 2010).

This chapter examines the way that children's rights are recognized in children's work through law and policy, the nature of children's work, the conditions which influence the effects of work, the nature of children's work, the relation between work and education, and children's participation rights in work.

7.1 THE INTERNATIONAL LABOUR ORGANIZATION, THE UNITED NATIONS CONVENTION ON THE RIGHTS OF THE CHILD AND CHILDREN'S WORK

The first organization to attempt to influence policy about children's paid work was the International Labour Organization (ILO), which involves collaboration between government, industry, and labor to provide a democratic alternative to socialism (Myers, 2001). The ILO introduced a Minimum Age Convention (MAC, No. 138) in 1973 to prohibit children under 15 years from engaging in any economic activity, except for work associated with training, or on small family farms producing for local consumption (ILO, 2015a). It permits children to do safe, part-time, "light" work at age 13, while in the poorest countries at age 12. Although based on protecting children from work that might interfere with their childhood, the convention was also, in part, based on fears that children's labor would interfere with adult jobs and incomes. Myers (2001) describes ILO MAC, No. 173 as an attempt to globalize Northern ideas and values, which is anachronistic in most developing countries, where children are mainly employed in agriculture, and social welfare laws and labor inspection are often precarious and ineffective. Currently, 168 countries have ratified MAC, No. 173, including only two Anglo countries, Ireland and the United Kingdom, and excluding Australia, Canada, New Zealand, and the United States. China, Brazil, Ethiopia, Pakistan, the Philippines, and Vietnam have ratified but not Bangladesh or India (ILO, 2015a). Myers argues that ratifying Convention 138 is a cheap price to pay for low-income countries for the money and technical assistance offered by the ILO. It has also been widely criticized because:

> The MAC embodies a developmental view of childhood as a time of dependency, schoolwork, play and freedom from paid work and responsibility, of "becoming" and preparation for adulthood. (Gasson, Calder, Diorio, Smith, & Stigter, 2015, p. 166)

Nieuwenhuys (2009) has linked the regulation of child labor with world trade, because when developing countries do not comply with regulations, the World Trade Organization can boycott those who do not comply, thereby protecting cheap products from the developing world entering the developed world and threatening jobs. She cites the example of the Harkins Bill, a U.S. bill to boycott products produced by child labor.

Although the bill was never passed, it had dramatic consequences, because Bangladeshi garment manufacturers felt threatened and dismissed 50,000 children from their jobs in the industry. Instead of returning to school, as U.S. advocates had intended, the children moved from safe well-paid jobs in the garment industry to more poorly paid and dangerous work, such as brick chipping and rickshaw pulling. This was argued to be a case of misguided good intentions and consequences of applying Western assumptions to developing countries (Boyden, 1997). The suppression of child labor is not an effective way of improving children's welfare unless substitute sources of income and support for education and poverty alleviation are provided.

The United Nations Convention on the Rights of the Child (UNCRC) also addresses the issue of children's paid work, but rather than excluding children from work altogether it seeks to protect them from exploitation and harm to their health, and is more accommodating of diversity than the ILO MAC (Myers, 2001). Article 32 of the UNCRC asserts:

> The right of the child to be protected from economic exploitation and from performing any work that is likely to be hazardous or to interfere with the child's education, or to be harmful to the child's health or physical, mental, spiritual, moral or social development. (UNCRC, 1989, Article 31, para 1)

The second part of Article 32 says that a minimum age for working as well as appropriate regulation of hours and conditions should be mandated. The UNCRC acknowledges that even if children must work because of the needs of their families, they should not have to engage in harmful work. Other articles in the Convention about the right to education (Articles 28 and 29), the right to rest, and leisure (Article 31), and the right to protection from abuse and maltreatment (Article 19) provide a balance and suggest the conditions under which children should work. Moreover, Article 12 recognizes children's right to have a say in decisions about their work, a right that opens opportunities for working children to participate and influence decisions about their work.

> It was increasingly clear that the ILO, stuck with an uninspiring child labor convention and competing with the more compelling vision and broader authority of the CRC, stood to lose its international leadership on child labor issues. It responded to this challenge in a highly creative and socially constructive manner, proposing an

altogether new convention to focus world attention and resources with priority on "the worst forms of child labor." (Myers, 2001, p. 51)

The content and style of the 1999 ILO Convention 182 (1999) is different from the MAC, focusing on obviously *harmful* forms of child labor, including slavery (the sale and traffic of children and forced labor), prostitution, illicit activities (drugs or drug production), and any other work likely to adversely affect children's health. These forms of labor are clearly indefensible and reflect a global consensus as illustrated by ILO 182 being the first ever ILO convention adopted by a unanimous vote (Myers, 2001). Ratifying countries are required to remove children from harmful labor and to provide education, training, or other alternatives to inappropriate work. Recommendation 190 recommends provision for children's participation in public decisions affecting them, making it much more compatible with the UNCRC. The ILO Convention 182 has been ratified by 179 countries, including all of the Anglo and European countries, and many developing countries (but not India) (ILO, 2015b). According to the ILO, the global numbers of children in child labor has declined by one-third since 2000, but there are more than 85 million still in hazardous work compared to 171 million in 2000, and the largest number of these are still in Asia, the Pacific, and sub-Saharan Africa (ILO, 2015c).

Whether these conventions have had an impact on children's work depends on how different countries have taken them into account in their domestic legislation and policy. It is interesting that the United States, which has signed but not ratified the UNCRC, has ratified ILO Convention 182, and two optional protocols to the UNCRC, on "the Involvement of Children in Armed Conflicts" and "the Sale of Children, Child Prostitution and Child Pornography" (Heesterman, 2005). In California, child labor laws were designed to help young people gain work experience while safeguarding their education and health. Legislation in the UK was amended in 1997 and employment there is regulated by a patchwork of statues and local by-laws. In contrast, in the Netherlands, a completely new 1995 Working Times Act was introduced. While a ban on child labor for 13- and 14-year-olds was included, the legislation also stipu-lated standards of work for children similar to that of adults, including paid holidays, freedom from sexual exploitation, provision of rest periods, workplace tuition, and minimum wages. All three countries had minimum age legislation, linked to the end of compulsory schooling. Heestserman looks at how well these laws were enforced in the three countries and found that the Netherlands had the most effective regime, because of its greater focus on enforcement. There were 400 labor inspectors in the Netherlands compared to less than 100 in California, even though its population is half the size. Heestserman concludes that ratifying children's rights conventions does not necessarily result in improved protection of children. The Netherlands was the only country examined by Heesterman, where serious attention had been given to the conditions of children's work, so that these were comparable with adult conditions.

Unlike most other OECD countries, New Zealand has no legislated minimum age for children carrying out paid work, but there are restrictions on dangerous and hazardous work and working during school hours (Gasson et al., 2015). Although minimum age legislation exists in the UK requiring that children must obtain a work permit from local authorities to work, this requirement is generally ignored. The most important task in protecting children's rights within the workplace is to ensure that their work conditions are fair, safe, and protected from exploitation. It appears that neither the UK nor New Zealand and many other countries have ensured that children are protected in work situations. One study shows that signing on to the UNCRC was associated with more child labor, suggesting that stronger antichild labor laws could increase child labor in certain sectors (Doytch, Thelen, & Mendoza, 2014). Banning children's work below a certain age does not address the necessity of improving their conditions of work.

7.2 CONDITIONS OF WORK

A comprehensive review of the contexts of children's work and their influence on well-being was carried out by Martin Woodhead (2004b). He argues that:

> The extent to which work constitutes a risk to children's well-being is conditional on a whole range of circumstances, not just on the nature of work itself. (p. 323)

According to Woodhead, the question is what kinds of work, and in what kinds of situation, are most likely to cause children harm. The physical hazards of some types of work are obvious. For example, children in Mali's gold mines work in extremely harsh conditions, where children as young as six have to dig mining shafts, pull up heavy ore, work underground, and remain exposed to mercury. Tobacco farming in Kazakhstan is another worst form of child labor, with children doing hard physical work for long hours in very hot conditions, exposed to hazardous pesticides and to the absorption of nicotine through the skin, as well as poor access to water, sanitation, and nutrition (Doytch et al., 2014).

Even with hazardous work, Woodhead argues that it is important to weigh up the risks against the benefits, since the hazards have to be considered in the wider context of children's life situations. Harm is relative, since survival might necessitate involvement in work that is harmful. If such work was prohibited, it could lead to greater poverty and deprivation for the families concerned (Bourdillon, 2006).

It is not straightforward to determine how children's physical health and well-being is affected by work. Woodhead cites an 18-country study of health hazards which failed to find consistent evidence linking children's work with ill-health (O'Donnell et al., 2002, cited by Woodhead, 2004b, p. 328). Data from five countries showed that working children were at risk of health problems, but in another five countries working children were the healthiest.[1] Children's working situations including their treatment by their employers, family circumstances, and the extent of regulation and super-vision of child work, as well as age, gender, and ethnicity, are important determinants of whether work is harmful. The effect of children's work is also mediated by cultural beliefs and expectations surrounding the value of children's work. If children's work is valued, their self-worth is likely to be enhanced, but if it is not, children may feel stigmatized. Rather than dismissing children's work as necessarily harmful,

> [i]t is more useful to see work situations of children as a continuum, containing harmful and beneficial influences. In this view, work is not fundamentally different from other activities such as sport or even school, which can also hurt children, but which bestow undoubted benefits. (Bourdillon, 2006, p. 1213)

Woodhead shows that the following factors positively impact on children's well-being at work:

- Secure relationships and consistent settings
- Sensitive, consistent guidance by responsible adults
- Opportunities for positive peer relations and mutual support

---

[1] Regarding children's work as a unitary phenomenon rather than one with many qualitative differences is, in my view, a mistake, akin to the older research assuming that "day-care" was inevitably harmful for children. Recent research has established that it is the *quality* of day care that influences outcomes for children.

- Safe healthy environments with opportunities for rest, learning and play
- Regulated protection of fair work, such as through contracts
- Family respect for children's work and well-being
- Opportunities for participation in school and other community settings

One small-scale qualitative study in New Zealand suggests that parent support is one condition that sustains children's paid work (Gasson et al., 2015). This study shows several examples of the way parents support their children's work, for example, by drawing newspaper advertisements to their attention, using parental friendship networks to gain access to work opportunities, transporting their children to and from work and occasionally actually doing the work. Parents scaffold children's working lives and help them to become capable and responsible.

On the other hand, major potential hazards from children working include the following:

- Disruptions to supportive relationships
- Monotonous, under stimulating, or illegal work
- Negligent, harsh, or inconsistent treatment (including physical and sexual abuse)
- Isolation from or rejection by peers
- Adverse working conditions such as exposure to toxins or lack of safety
- Financial or job insecurity, and lack of job protection
- Unreasonable parent expectations and coercive treatment
- Incompatibility of work with school (Woodhead, 2004b)

These hazards are linked to negative outcomes for children, including delayed development, narrower cognitive skills, insecurity, low self-confidence, feelings of worthlessness and failure, hopelessness, apathy, and stress, trauma, fear, and anxiety. Many working children across the globe have work that is unhealthy, exploitative, and abusive, and children are denied education, so intervention is necessary to protect these children's rights. Unfortunately, there is little relevant research on the conditions of children's work, and despite the ILO and UNCRC conventions, regulatory efforts have only been partially effective.

Even within the developed world, there is evidence that children can be treated unfairly. According to Gasson et al.'s New Zealand (2015) study, employers gave children a month's trial without paying them, expected children to work unreasonably long hours, did not give them contracts or provide breaks, and paid children rock bottom wages. Many other similar examples of work being unsafe, unregulated, and receiving unfair wages and conditions are reported in Europe (Frederiksen, 1999; Leonard, 2002; Liebel, 2004; Mizen, Pole, & Bolton, 2001).

Children's invisibility in work settings and the perceived lesser value of their work leads to lack of government action to improve their working conditions (Gasson & Linsell, 2010). Wherever children work they are likely to be paid less and powerless to change their circumstances. Children are also often unaware of the rights that they do have, such as holiday pay, sick pay, or breaks. Legislation tends to focus on the protection of under-age children from working, rather than improving children's conditions of work. Children should have equal rights as adults when they do similar work, and their working conditions should be monitored to ensure this. Employers often have little economic interest in improving children's work conditions. The prohibition of underage children's work in many countries makes improvement of working conditions difficult, because this could be construed as legitimizing children's work (Liebel, 2004).

Some suggestions for improving the conditions of children's work include shortening work hours so that children can go to school, paying children a fair wage, providing health and safety measures (and making children familiar with them), providing protective clothing, social services, and infrastructure (such as meals and health services), as well as training and recreational facilities (Marcus, 1998, cited by Liebel, 2004, p. 233).

7.3   THE NATURE OF CHILDREN'S WORK

Children's paid work in the minority world generally takes place outside school hours and is usually light or casual work, unlikely to adversely affect children's health.

> The search for paid work is today an expression of children's own wishes, and is almost always based on their own decisions. It shows that it is part of a widespread attitude on the part of children today not to leave the possibility of working to adults, but to claim it for themselves. (Liebel, 2004, p. 122)

Ginny Morrow (1994) found that children's paid work in the UK fell into four main categories: *wage labor*, such as newspaper delivery, the service sector, retail, catering, or service sectors; *marginal economic activities or"self-employment,"* such as baby-sitting, car-washing, and other odd jobs; *nondomestic family labor*, such as working in family businesses such as farm work or shops; *domestic labor*, such as caring activities, house maintenance and repair, and car maintenance. Children in Morrow's study were working because they wanted to, in order to allow them access to consumer goods, feel more grown-up and have something to do outside school. In Germany, the most common type of paid work was delivering newspapers, but children were also involved in babysitting, car-washing, serving in shops and restaurants, cleaning, simple office work, or door-to-door selling (Liebel, 2004). In the UK children's work is mainly unskilled and around the edges of the formal labor market, for example performing simple and repetitive manual tasks like packing clothes, chocolates, or sweets, picking fruit and doing light assembly work. Service works like kitchen hand work tended to be dirty, hot and arduous (Mizen et al., 2001). In southern and eastern Europe, children were likely to be used as cheap and flexible labor, with links to the mainstream economy. For example, in the Portuguese textile, clothing, and shoe industry, many 14- to 18-year-olds were regularly employed because they only had to be paid 75 percent of the minimum wage. In Italy, children commonly worked in small industrial workshops or in agriculture (Liebel, 2004).

In New Zealand, Gasson and Linsell (2010) found that delivery work was the most frequent type of paid work done by children, with 32 percent 11- to 15-year-olds involved in it. Next was service work including food preparation, cleaning, babysitting, and retail work (18 percent). Only 8 percent of children were involved in agricultural work (such as fruit picking and farm laboring), though it should be noted that the sample came from an urban area. Liebel (2004) reports that in the United States, most young people are employed in the retail and service industries, with older students more likely to hold formal jobs and young students doing informal jobs like babysitting, gardening or newspaper delivery. Agriculture, the least regulated sector in the U.S. economy, was one area where children performed the same work as that done by adults, and farm children took on increasing responsibility for farm occupations. Many children from Latin American origin were working in agriculture, often the children of migrant and seasonal farm workers.

7.4 WORK AND SCHOOL

One of the main arguments against allowing children to work is that it will interfere with their education, which is an important right. While the idea of children helping out at home is not controversial in the developed world, paid work is usually thought to prevent children from serious engagement in school. Part-time and holiday paid work, however, is very typical of many children's childhoods in western countries and there is little evidence that this work adversely affects schooling (Bourdillon, 2006; Gasson & Linsell, 2010; Liebel, 2004).

Qvortrup (2001) argues that participation in compulsory schooling by children should be regarded as socially necessary work, since it contributes to the building of future human capital and future economies. Going to school is a futuristic contribution to the world of work through qualifying children to contribute to work later on, according to Morrow (2010). The emphasis on schooling during childhood is partly a result of the fact that the nature of work has changed from traditional trades and crafts to jobs that require literacy and numeracy. The state invests in children's education because it secures the future functioning of the economy, rather than as a free gift to children. Because the state only pays about 10 percent of the costs of education, parents pay a major role in building human capital. Close (2009) takes Qvortrup's argument a step further, and argues that since children are compelled to go to school and be educated under the supervision of others, that this is a type of unpaid and forced labor, however benign schooling might appear.

Children are therefore engaged in productive human labor and make a fundamental contribution to society while they are still at school, even though they have little control over their schooling and receive no financial reward. School and paid work, however, are still considered to be separate spheres. Keeping children out of work and in school, however, is not just motivated by concern for children, but for the building of future societies and economies.

There is little evidence that many children in the developed world are driven to work by poverty, since middle-class children are more likely to do paid work than poor children. For example, in Morrow's (1994) study of UK 11 to 16-year-old children, twice as many children from affluent families than from poorer families worked. Frederiksen (1999) found that in Denmark poorer children were discouraged from working because their family benefits were reduced, so it was more often better off children who worked. In New Zealand, children from Māori and Pasifika ethnicities (generally of lower income) were less likely to be employed than European children, and children from low docile[2] (poorer area)

---

[2] A docile is any of the nine values that divide a set of data into ten equal parts, so that each part represents 1/10 of the sample or population.

schools were less likely to be employed than children from high docile schools (Gasson & Linsell, 2010).

U.S. research suggests that up to 10 hours of outside paid work a week does not affect the performance of children at school, and that time in paid employment is generally taken from passive activities like watching TV or hanging out with friends rather than school work (Mortimer, 2003, cited by Bourdillon, 2006, p. 1217). Boys who had worked for less than 20 hours a week while at school, were actually more likely than those who had not worked to continue with their education, obtain university degrees and find well-paid jobs. A New Zealand study found that Year 11 students who were in paid employment, achieved more school credits than those who were unemployed or played sport. The research suggests that paid work is compatible with schooling, can provide learning opportunities, and open pathways to positive future outcomes, provided it does not exceed a threshold between 10 and 20 hours (Gasson & Linsell, 2010).

Paid work in developing countries is however a different matter. In contrast to the developed world, children's work usually contributes to family income and cannot be done without (Liebel, 2004). A major UK research project, Young Lives, carried out in India, Vietnam, Peru, and Ethiopia, show that children regularly drop out of school because of their need to work to support their families, frequently for agricultural, or domestic work (Murray, 2012). In Ethiopia in 2009, more than 90 percent of 8 year-olds and 98 percent of 15 year-olds participated both in paid or unpaid work. The reasons for dropping out of school included to participate in domestic and agricultural work (38.6 percent of boys and 6.4 percent of girls); because of illness or disability (12.2 percent of girls and 15.4 percent of boys); and to look after younger siblings (16 percent of girls and 1.3 percent of boys) (Murray, 2012). The three main reasons for leaving school in Andhra Pradesh (India) were not wanting to go to school because of lack of interest (15.9 percent), to earn money (15.5 percent), and to contribute to domestic or agricultural work at home (13.6 percent) (Morrow, 2013a).

Longitudinal case studies of children growing up in poverty in Andhra Pradesh (India) from the Young Lives study, illustrates the place of work in children's lives, and its conflict with education (Morrow, 2013a). Bhavana at age of 13 years was responsible for cooking for other family members who worked in construction and road building. By 16 years, she also worked in construction and road building as well as doing seasonal agricultural work (harvesting groundnuts). Her work was hard and involved carrying bricks, stones, cement, and water. She worked because "one must earn a good name among people" and if she didn't work hard, she would lose respect (p. 94). Subbaiah at the age 15 did some farm work for his family while attending school, took cattle to graze, harnessed buffalo, and irrigation work. Three years later he had left school, learned to plow and spent most of his time grazing cattle, although previously he had said he wanted to be a doctor. Another boy, Ranadeep, had planned to open a shop, but he had failed his exams and had to drop the idea because of family debt problems. Children's participation in work and schooling is intricately bound up with family responsibilities. While, children aspire to better jobs and to an education, these aspirations are mediated by their immediate responsibilities to their families. Children value family relationships and the ability to care for their parents (Morrow, 2013a, 2013b).

> There seems to be a moral economy of paying debts of gratitude to parents, of intricate connections between material and social values within the context of kinship, which fosters intergenerational mutuality. (Morrow, 2013b, p. 266)

One of the factors that keep children in the developing world in work and out of school is the quality of education. There has been an unprecedented global push toward getting more children into school, but this effort is unwarranted if schooling is of poor quality. The Young Lives study shows that the quality of education in poor countries is often low, and that schools lack flexibility when children have to be absent because of the demands of seasonal work, parental illness, and domestic responsibilities. Thirty percent of children in Andhra Pradesh dropped out because they did not want to go to school or were not interested in school. Some children talked about being scared of school and being mistreated by teachers (Morrow, 2013a). Schools were often inflexible and unwilling to accommodate children's absences and help them to stay at school. An Ethiopian girl, Shonah, had to drop out of school when her mother became ill, to take care of domestic duties, so returned to school and had to start Grade 1 for the third time. After her mother died, she became ill herself with malaria, and after previous absences the school would not allow her to return to school (Murray, 2012). Flexible schools that are tolerant of children's obligations, provide extra tutorials for missed classes allow children to stay at school and combine this with work, are necessary in developing countries.

Harika's story shows how it is possible to combine demanding home and paid work duties with school. Harika was an only daughter, whose father was immobile because of an accident. Her mother worked in the fields, while Harika did most of the household work. She managed to go to school with difficulty especially when it was the peak season in the cotton fields. Her daily routine was as follows:

> I wake up at 6 o'clock in the morning and sweep the floor. I wash the dishes. I will bring water, I will brush my teeth ... drink the tea .... I do study for a while and after studying .... I go to the [fields]. After doing the crossing work, I come back at 11 o'clock and take a bath. I still study for some time and come to school at 2 o'clock ... after eating lunch. I will come to school and write the exam and go back home at 4.30 pm. After going I will press the cotton and sweep the floor and cook the food for night. (Harika aged 13 years, Morrow, 2013b, p. 262)

Despite this incredibly demanding life, Harika wanted to become a teacher, and obtained a scholarship to continue schooling. She later stopped working in the fields and only did domestic chores like washing dishes and cooking because she had to study. Although her parents did not want her to stay in school, they later agreed to support her doing so. Although she decided that now she wanted to be a doctor, she saw gaining educational qualifications as a way of getting an educated husband and as a route out of poverty (Morrow, 2013b).

Children also combine work and school in developed countries, as illustrated by Zadie's story, this time less positive as far as continuing with education is concerned (Stainton Rogers, 2009). Zadie was 14 years old and her teachers were critical of her behavior as being infantile, and she was contemptuous of her teachers, bored with school and could not wait to leave. Yet at home Zadie was a highly responsible young woman. Her father left home when she was 11, and she now looked after her little sister Sally and her wheel chair bound mother. Every day she gave Sally her breakfast and got her ready for school, before helping her mother get dressed. She shopped on the way home from school and cooked for the family. She tidied the house and did the washing and ironing, then put Sally to bed and read her a story. Other people provided some help such as a home help two mornings a week, and a visit from a social worker to Zadie's Mum every couple of months, but Zadie was the main caregiver. Stainton Rogers argues that Zadie's strengths and resilience should be recognized and celebrated, but that she is deserving of a great deal more help. Social services could provide better support for her and school could be better adapted to her situation.

This section has shown how essential it is to see work within the context of the whole of children's everyday lives. In the west, work may not be incompatible with school, provided it is restricted in hours, and can be worthwhile, provided that work conditions are fair and safe. Work in developing countries is a necessity to keep families out of poverty though many children also attend school at the same time, but often sporadically and subject to family circumstances. Opportunities for quality education are much more limited and education also may also not lead to better jobs, so children are forced into staying in low skilled work.

7.5 CHILDREN'S PARTICIPATION RIGHTS IN WORK

Concern about children's work has stemmed largely from a wish to protect children from being the victims of exploitation and abuse in work. Sometimes well-intentioned policies to protect children can have harmful effects, as was illustrated by earlier efforts to ban children from working below a certain age, which led to children losing good jobs and taking on more dangerous ones. Children's work is frequently a "discourse of child concern" that constructs children as vulnerable and at risk. Such discourses frequently add children's problems by stigmatizing them and exacerbating social exclusion (Stainton Rogers, 2009). By listening to children's perspectives and seeing children's situation in the holistic context of their culture and everyday life, and recognizing their strengths, we can learn what matters for children, and if intervention is necessary, and work with children to implement change.

Children's participation rights in paid work have largely been ignored, and children have only rarely been given the opportunity to have an input into the debate about their work, or to have work considered from their perspectives. They have the right to have their views about work taken into account, and to provide and receive information about their work, as stated in Articles 12 and 13. They are not simply the objects of adult concern to be molded into roles determined by others, but are citizens and participants in society, and working is one of the ways that they participate. Moreover if attention is paid to how children experience their working lives, policy on children's work will be much better informed by children's realities.

Children should be viewed as subjects and social actors who, through their productive work, contribute to society and their families, and deserve recognition for this (Liebel, 2004). Children's work does not necessarily involve abuse and exploitation, as is so often assumed by advocates in western countries. If children's work is taken seriously, then children should have working conditions and pay consistent with human dignity and respect for their personhood. Children's agency, sense of responsibility, and self-confidence can be enhanced by their participation in work, if it is under favorable conditions.

Money rather than necessity is most often the motivation for children in the developed world to work. They often work to be able to buy things with their own money.

I'm in it for the money. ... I thought I would be in it just to meet new people and that it would be exciting a new job, I thought that at first, for the first few weeks, but now it's just about the money. (Amy, 15 years from the Midlands)

I haven't got any bills to pay, I just like money and I can do whatever I want with it. And that's why I work ... nobody trying to take the money away from me. (Jason from East Anglia, 15 years, p. 46)

... it's so that I can do things like go to the cinema and go out with my mates. I want to go places that I wouldn't be able to otherwise, that's the reason for having money. Not just to save it or hoard it or anything. (Ian from East Anglia, 15 years, Liebel, 2004, pp. 45–46)

Working children in Morrow's (1994) study spent their money on toys, sweets and other children's products, while others were working to save for holidays, a TV, and a car. Earning money meant that Danish children could buy jeans, shoes, cigarettes and music (Frederiksen, 1999). One Danish boy said working made you think about money in a different way. He said that it was hard to buy a bag of wine gums when you knew that it would take you 45 minutes to earn the money. Although children did not usually give the money to their parents, they were expected to cover expenses like clothes, sports activities and pocket money. In New Zealand, children were encouraged by some parents to save at least part of their earnings, and parents thought that working helped children to learn to manage their money (Gasson et al., 2015). Working children spend money on extracurricular activities enjoyed by wealthier peers—such as scuba diving, dancing lessons or overseas trips (with clubs) (Gasson & Linsell, 2011). This enables them to have a sense of belonging and keep up with their peer groups.

Children's accounts of their work show that it often involves a great deal of responsibility. In Morrow's study, a 15-year-old boy worked in an ice factory and acted as a store man and a factory worker. He operated a pump truck and a forklift truck, shifted pallets and stored them on top of each other.

> Evenings and weekends I help my parents run their company. They run a towing service. I help my dad out in the motor, so I can end up anywhere in the country, doing a job .... If we are towing a toilet block or office block, I will help, hook the trailer on, the lighting board to the unit. (Morrow, 1994, p. 133)

Many children were involved in sibling caretaking and some looked after grandparents. Other children (usually girls) did paid babysitting for neighbors or friends. This quote is from a 15-year-old girl and illustrates the extent of her responsibilities:

> Most of my nights from 8.00 till 12.00 I babysit for different families. I have six baby-sitting jobs. I enjoy doing it as I love to be with them. The youngest is six weeks, which I've looked after ever since it was born and the oldest is 12. So I get quite a lot of money but I don't do it because of that. I get on well with the children and I can communicate with them. (Morrow, 1994, p. 136)

Even newspaper delivery, which is often thought to be light, unskilled, and particularly suitable for children, demands important skills and responsibilities (Leonard, 2002). Children have to manage their time, make sure that the papers go to the right address, collect weekly payments, give correct change and balance books at the end of the week. Such work is usually unregulated and unmonitored, and involves very low pay and poor working conditions.

Children's work can also be demanding and risky. Leonard (2002) found that teenagers in Belfast who delivered newspapers, worked for five or six hours a week before school, had to lift heavy bags of newspapers (sometimes leading to sore backs or falls), face traffic dangers, confront dangerous dogs, and get fingers caught in letterboxes. One child felt frightened and vulnerable when delivering newspapers on dark mornings. Parents in Gasson et al.'s (2015) study found that some children needed support in their delivery work. The continuous commitment was difficult and they felt like giving up, so parents stepped in to support them. In one case a father took over the boy's paper run for a few weeks to give him time to decide if he wanted to continue.

Accounts of work from children in developing countries suggest that most children have no choice but to work, and that it is a normal part of growing up. A child working as a porter in Bangladesh said: "a domestic worker has to work even if he doesn't want to" (Woodhead, 1999, p. 34), and another young person from the Young Lives study said "… we work for our stomach. If we don't work, there is no food, no clothes" (Woodhead, 2004b, p. 366). Moreover, the working conditions are usually described as harsher and more dangerous than in the developed world. For example:

> A porter gets beaten by customers … we too get beaten … but then it is only from one person [the child's employer] not from the public.

> In the garment factory there are times when you are scolded. But that is to help you learn the skill. Whereas in domestic helping they beat us … not for our own good. (Children's comments, Woodhead, 2004b, p. 366)

Young people have shown that they are articulate and knowledgeable about the matters that affect them, and can take actions to improve their own lives. This is demonstrated by the rise of working children movements since the 1980s. In these movements, young people collaborate to protect their rights, and acquire "collective self-awareness," negotiate and resist exploitation (Liebel, 2004, p. 12). Working children's movements are becoming increasingly important in international debates and actions on child labor. The children involved are usually between the ages of 12 and 16, often migrants from the country, working in the informal sectors of the economy in urban areas. Working children's organizations typically draw on the UNCRC, often reworded to adapt to their situations, and supplemented by further rights. African children demanded: the right to vocational training, to stay in their village and not move away, to carry out work safely, access to justice, sick leave, to be respected, to be listened to, to light work adapted to age, to healthcare, to read and write, to have fun and play, to express themselves and to organize (Liebel, 2004).

"We are against exploitation at work but we are for work with dignity with hours adapted so that we have time for education and leisure" (Kundapar Declaration, 1996, cited by Miljeteig, 2005, p. 124). Working children's movements assert their right to work, and that they are not just passive victims of exploitation. They take an activist approach, supporting empowerment of the poor and marginalized, are often distrustful of government initiatives, and democratically organized. They aim to support each other in their daily lives and organize small focus groups for discussion and informal training in literacy and vocations skills. Such groups have been prominent at community and national level and have effectively contrasted themselves with the typical "picture of working children as sad and suffering victims, unable to protect themselves" (p. 127). Miljeteig describes the organizations as like living laboratories for participation rights and democracy. One young person spoke at an international conference and said:

> They said they want to abolish child labour, put children in schools because children have to go to school, have to play, and that if a child works then he or she is no more a child, while we have organized ourselves to fight against poverty and improvement of our working conditions. (Faye, in Miljeteig, 2005, p. 131)

If working children's participation rights are to be respected, it is important that these initiatives and organizations are acknowledged and supported, and that dialogues reflecting mutual respect, are established with them. Opportunities for working children's groups to present and be heard at international conferences are important, to enlist support for improving their conditions of work and help make schools more flexible so that children's aspirations to work and be educated are achieved. Working children are valuable partners in bringing about reforms to children's work.

7.6 SUMMARY

While children's work in the developing world tends to have been invisible and unrecognized, this chapter has shown that children's work is an important part of the productivity of nations, throughout the world. It is also a normal part of growing up for most children in the majority world, and for a large percentage of older children in the minority world. The idea that children below a minimum age should be prohibited from work stems from the construction of childhood as a time for play, socialization and learning, and this is a Western idea that is not applicable in the majority world. Moves to ban children's work have had some unintended negative consequences in the developing world. While work for children in western nations tends to be part-time and outside of school hours, work for children in developing countries is often a necessity for the survival of families and communities.

Children, however, have the right not to be exposed to work that is dangerous, harmful to their health or exploitative, and these rights are enshrined in the UNCRC and in the most recent ILO Convention 182.

Despite widespread ratification of the UNCRC and ILO Convention 182, children's work is largely unregulated and unmonitored. The Netherlands is an example of a country that has legislated children's conditions of work and takes care to monitor and regulate their work.

A variety of conditions of children's work may either protect their well-being or expose them to risk. Work can be hazardous to children's health through exposure to toxins, heavy labor, lack of protection from heat, cold, or machinery, or abusive treatment by employers. Children's well-being at work is enhanced when they have secure relationships, sensitive adult guidance, opportunities for positive peer relationships, regulated conditions and pay, and opportunities to continue in education. The extent to which their families and communities support and respect their work is also important. On the other hand, children's well-being suffers if they have boring or illegal work, negligent or inconsistent treatment, isolation from peers, lack of safety, job insecurity, and inability to go to school.

While schoolwork is a form of unpaid child work, paid work should not prevent children from going to school. Most work in the minority world takes place outside school hours, but in the majority world children have difficulty remaining in school when there are family domestic or business obligations, or they or their parents are ill. (Such obligations can also occur also in the majority world.) Children's work is often a moral obligation to older generations and an important component of the local economy, and children often sacrifice their education to meet these obligations. However, when school is inflexible or of low quality, it does not cater for children's family obligations, nor does it prepare them for participation in more skilled work. Work has to be seen in the holistic context of children's everyday lives within their larger societies.

In order to achieve reforms to the conditions of children's work, it is necessary to take children's views seriously and allow them to have an input into debate about work. Protectionist assumptions about children's vulnerability within work have dominated the discourse about children's work. Yet children are responsible and active subjects in their working lives, not mere dependents. They have the right to dignity and respect within work, and their views should be listened to and taken into account. Working children's movements have sprung up in the developing world enabling children to support each other in work and work together to achieve change. These movements demonstrate young people's agency as well as their ability to work within democratic organizations.

CHAPTER 8

Conclusion—Drawing the Threads Together

Rights without remedies are of symbolic importance, no more. And remedies themselves require the injection of resources, a commitment on behalf of all of us that we view rights with respect, that we want them to have an impact on the lives of all people, and not just the lives of the powerful and privileged, who are often the first to exploit rights for their own purposes.

—(Freeman, 2007, p. 8)

There are a number of themes that hold the chapters in this book together, and I will outline them in this final chapter.

8.1 THE PRINCIPLES AND HOLISTIC APPROACH OF THE UNCRC

The UNCRC provides a holistic, unifying vision of children's rights and childhood, and provides child advocates, professionals working with children, and policy-makers, with a direction and moral imperative for improving policies and practices for children. It is impossible to see one article of the convention in isolation from the others. Unless children's rights to be healthy are realized, for example, they are unlikely to be benefit from education and reach their full potential, to enjoy their rights to play and recreation, or to be able to have a say in decisions that affect them. For children in child protection systems, ensuring their rights to be healthy, and to be educated is a priority, and rather than permitting children in state care to experience poor access to health care and low expectations about their achievement, special efforts have to be made to provide them with a level playing field. Being able to have their voices heard and acted on is a bedrock right for all children, because if we help children formulate their views and listen to their perspectives on their lives, we are more likely to develop policies that will enhance their well-being. Finding, for example, that some children experience school as a negative and even frightening experience, tells us that if we want children to stay in school and have a better chance in life, we have to improve the quality of their education. Making especial efforts to find ways of listening to the views of younger children, or children with disabilities, even though it requires extra efforts and ingenuity, is essential to support their right to be heard.

The first principle of the convention is that of universality and respect for diversity. Rights are for all children, regardless of age, gender, ethnicity, disability, religion, sexuality, or any other difference. Families are more diverse than ever before in history, and the context of children's lives in these heterogeneous families has to be taken into account in catering for their rights. The world is unfortunately full of inequalities, and in many countries, inequalities are increasing. In every domain of children's rights, family resources (both economic and other) either help or hinder the realization of their rights, because children are vulnerable to harm. There is a very strong relationship between income and a large variety of indicators of children's rights and well-being: including educational achievement, health status, access to preschool or school, and exposure to abuse and neglect. Inequalities due to child characteristics such as gender, disability or immigration status are also a violation of rights. Girls have as much right to an education as boys, disabled children as nondisabled children, and refugee children as resident children. Children also have a right to their own language, so indigenous children's language rights should be catered for, and every effort made to support immigrant or refugee children's languages.

The second principle of best interests is in some ways controversial, because what is in children's best interests is an issue for human judgment, and a very subjective concept. Research can make a contribution here, and provide guidance about what is in children's best interests, although it does not always provide definitive answers. Research can have some input into the big issues of the impact of corporal punishment on children's attachment to their parents and relationship with peers; the nature of quality early childhood education; the effect of bullying on children's self-concept; the value of contact with birth parents for children in state care; the impact of neighborhood environments on children's health; and the relationship between children's work and their school achievement. Nevertheless, the difficulty with research is that it is not always generalizable to local situations and individual children, so the specific situation must still be carefully considered. For example, while it may generally be the case that children in divorced families benefit from contact with both parents, there are examples where such contact is not so beneficial (as when there is abuse or violence from one parent).

The third principle, of the right to survival and development, is a theme that cuts across many of the chapters in this book. I have shown, for example, that there is a profound impact of reciprocal, responsive, sensitive, and loving relationships with adults at home and in early childhood education, on children's long-term development. Universal public health approaches to child protection and health are positive for children, for example, providing good maternal and infant health care has a powerful impact on children's survival. Improving the conditions of children's work can ameliorate any harmful effects, but banning children below a certain age from working can result in harm. Excluding children from school is likely to have negative consequences for children's development, so schools need to work at ways to make school relevant and responsive to all children, to support their continued engagement. The final principal of respect for the views of the child and support for their participation gets a subheading of its own, Children's Citizenship, later in this chapter.

8.2 CONSTRUCTIONS OF CHILDREN AND CHILDHOOD

Another theme that is repeated throughout this book is that childhood is socially constructed through discourses. Childhood does not have a fixed universal meaning, but it changes in different historical times and in different cultural settings. In the past developmental psychology has, at least in Western countries, had a strong impact on how we see children, what we expect of them at different ages, and what are regarded as the appropriate ways for them to act, and for us to treat them. Childhood Studies theory rejects a construction of the child as incompetent, vulnerable and dependent, and moving through stages toward an end point of rationality. Instead it proposes that the child is agentic, responsible, knowledgeable, and an active participant and partner in social interactions. Hence a gradual change in how childhood is constructed is currently taking place. Many families have become more democratic and do not expect unquestioning obedience from children. Children are expected to internalize family rules, rather than be subjected to arbitrary or cruel discipline. Children are more often recognized as playing a responsible role in families, often taking care of siblings, parents or grandparents, and contributing to family income. The relationship of children with their families is reciprocal. Rather than passive children being socialized into adulthood by their families, children co-construct meanings within their family and community settings, and have a unique individual contribution to make to their families.

In education, the way children are portrayed in pedagogy has an important impact on how teachers relate to them. For example, in the Italian Reggio Emilia programs children are seen as rich, strong, powerful and competent, and in the New Zealand *Te Whāriki* model, children are viewed as active learners who choose, plan, challenge, and engage with learning. Positioning children as authoritative learners builds children's motivation and self-confidence and encourages them to take responsibility for their own learning. In contrast, when deficit models of families and children are used to explain away the poorer achievement of indigenous or minority students, the messages in these discourses are internalized by students and alienate them from education. Similarly when disabled students or children in state care face stigmatization through labeling and segregation, it is not surprising that they disengage from school.

Discourses of risk and vulnerability have particular dangers for children, and examples can be seen in child protection systems, concerns about working children and children with chronic health conditions. If children are seen as sad and suffering victims of their condition or situation, then their resilience and ability to cope are undermined. Too great a focus on protecting vulnerable children, fails to recognize children's agency, restricts their freedom and privacy, and disempowers them. In child protection systems, managerialist approaches tend to be authoritarian and coercive, and fail to focus on supporting children (or families) to deal with difficult circumstances. When social workers become bound up in performance management and standardized procedures, forming relationships with children and families takes a back seat, and the rights of children are ignored. Similarly, in the provision of health services, if children are not recognized as knowing and active agents, their ability to demonstrate healthy self-care is diminished. Doctors and nurses, who take the time to speak directly to children and explain their illness to them, are more effective in supporting children's return to health, than those who assume children are incapable of understanding. Moral panics about issues such as childhood obesity are another kind of discourse that result in partial and distorted concerns.

Working children are particularly subject to risk and vulnerability discourses, since work in the developed world is not regarded as a normal activity for children, despite the huge numbers of children working across the globe. Children can, of course, be exploited and badly treated in work, but in order to address these problems it is more appropriate to treat children as rights holders who deserve fair conditions of work, and fight to improve those conditions, rather than to prevent them working altogether.

8.3   SOCIOCULTURAL CONTEXTS FOR CHILDREN'S RIGHTS

We come to know our worlds through participation in social processes, and in communication with others within our cultures. Although Childhood Studies theory highlights the importance of children's agency, children do not acquire agency as lone individuals. Social processes are the source of agency, since children acquire their knowledge of themselves and their cultures, through social relationships with other people, culture and the tools of culture. Identity or knowing who you are is a fundamental characteristic of being human, and this is profoundly influenced by the culture that surrounds us. Positive cultural belonging helps to make children resilient, and respect for children's cultural background is an important aspect of recognizing their rights. Cultural meanings are important in many of the issues that have been traversed in this book. For example, there are a variety of cultural meanings of being healthy, children working, getting a good education, being responsible for your family, and acceptable ways to treat your children. It is therefore essential that children's rights are not decontextualized but placed within the cultural context where they are being applied. For example, a family can mean different things in cultural contexts, so it is inappropriate to judge all families and children through the lens of a nuclear family model.

Another aspect of sociocultural theory that is particularly relevant to the issue of children's rights is that adults can provide guidance and support (scaffolding) for children as they come to formulate their views, and express them. There are many examples throughout the book of the way that adults can scaffold children's experiences such as: parents helping children to internalize control of their own behavior; teachers talking to children, building on their interests and positioning them as authoritative learners; lawyers helping children to decide the type of residence and contact they have with parents; parents helping their children with their work commitments; social workers or children's rights advocates explaining child protection procedures and making sure that children in care have access to education and health services; doctors and nurses asking children about their symptoms or their levels of pain, explaining their treatments, and helping them take control of their own bodies. In order to be effective, adult guidance depends on warmth, reciprocity and balance of power, where adults are sensitive to what children know and can do, and can provide help, but only where it is needed. Ordinary conversations where children have the chance to initiate talk as well as respond are an effective way for adults to scaffold children's understanding. Adult guidance can be gradually phased out as children become better able to act independently without support.

It is not just adults who scaffold children's learning and coping, but other children and young people provide such support for each other. From an early age children negotiate and collaborate over activities and explorations, and working together has the advantage of integrating different perspectives and experiences to elicit new insights and solve problems. Friends are often the most effective support for other children when they struggle with difficulties, such as being bullied at school, being excluded or discriminated against, becoming ill, or having difficulties at home because of disputes between parents. Beyond providing personal support, peers working together can empower each other to bring about change in the systems that affect each others' lives. The best example of this in the book is the organizations of working children who have fought to continue working, but for the right not to be exploited and unfairly treated at work, and work together to improve their lives. For example, working children from the Ivory Coast collaborated with local health authorities to set up a scheme for working children to gain access to hospital consultations at the same price as school children (Miljeteig, 2000). Peer mediation processes at school for dealing with bullying is another example of children working together to support and guide each other.

8.4   CHILDREN AS CITIZENS

The fourth, and arguably the most progressive principle and a fundamental requirement of the UNCRC, is that children should have the right to have their views listened to, and taken seriously and to be treated as citizens, a theme that permeates this book. Inherent in citizenship is being accorded recognition, dignity and respect. Being a citizen implies that you are a part of a group, community and society, in which there are mutual obligations and a sharing of common interests (Smith & Bjerke, 2009). Citizenship involves having rights, but also having obligations to others. If children are treated as citizens, they are believed to have agency and decision-making capability, and not to be the passive objects of decisions made about them by others. Children as citizens are expected to be responsible and able to carry out tasks in their own and other people's interests.

I have argued that fairness and justice can be expected for children as citizens in how they are treated in families, at school and preschool, in child protection systems, in the workplace, and in health services. For example, children may be treated unfairly by being excluded from school without procedures that respect natural justice, children in child protection systems may be denied privacy and prevented from having a say in where they live or go to school, children may not get health-care when their families lack health insurance, and children may be exploited in the workplace. Being citizens means being accorded dignity and respect, and not subject to unfair, humiliating, or painful treatment. Corporal punishment at home, school or the workplace obviously completely denies children dignity and respect and does not accord children citizenship status.

Being treated like citizens, means that children should have the opportunity to express their views, to have access to information, and to have an input into decisions. Throughout the book, I have attempted to find out the views of children through relevant research on the topics I have covered. It is well worth finding out what children think or understand, not just because it recognizes their rights, but because it helps us to understand how they are affected by their treatment from parents, teachers, social workers, doctors, nurses, lawyers and employers, and what policy or practice is likely to work best to help them. Children experience a different reality from the adults who play a part in their lives. It took research on children's perspectives on their parents' separation or divorce, for example, to help adults understand how children's lives are transformed by marital transitions, and to develop laws and practices that are more respectful of their right to have their views listened to and taken into account. Research on children with chronic health conditions demonstrated to health professionals that these children were capable of understanding their condition, communicating with professionals, and having a part in decisions about their treatment. In education at the early childhood or school level, teachers who know children well and have worked on developing respectful, responsive relationships with them are more likely to help children to become lifelong learners.

Finally, being a citizen implies the necessity of making children's issues visible and making children's interests and rights a priority. Too often in the past children have been invisible and voiceless, and treated entirely as incompetent beings on the way to completion as adults. Children are citizens in the present not just waiting to be citizens in the future. Being a citizen is a dynamic ongoing process in which children are social partners with adults, so that they should be included and involved in contributing to their societies and communities.

8.5   THE ROLE OF RESEARCH

This book has relied on evidence from research to support arguments on what needs to change before children's rights can be realized. In my view it is very important that policies and practices are evidence-based, rather than relying on politics or theory. Researcher, Judith Ennew, argued that: "The greatest violation of children's rights is that we do not know enough about them or care enough to find out more" (Ennew, 2011, p. 154). I have argued elsewhere (Smith, 2015c) that good quality research from diverse multimethod research paradigms and a variety of disciplines is necessary, to contribute to implementing children's rights. While randomized control trials or large scale surveys may be suitable to answer some questions about whether interventions work on a large scale, qualitative research and formative evaluation is equally important to help us understand why policies and practices work or not, and to access the perspectives of participants in research.

There have been widespread political changes with the global shift toward neoliberalism, and these have usually affected children adversely. For example, unregulated poor quality services provided by profit-making entities, which rely on market forces to control quality, has led to appalling levels of quality in many early childhood services. There is a great deal of evidence to show the harmfulness of such poor quality for children's development, yet these practices persist and harm to children is tolerated. Examples of cuts to other services, such as health, education and child protection systems, are seen throughout the book, despite evidence that not only do they affect children adversely, but that they will lead to costs to society in the future. For example, if children from poor families are excluded from school and not engaged in education, their chances of obtaining skilled employment later on, mean that they may have to rely on welfare benefits in the future. But how much energy and resources are put into improving the capacity of schools to engage all children, or to programs like the Australian *Hands on Learning* Project (see Chapter 4)? If children live in unhealthy houses, do not get nutritious food, have poor access to medical care, this affects their lifelong health and becomes an ongoing cost to the country. Yet poor families in many parts of the developed and developing world have limited access to healthy environments or health services, for themselves and their children. While millions of dollars are spent on research about the effects of poverty, how many of the implications and recommendations of these research projects are put into practice?

Not only is it important to ensure that research on children's rights is prioritized and funded but it is also necessary to optimize the uptake of such research. The diffusion of research knowledge depends on such factors as the relationships between researchers and the end users, and the understanding that researchers have of the situation on the ground for people in services and agencies (customers and providers). Researchers have to be sensitive to local contexts, develop relationships with users, and be reliable in delivering what was promised. They need also to be good communicators, and find ways (other than through scientific journals) of tailoring the dissemination of research findings to different audiences. Skills in the use of such methods as the Internet, outside forums, informal conversations, the news media, YouTube videos and tailored professional development programs, are essential to get the best value out of quality research. It is up to politicians and governments, however, to implement good laws and policies, and to provide proper resources for their implementation, if conditions for children are to improve.

Education about children's rights is a fundamental factor in changing attitudes and promoting practices that support children's rights. Parents and professionals spend a great of their lives interacting and working with children, so they have awesome power to affect children's lives. Their understanding of the things that children are entitled to in their lives make a big difference, and therefore I believe that children's rights education should be a core component of professional preservice and ongoing education for teachers, doctors, nurses, police, social workers, lawyers, and any other professionals who impact on the lives of children. For children too, it is important to know about and understand human rights. Children, who understand rights, know that rights are not just for themselves, but also for other children. Children can act as change agents and advocates to promote rights and to fight against injustices that deny children's rights. Education about human rights is an important way of them learning about democracy. More is likely to be learned within the context of democratic processes at school, however, than through didactic teaching and formal civics lessons.

8.6 FINAL WORD ON THE ROLE OF THE UN CONVENTION

This book has drawn heavily on the principles and articles of the 1989 UNCRC to write about various aspects of children's rights, even though the convention does not provide the last word on these issues, and must respond dynamically to the issues and situations faced by children in a changing world. The UNCRC can play an important role in ensuring that the principles and articles are converted into concrete actions within ratifying countries. The UNCRC is a groundbreaking document, the most rapidly and widely ratified of all UN treaties, that helps us set goals for what ought to be achieved for children, and to assess progress in reaching those goals. Universal ratification of the treaty could be achieved if the U.S. was to ratify, enabling it to review its own progress, and utilize the expertise of the UN Committee on the Rights of the Child (CRC) to monitor implementation. The whole process of reporting to the CRC involves gathering data from a wide range of government ministries and departments, and this process itself helps to raise awareness of issues and concerns, and encourages openness and transparency. NGOs can play an important role by providing independent reports, and coordination between different NGOs over this process, helps build alliances for children's rights. Concluding observations from the CRC provide feedback and specific recommendations for each country, although follow-up and implementation is left to governments and NGOs. "Full implementation of the CRC remains a huge challenge for everyone" (Doek, 2011, p. 115). Despite difficulties, much can be achieved.

> The mainstreaming of children's rights is a deeply political project with potentially transformative consequences for the way in which children are viewed and engaged with by all actors in society .... It is this potential that inspires and motivates advocates for children to actively embrace the rights based approach as a means of making the invisible visible, giving the silenced a voice, redirecting scarce resources to meet children's health, educational, housing, nutritional and development needs and holding the state, and indeed the international community, accountable when they fail to meet the standards. (Tobin, 2011, p. 89)

REFERENCES

Ahrons, C. R. (2007). Family ties after divorce: Long-term implications for children. *Family Process, 46*(1), 53–65. doi:10.1111/j.1545-5300.2006.00191.x

Alanen, L. (2009). Generational order. In J. Qvortrup, W. A. Corsaro, & M-S. Honig (Eds.), *The Palgrave handbook of childhood studies* (pp. 159–174). London, UK: Palgrave-McMillan.

Alderson, P. (2001). Life and death: Agency and dependency in young children's health care. *Childrenz Issues, 5*(1), 23–27. Retrieved from: http://research.ioe.ac.uk/portal/en/publications/life-and-death-agency-and-dependency-in-young-childrens-health-care%28024548cb-98c1-4ec4-87a0-01ab33d3810c%29/export.html

Alderson, P. (2002). Young children's health care rights and consent. In B. Franklin (Ed.), *The new handbook of children's rights: Comparative policy and practice* (pp. 155–167). London and New York, NY: Routledge.

Alderson, P. (2015). Reforms to healthcare systems and policies: Influences from children's rights. In A. B. Smith (Ed.), *Enhancing children's rights: Connecting research, policy and practice* (pp. 17–32, Chapter 2). Basingstoke, UK: Palgrave MacMillan.

Alderson, P., Hawthorne, J., & Killen, M. (2005). The participation rights of premature babies. *International Journal of Children's Rights, 13*(1/2), 31–50. doi:10.1163/1571818054545231

Alderson, P., & Montgomery, J. (1996). *Health care choices: Making decisions with children.* London, UK: Institute for Public Policy Research.

Amato, P. R. (2010). Research on divorce: Continuing trends and new developments. *Journal of Marriage and the Family, 72*(3), 650–666. doi:10.1111/j.1741-3737.2010.00723.x

Anning, A. (2004). The co-construction of an early childhood curriculum. In A. Anning, J. Cullen, & M. Fleer (Eds.), *Early childhood education: Society and culture* (pp. 57–68). London, UK: Sage Publications.

Anyan, S. E., & Pryor, J. (2002). What is in a family? Adolescent perceptions. *Children & Society, 16*(5), 306–317. doi:10.1002/chi.716

Archard, D. (2012). Children's rights. In T. Cushman (Ed.), *Handbook of human rights* (pp. 324–332). Abingdon, Oxon and New York, NY: Routledge.

Archard, D., & Skivenes, M. (2009). Hearing the child. *Child and Family Social Work, 14*(4), 391–399.

Asher, I. (2008, October 29). *Improving our poor child health outcomes – what more can New Zealand do?* Keynote address to Paediatric Society of New Zealand Annual Scientific Meeting, Waitangi. Retrieved July 3, 2015 from www.paediatrics.org.nz/files/PSNZ%20Asher%20Child%20Health%20Oct%202008%20formatted.pdf

Asher, I. (2015, May 14). *More income is required to improve the health of poor children.* Briefing Papers. Child Poverty Action Group. Retrieved July 2, 2015 from http://briefingpapers.co.nz/2015/05/more-income-is-required-to-improve-the-health-of-poor-children/

Attiah, K. (2014, November 21). Why won't the U.S. ratify the U.N.'s child rights treaty? *The Washington Post.* Retrieved March 11, 2015 from http://www.washingtonpost.com/blogs/post-partisan/wp/2014/11/21/why-wont-the-u-s-ratify-the-u-n-s-child-rights-treaty/

Atwool, N. (1999). New Zealand children in the 1990s: Beneficiaries of new right economic policy. *Children & Society, 13*(5), 380–393. doi:10.1111/j.1099-0860.1999.tb00133.x

Atwool, N. (2010). *Children in care: A report into the quality of services provided to children in care.* Wellington , New Zealand: Office of the Children's Commissioner.

Australian Human Rights Commission. (2014). *Inquiry into childcare and early childhood learning: Submission to the productivity commission.* Sydney: Australian Human Rights Commission.

Baiyee, M., Hawkins, C., & Polakow, V. (2013). Children's rights and educational exclusion. In B. Swadener, L. Lundy, J. Habashi, & N. Blanchet-Cohen (Eds.), *Children's rights and education* (pp. 39–62). New York, NY: Peter Lang.

Barbarin, O., & Aikens, N. (2015). Overcoming the educational disadvantages of poor children: How much do teacher preparation, workload and expectations matter? *American Journal of Orthopsychiatry, 85*(2), 101–105. doi:10.1037/ort0000060

Barber, J., & Delfabbro, P. (2004). *Children in foster care.* London, UK and New York, NY: Routledge.

Barber, J., & Delfabbro, P. (2005). Children's adjustment to long-term foster care. *Children and Youth Services Review, 27*(3), 329–340. doi:10.1016/j.childyouth.2004.10.010

Barnes, V. (2012). Social work and advocacy with young people: Rights and care in practice. *British Journal of Social Work, 42*(7), 1275–1292. doi:10.1093/bjsw/bcr142

Barnett, W. S. (1995). Long-term effects of early childhood programs on cognitive and school outcomes. *The Future of Children, 5*(3), 25–50. doi:10.2307/1602366

Barnett, W. S., & Ackerman, D. J. (2006). Costs, benefits, and long-term effects of early care and education programs: Recommendations and cautions for community developers. *Community Development, 37*(3), 86–100. doi:10.1080/15575330609490209

Bartholet, E. (2011). Ratification by the United States of the Convention on the Rights of the Child: Pros and cons from a child's rights perspective. *Annals of the American Association of Political and Social Science, 633*(1), 80–101. doi:10.1177/0002716210382389

Bartle, C. (2002). Breast milk, breastfeeding and the developing brain. *Childrenz Issues, 6*(2), 39–43. Retrieved from http://search.informit.com.au/document-Summary;dn=458463665021176;res=IELFSC

Bartle, C., & Duncan, J. (2010). Food for thought: 'Breastfeeding and early childhood education services' [online]. *Early Childhood Folio, 14*(2), 31–36. Retrieved from http://search.informit.com.au/documentSummary; dn=310886420866953;res=IELHSS

Berger, L. M., & Shook Slack, K. (2014). Child protection and child well-being. In A. Ben-Arieh, F. Casas, I. Frønes, & J. Korbin (Eds.), *Handbook of child well-being* (pp. 2965–2992). Dordecht: Springer. doi:10.1007/978-90-481-9063-8_120

Berrueta-Clement, J. R., Schweinhart, L. J., Barnett, W. S., Epstein, A. S., & Weikart, D. P. (1984). *Changed lives: The effects of the Perry Preschool Program on youths through age 19.* Ypsilanti, MI: High Scope Press.

Bessell, S. (2011). Participation in decision-making in out-of-home care in Australia: What do young people say? *Children and Youth Services Review, 33*(4), 496–501. doi:10.1016/j.child.youth.2010.05.006

Bishop, R., & Berryman, M. (2006). *Culture speaks: Cultural relationships and classroom learning.* Wellington, New Zealand: Huia Publishers.

Bishop, R., Berryman, M., Cavanagh, T., & Teddy, L. (2009). *Te Kotahitanga*: Addressing educational disparities facing Māori students in New Zealand. *Teaching and Teacher Education, 25*(5), 734–742. doi:10.1016/j.tate.2009.01.009

Bishop, R., Berryman, M., Wearmouth, J., Peter, M., & Clapham, S. (2012). Professional development, changes in teacher practice and improvements in indigenous students' educational performance: A case study from New Zealand. *Teaching and Teacher Education, 28*(5), 694–705. doi:10.1016/j.tate. 2012.02.002

Blair, A. (2005). The invisible child in education law. In J. Goddard, S. McNamee, A. James, & A. James (Eds.), *The politics of childhood* (pp. 166–184). Basingstoke, UK: Palgrave MacMillan.

Boothby, N., Balster, R. L., Goldman, P., Wessells, M. G., Zeanah, C. H., Huebner, G., & Garbarino, J. (2012). Coordinated and evidence-based policy and practice for protecting children outside of family care. *Child Abuse & Neglect, 36*(10), 743–751. doi:10.1016/j.chiabu.2012.09.007

Boston, J., & Chapple, S. (2014). *Child poverty in New Zealand.* Wellington, New Zealand: Bridget Williams Books.

Bourdillon, M. (2006). Children and work: A review of current literature and debates. *Development and Change, 37*(6), 1201–1226. doi:10.1111/j.1467-7660.2006.00519.x

Boyden, J. (1997). Childhood and the policy makers: A comparative perspective on the globalization of childhood. In A. James & A. Prout (Eds.), *Constructing and reconstructing childhood: Contemporary issues in the sociological study of childhood* (2nd ed., pp. 190–215). London, UK: The Falmer Press.

Bronfenbrenner, U. (1979a). *The ecology of human development.* Cambridge, MA: Harvard University Press.

Bronfenbrenner, U. (1979b). Who cares for children? *Delta, 25,* 2–15.

Bradley, M., & Aldgate, J. (1994). Short-term family based care for children in need. *Adoption and Fostering, 18*(4), 24–29. doi:10.1177/030857599401800406

Bradley, R. H., & Corwyn, R. F. (2002). Socioeconomic status and child development. *Annual Review of Psychology, 53*(1), 371–399. doi:10.1146/annurev.psych.53.100901.135233

Bruner, J. (1995). Foreword: From joint attention to meeting of minds: An introduction. In C. Moore & P. J. Dunham (Eds.), *Joint attention: Its origins and role in development* (pp. 1–14). Hillsdale, NJ: Lawrence Erlbaum Associates.

Burman, E. (2008). *Deconstructing developmental psychology* (2nd ed.). Hove, UK and New York, NY: Routledge.

Burrows, L. (2011). 'I'm proud to be me': Health, community and schooling. *Policy Futures in Education, 9*(3), 341–352. doi:10.2304/pfie.2011.9.3.341

Burrows, L., & Wright, J. (2004). The good life: New Zealand children's perspectives on health and self. *Sport, Education and Society, 9*(2), 193–205. doi:10.1080/1357332042000233930

Burrows, L., Wright, J., & McCormack, J. (2009). Dosing up on food and physical activity: New Zealand children's ideas about 'health'. *Health Education Journal, 68*(3), 157–169. doi:10.1177/0017896909339332

Bussman, K-D., Erthal, C., & Schroth, A. (2011). Effects of banning corporal punishment in Europe: A five-nation comparison. In J. Durrant & A. B. Smith (Eds.), *Global pathways to abolishing physical punishment: Realizing children's rights* (pp. 299–322). New York, NY: Routledge.

Caldwell, B. (1989). All day kindergarten—Assumptions, precautions, and overgeneralizations. *Early Childhood Research Quarterly, 4*(2), 261–266. doi:10.1016/s0885-2006(89)80007-9

Cameron, R. J., & Maginn, C. (2009). *Achieving positive outcomes for children in care.* Los Angeles and London: Sage.

Camilli, G., Vargas, S., Ryan, S., & Barnett, W. S. (2010). Meta-analysis of the effects of early education interventions on cognitive and social development. *Teachers College Record, 112*(3), 579–620. http://www.tcrecord.org/library ID Number 15440

Campbell, M. (2005). Cyber bullying: An old problem in a new guise? *Australian Journal of Guidance and Counselling, 15*(1), 68–76. doi:10.1375/ajgc.15.1.68

Campbell, F. A., Pungello, E. P., Burchinal, M., Kainz, K., Pan, Y., Wasik, B. H., . . . Ramey, C. T. (2012). Adult outcomes as a function of an early childhood educational program: An Abecedarian Project follow-up. *Developmental Psychology, 48*(4), 1033. doi:10.1037/a0026644

Cannella, G. (1997). *Deconstructing early childhood: Social justice and revolution: Rethinking early childhood.* New York, NY: Peter Lang Publishing.

Cantwell, N. (2011). Are children's rights still human? In A. Invernizzi & J. Williams (Eds.), *The human rights of children: From vision to implementation* (pp. 37–60). Farnham, UK: Ashgate.

Cappadocia, M. C., Craig, W. M., & Pepler, D. (2013). Cyberbullying: Prevalence, stability, and risk factors during adolescence. *Canadian Journal of School Psychology, 28*(2), 171–192. doi:10.1177/0829573513491212

Carpenter, D., Stover, A., Slota, C., Ayala, G. X., Yeatts, K., Tudor, G., . . . Sleath, B. (2014). An evaluation of physicians' engagement of children with asthma in treatment-related discussions. *Journal of Child Health Care, 18*(3), 261–274. doi:10.1177/1367493513489780

Carr, M. (1997). *Learning Stories.* Position paper 5. Project for Assessing Children's Experiences. Department of Early Childhood Studies, University of Waikato.

Carr, M. (1998). *Assessing children's experiences in early childhood: Final report to the Ministry of Education. Part two: Case Studies.* Wellington: Ministry of Education.

Carr, M. (2001). *Assessment in early childhood settings: Learning stories.* London, UK: Paul Chapman.

Carr, M., Hatherly, A., Lee, W., & Ramsey, K. (2005). Te Whāriki and assessment: A case study of teacher change. In J. Nuttall (Ed.), *Weaving 'Te Whāriki': Aotearoa New Zealand's early childhood curriculum document in theory and practice* (pp. 187–214). Palmerston North, New Zealand: Dunmore Press.

Carr, M., Smith, A. B., Duncan, J., Jones, C., Lee, W., & Marshall, K. (2010). *Learning in the making: Disposition and design in early education.* Rotterdam and New York, NY: Sense Publishers.

Cashmore, J. (2002). Promoting the participation of children and young people in care. *Child Abuse and Neglect, 26*(8), 837–847. doi:10.1016/s0145-2134(02)00353-8

Cashmore, J., & Parkinson, P. (2007). What responsibility do courts have to hear children's voices. *International Journal of Children's Rights, 15*(1), 43–60. doi:10.1163/092755607x181694

Castro, C. (2010). An overview of child labour statistics. In A. Fassa, D. Parker, & T. Scanlon (Eds.), *Child Labour: A public health perspective* (pp. 7–24). Oxford, UK: Oxford University Press.

Cherlin, A. J. (2010). Demographic trends in the United States: A review of research in the 2000s. *Journal of Marriage and the Family, 72*(3), 403–419. doi:10.1111/j.1741-3737.2010.00710.x

Cicchetti, D., Toth, S. L., & Hennessy, K. (1989). Research on the consequences of maltreatment and its application to educational settings. *Topics in Early Childhood Special Education, 9*(2), 33–55. doi:10.1177/027112148900900204

Clark, R. M. (2010). *Childhood in society for early childhood studies.* Exeter: Learning Matters.

Close, P. (2009). Making sense of child labour in modern society. In J. Qvortrup, K.B. Rosier & D.A. Kinney (Eds.), *Structural, Historical, and Comparative Perspectives (Sociological Studies of Children and Youth, Volume 12)* (167–194). Emerald Group Publishing Limited. doi:10.1108/s1537-4661(2009)0000012012

Cohen, C. P. (1995). Children's rights: An American perspective. In B. Franklin (Ed.), *The handbook of children's rights: Comparative policy and practice* (pp. 163–175). London, UK: Routledge.

Connors, C., & Stalker, K. (2007). Children's experiences of disability: Pointers to a social model of childhood disability. *Disability & Society, 22*(1), 19–33. doi:10.1080/09687590601056162

Craig, W., Harel-Fisch, H., Fogel-Grinvald, H., Dostaler, S., Hetland, J., Simons-Morton, B., & HBSC Bullying Writing Group. (2009). A cross-national profile of bullying and victimization among adolescents in 40 countries. *International Journal of Public Health, 54*(S2), 216–224. doi:10.1007/s00038-009-5413-9

Dahlberg, G. (2009). Policies in Early Childhood Education and Care: Potentialities for agency, play and learning. In J. Qvortrup, W. A. Corsaro, & M-S.. Honig (Eds.), *The Palgrave handbook of childhood studies* (pp. 228–237). Basingstoke, Hampshire: Palgrave MacMillan.

Daly, D., & Dowd, T. P. (1992). Characteristics of effective, harm-free environments for children in out-of-home care. *Child Welfare, 71*(6), 487–496. http://www.ncbi.nlm.nih.gov/pubmed/1424944

Davies, H. (2012). Affinities, seeing and feeling like family: Exploring why children value face-to-face contact. *Childhood, 19*(1), 8–23. doi:10.1177/0907568211400453

Desai, M. (2010). *A rights preventative approach for the psychological well-being in childhood.* Dordrecht, Netherlands: Springer.

Dixon, R., & Nussbaum, M. C. (2012). Children's rights and a capabilities approach: The question of special priority. *Cornell Law Review, 97*, 549–594. Retrieved from http://chicagounbound.uchicago.edu/cgi/viewcontent.cgi?-article=1056&context=public_law_and_legal_theory

Dobbs, T. (2005). *Insights: Children and young people speak out about family discipline.* Wellington, New Zealand: Save the Children New Zealand.

Dobbs, T. (2007). What do children tell us about physical punishment as a risk factor for child abuse. *Social Policy Journal of New Zealand, 30*, 145–162. Retrieved from http://www.msd.govt.nz/about-msd-and-our-work/publications-resources/journals-and-magazines/social-policy-journal/spj30/30-children-physical-punishment-risk-factor-child-abuse-p145-162.html

Dobbs, T., Smith, A. B., & Taylor, N. (2006). 'No, we don't get a say, children just suffer the consequences': Children talk about family discipline. *International Journal of Children's Rights, 14*(2), 137–156. doi:10.1163/157181806777922694

Doek, J. (2011). The CRC: Dynamics and directions of monitoring its implementation. In A. Invernizzi & J. Williams (Eds.), *The human rights of children: From vision to implementation* (pp. 99–116). Farnham, UK: Ashgate.

Doytch, N., Thelen, N., & Mendoza, R. (2014). The impact of FDI on child labor: Insights from an empirical analysis of sectoral FDI data and case studies. *Children and Youth Services Review, 47,* 157–167. doi:10.1016/j.childyouth.2014.09.008

Duncan, G., Ziol-Guest, K. M., & Kalil, A. (2010). Early-childhood poverty and adult attainment, behavior, and health. *Child Development, 81*(1), 306–325. doi:10.1111/j.1467-8624.2009.01396.x

Durrant, J. (2011). The empirical rationale for eliminating physical punishment. In J. Durrant & A. B. Smith (Eds.), *Global pathways to abolishing physical punishment: Realizing children's rights* (pp. 42–63). New York, NY: Routledge.

Durrant, J., & Ensom, R. (2012). Physical punishment of children: Lessons from 20 years of research. *Canadian Medical Association Journal, 184*(12), 1373–1377. doi:10.1503/cmaj.101314

Earls, F. (2011). Children: From Rights to Citizenship. *Annals of the American Association of Political and Social Science, 633*(1), 6–16. doi:10.1177/0002716210383637

Economist Intelligence Unit. (2012). *Starting well: Benchmarking early education across the world. A report from the Economist Intelligence Unit.* Commissioned by the Lien Foundation. Retrieved from www.economistinsights.com/leadership-talent-innovation/analysis/starting-well/fullreport

Ennew, J. (1995). Outside children: Street children's rights. In B. Franklin (Ed.), *The handbook of children's rights: Comparative policy and practice* (pp. 201–214). London, UK: Routledge.

Ennew, J. (2011). Has research improved the human rights of children? Or have the information needs of the CRC improved data about children? In A. Invernizzi & J. Williams (Eds.), *The human rights of children: From vision to implementation* (pp. 133–158). Farnham, UK: Ashgate.

Epstein, A. S., Johnson, S., & Lafferty, P. (2011). The HighScope approach. In L. Miller & L. Pound (Eds.), *Critical Issues in the Early Years Series. Theories and approaches to learning in the early years* (pp. 101–118). London, UK: Sage.

Esping-Andersen, G. (2008). Childhood investments and skill formation. *International Tax and Public Finance, 15*(1), 19–44. doi:10.1007/s10797-007-9033-0

European Commission. (2011). *Early Childhood Education and Care: Providing all our children with the best start for the world of tomorrow.* Brussels, February 17, 2011, COM (2011).

Evans, G. W. (2004). The environment of child poverty. *American Psychologist, 59*(2), 77–92. doi:10.1037/0003-066x.59.2.77

Every Child Counts. (2010). *Eradicating child poverty in New Zealand.* Auckland, New Zealand: Every Child Counts Steering Group.

Expert Advisory Group on Solutions to Child Poverty. (2012). *Solutions to child poverty in New Zealand: Evidence for action.* Wellington, New Zealand: Office of the Commissioner for Children.

Fass, P. S. (2011). A historical context for the United Nations convention on the rights of the child. *Annals of the American Association of Political and Social Science, 633*(1), 17–29. doi:10.1177/0002716210382388

Featherstone, B., Morris, K., & White, S. (2014). A marriage made in hell: Early intervention meets child protection. *British Journal of Social Work, 44*(7), 1735–1749. doi:10.1093/bjsw/bct052

Fleer, M., & Richardson, C. (2004). Mapping the transformation of understanding. In A. Anning, J. Cullen, & M. Fleer (Eds.), *Early childhood education: Society and culture* (pp. 119–136). London, UK: Sage Publications.

Fox, S. E., Levitt, P., & Nelson, C. A. (2010). How the timing and quality of early experience influence the development of brain architecture. *Child Development, 81*(1), 28–40. doi:10.1111/j.1467-8624.2009.01380.x

Franklin, B. (1995). The case for children's rights: A progress report. In B. Franklin (Ed.), *The handbook of children's rights: Comparative policy and practice* (pp. 3–22). London, UK: Routledge.

Franklin, A., & Soper, P. (2005). Listening and responding? Children's participation in health care within England. *International Journal of Children's Rights, 13*(1), 11–29. doi:10.1163/1571818054545277

Frederiksen, L. (1999). Child and youth employment in Denmark: Comments on children's work from their own perspective. *Childhood, 6*(1), 101–112. doi:10.1177/0907568299006001008

Freeman, M. (1998). The sociology of childhood and children's rights, *International Journal of Children's Rights, 6*(4), 433–444. doi:10.1163/15718189820494175

Freeman, M. (2007). Why it remains important to take children's rights seriously. *International Journal of Children's Rights, 15*(1), 5–23. doi:10.1163/092755607x181711

Freeman, M. (2009). Children's rights as human rights: Reading the UNCRC. In J. Qvortrup, W. A. Corsaro, & M-S. Honig (Eds.), *The Palgrave handbook of childhood studies* (pp. 377–393). Basingstoke, Hampshire: Palgrave MacMillan.

Freeman, M. (2011). The value and values of children. In A. Invernizzi & J. Williams (Eds.), *The human rights of children: From vision to implementation* (pp. 21–36). Farnham, UK: Ashgate.

Freeman, M., & Saunders, B. (2014). Can we conquer child abuse if we don't outlaw physical chastisement of children? *International Journal of Children's Rights, 22*(4), 681–709. doi:10.1163/15718182-02204002

Gaffney, M., & Taylor, N. (2004, July). *Developing a more positive school culture to address bullying and improve school relationships: Case studies from two primary schools and one intermediate school.* Dunedin, New Zealand: Ministry of Social Development.

Gard, M. (2008). Producing little decision makers and goal setters in the age of the obesity crisis. *Quest, 60*(4), 488–502. doi:10.1080/00336297.2008.10483594

Garvis, S., & Austin, L. (2007). The forgotten children in Australian detention centres before 2005. *Australian Journal of Early Childhood, 32*(1), 19–23. http://www.earlychildhoodaustralia.org.au/wp-content/uploads/2014/06/AJEC0701.pdf

Gasson, R., & Linsell, C. (2011). Young workers: A New Zealand perspective. *International Journal of Children's Rights, 19*(4), 641–659. doi:10.1163/157181811x547272

Gasson, R., Calder, J., Diorio, J., Smith, A. B., & Stigter, J. R. (2015). Young people's employment: Protection or participation? *Childhood, 22*(2), 154–170. doi:10.1177/0907568214524456

Gershoff, E. T., & Bitensky, S. H. (2008). The case against corporal punishment of children: Converging evidence from social science research and international human rights law and implications for U.S. public policy. *Psychology, Public Policy and Law, 13*(4), 231–272. doi:10.1037/1076-8971.13.4.231

Gershoff, E. T., Purtell, K. M., & Holas, I. (2015). *Corporal punishment in US public schools: Legal precedents, current practices, and future policy.* New York, NY: Springer.

Gilligan, R. (2000). The key role of social workers in promoting the well-being of children in state care – a neglected dimension of reforming policies. *Children and Society, 14*(4), 267–276. doi:10.1002/1099-0860(200009)14:4<267::aid-chi629>3.0.co;2-e

Global Initiative to End All Corporal Punishment of Children. (2015). Retrieved November 13 from http://www.endcorporalpunishment.org/

Goelman, H., Forer, B., Kershaw, P., Doherty, G., Lero, D., & LaGrange, A. (2006). Towards a predictive model of quality in Canadian child care centers. *Early Childhood Research Quarterly, 21*(3), 280–295. doi:10.1016/j.ecresq.2006.07.005

González, N., Moll, L. C., & Amanti, C. (2005). *Funds of knowledge: Theorizing practices in households, communities and classrooms.* Mahwah, NJ: Lawrence Erlbaum Associates.

Graham, L. J., & Harwood, V. (2011). Developing capabilities for school inclusion: Engaging diversity through inclusive school communities. *International Journal of Inclusive Education, 15*(1), 135–152. doi:10.1080/13603116.2010.496208

Greeno, J. (2006). Authoritative, accountable positioning and connected, general knowing: Progressive themes in understanding transfer. *Journal of the Learning Sciences, 15*(4), 537–547. doi:10.1207/s15327809jls1504_4

Hall, E. L., & Rudkin, J. K. (2011). *Seen and heard: Children's rights in early childhood education.* New York, NY: Teachers College Press.

Hanson, K., & Nieuwenhuys, O. (2013). Introduction: Living rights, translations, social justice. In K. Hansen & O. Nieuwenhuys (Eds.), *Living Rights – Theorising children's rights in international development* (pp. 3–26). Cambridge, UK: Cambridge University Press.

Harcourt, D., & Hägglund, S. (2013). Turning the UNCRC upside down: A bottom-up perspective on children's rights. *International Journal of Early Years Education, 21*(4), 286–299, doi:10.1080/09669760.2013.867167

Heckman, J. J. (2011). Effective child development strategies. In E. Zigler, W. S. Gillam, & W. S. Barnett (Eds.), *The pre-K debates: Current controversies and issues* (pp. 2–8). Baltimore, MD: Paul Brookes Publishing Co.

Heesterman, W. (2005). Child labour and children's rights: Policy issues in three affluent societies. In J. Goddard, S. McNamee, A. L. James, & A. James (Eds.), *The politics of childhood: International perspectives, contemporary developments* (pp. 73–89). Basingstoke, UK: Palgrave Macmillan.

Helburn, S. W. (1995). *Cost, quality and child outcomes in child care centers: Technical Report.* Denver, CO: Department of Economics, Center for Research in Economic and Social Policy, University of Colorado at Denver.

Hemphill, S. A., & Schneider, S. (2013). Excluding students from school: A re-examination from a children's rights perspective. *International Journal of Children's Rights, 21*(1), 88–96. doi:10.1163/15718182-55680008

Hendrick, H. (2009). The evolution of childhood in Western Europe c.1400-c.1750. In J. Qvortrup, W. A. Corsaro, & M-S. Honig (Eds.), *The Palgrave handbook of childhood studies* (pp. 99–113). London, UK: Palgrave-McMillan.

Herztman, C., & Wiens, M. (1996). Child development and long-term outcomes: A population health perspective and summary of successful interventions. *Social Science Medicine, 43*(7), 1083–1095. doi:10.1016/0277-9536(96)00028-7

Hetherington, E. M. (2006). The influence of conflict, marital problem solving and parenting on children's adjustment in nondivorced, divorced and remarried families. In A. Clarke-Stewart & J. Dunn (Eds.), *Families count: Effects on child and adolescent development* (pp. 203–237). New York, NY: Cambridge University Press.

Hill, M., & Tisdall, K. (1997). *Children and Society.* London, UK and New York, NY: Longman.

Holzman, L. (1995). Creating developmental learning environments: A Vygotskian perspective. *School Psychology International, 16*(2), 199–212. doi:10.1177/0143034395162009

ILO. (1999). *Convention concerning the prohibition and immediate action for the elimination of the worst forms of child labour.* Retrieved July 28, 2015 from http://www.ilo.org/public/english/standards/relm/ilc/ilc87/com-chic.htm

ILO. (2015a). *Ratifications of C138 - minimum age convention, 1973 (No. 138).* Retrieved July 27, 2015 from http://www.ilo.org/dyn/normlex/en/f?p=1000:1 1300:0::NO:11300:P11300_INSTRUMENT_ID:312283

ILO. (2015b). *Ratifications of C182 - worst forms of child labour convention, 1999 (No. 182).* Retrieved July 28 from http://www.ilo.org/dyn/normlex/en/f?p=NORMLEXPUB:11300:0::NO::P11300_INSTRUMENT_ID:312327

ILO. (2015c). *Child labour.* Retrieved July 28 from http://www.ilo.org/global/topics/child-labour/lang--en/index.htm

Irwin, L., Johnson, J., Henderson, A., Dahinten, V., & Hertzman, C. (2006). Examining how contexts shape young children's perspectives of health. *Child Care, Health and Development, 33*(4), 353–359. doi:10.1111/j.1365-2214.2006.00668.x

James, A. (2009). Agency. In J. Qvorturp, W. A. Corsaro, & M-S. Honig (Eds.), *Childhood studies* (pp. 34–45). New York, NY: Palgrave Macmillan.

Jamieson, L., & Highet, G. (2013). Troubling loss? Children's experiences of major disruptions in family life. In J. Ribbens McCarthy, C-A. Hooper, & V. Gillies (Eds.), *Family troubles? Exploring change and challenges in the family lives of children and young people* (pp. 135–150). Bristol, UK: Policy Press.

John, M. (2003). *Children's rights and power: Charging up for a new century.* London, UK: Jessica Kingsley.

Jones, P., & Welch, S. (2010). *Rethinking children's rights: Attitudes in contemporary society.* New Childhood Series. London, UK: Bloomsbury.

Karagianni, P., Mitakidou, S., & Tressou, E. (2013). What's right in children's rights? The subtext of dependency. In B. Swadener, L. Lundy, J. Habashi, & N. Blanchet-Cohen (Eds.), *Children's Rights and Education* (pp. 82–98). New York, NY: Peter Lang.

Karoly, L. A., Greenwood, P. W., Everingham, S. S., Hoube, J., Kilburn, M. R., Rydell, C. P., Sanders, M., and Chiesa, J. (1998). *Investing in our children: What we know and don't know about the costs and benefits of early childhood interventions.* Santa Monica, CA: Rand Corporation.

Karoly, L. A., Kilburn, M. R., & Cannon, J. S. (2005). *Early childhood intervention: Proven results, future promises.* Santa Monica, CA: Rand Corporation.

Kassem, D. (2010). Life as a looked-after child: The parent of last resort. In D. Kassem, L. Murphy, & E. Taylor (Eds.), *Key Issues in Childhood and Youth Studies* (pp. 96–107). Abingdon, Oxon: Routledge.

Kaufman, N. H. (1990). *Human rights treaties and the senate: A history of opposition.* Chapel Hill, NC: The University of North Carolina Press.

Kelly, B. (2005). "Chocolate... makes you autism": Impairment, disability and childhood identities. *Disability & Society, 20*(3), 261–275. doi:10.1080/09687590500060687

Kelly, J. B. (2007). Children's living arrangements following separation and divorce: Insights from empirical and clinical research. *Family Process, 46*(1), 35–52. doi:10.1111/j.1545-5300.2006.00190.x

Kennedy, A. (2010). Children and the notion of risk: The nanny state? In D. Kassem, L. Murphy, & E. Taylor (Eds.), *Key Issues in Childhood and Youth Studies* (pp. 75–85). Abingdon, Oxon: Routledge.

Kerber-Ganse, W. (2015). Eglantyne Jebb – a pioneer of the convention on the rights of the child. *International Journal of Children's Rights, 23*(2), 272–282. doi:10.1163/15718182-02302003

Kilkelly, U., & Donnelly, M. (2011). Participation in health care: The views and experiences of children and young people. *International Journal of Children's Rights, 19*(1), 107–125. doi:10.1163/157181810x522379

Lagaay, M., & Courtney, L. (2013). *Time to listen: Independent advocacy within the child protection process.* London, UK: National Children's Bureau.

Lally, R. J., Mangione, P., & Honig, A. S. (1988). The Syracuse University Family Development Research Program: Long-range impact of an early intervention with low-income children and their families. In D. Powell (Ed.), *Parent education as an early childhood intervention: Emerging directions in theory, research and practice* (pp. 79–104). Norwood, NJ: Ablex Publishers.

Lamb, M. (1998). Nonparental child care: Context, quality, correlates and consequences. In I. E. Sigel & K. A. Renninger (Eds.), *Handbook of child psychology* (Vol. 4, pp. 73–144). New York, NY: Wiley.

Landry, S. H., Zucker, T. A., Taylor, H. B., Swank, P. R., Williams, J. M., Assel, M., Crawford, A., Huang, W., Clancy-Menchetti, J., Lonigan, C. J., Phillips, B. M., Eisenberg, N., Spinrad, T. L., de Villiers, J., de Villiers, P., Barnes, M., Starkey, P., Klein, A. (2014). Enhancing early child care quality and learning for toddlers at risk: The responsive early childhood program. *Developmental Psychology, 50*(2), 526–541. doi:10.1037/a0033494

Lansdown, G. (1994). Children's rights. In B. Mayall (Ed.), *Children's childhoods: Observed and experienced* (pp.33–44). London, UK: Falmer Press.

Lansdown, G., Jimerman, S. R., & Shahroozi, R. (2014). Children's rights and school psychology: Children's right to participation. *Journal of School Psychology, 52*(1), 3–12. doi:10.1016/j.jsp.2013.12.006

Landsman, M. J., & Boel-Studt, S. (2011). Fostering families' and children's rights to family connections. *Child Welfare, 90*(4), 19–40. Retrieved from http://www.ncbi.nlm.nih.gov/pubmed/22413378

Laughlin, L. (2014). *A child's day: Living arrangements, nativity, and family transitions: 2011 (Selected indicators of child well-being).* Household Economic Studies, United States Census. Retrieved from http://www.census.gov/content/dam/Census/library/publications/2014/demo/p70-139.pdf

Lengborn, T. (2000). *Ellen Key 1849-1926.* Retrieved March 5, 2015 from http://www.ibe.unesco.org/publications/ThinkersPdf/keye.pdf

Leonard, M. (2002). Working on your doorstep: Child newspaper deliverers in Belfast. *Childhood, 9*(2), 190–204. doi:10.1177/0907568202009002804

Liebel, M. (2004). *A will of their own: Cross-cultural perspectives on working children.* London, UK: Zed Books.

Liebel, M. (2012a). Hidden aspects of children's rights history. In M. Liebel, K. Hanson, & I. Saadi (Eds.), *Children's rights from below: Cross-cultural perspectives* (pp. 29–42). Basingstoke, UK: Palgrave McMillan.

Liebel, M. (2012b). Framing the issue: Rethinking children's rights. In M. Liebel, K. Hanson, & I. Saadi (Eds.), *Children's rights from below: Cross-cultural perspectives* (pp. 9–28). Basingstoke, UK: Palgrave McMillan.

Liebel, M., & Saadi, I. (2012). Cultural variations in constructions of children's participation. In M. Liebel, K. Hanson, & I. Saadi (Eds.), *Children's rights from below: Cross-cultural perspectives* (pp. 162–182). Basingstoke, UK: Palgrave McMillan.

Limber, S. P., & Flekkøy, M. G. (1995). *The UN Convention on the Rights of the Child: Its relevance for social scientists.* Ann Arbor, MI: Society for Research in Child Development.

Lindahl, M. (2008). Children's right to democratic upbringings. *International Journal of Early Childhood, 37*(3), 33–47. doi:10.1007/bf03168344

Lonne, B., Parton, N., Thomson, J., & Harries, M. (2009). *Reforming child protection.* London, UK: Routledge.

Lundy, L. (2012). Children's rights and educational policy in Europe: The implementation of the United Nations Convention on the Rights of the Child. *Oxford Review of Education, 38*(4), 393–411. doi:10.1080/03054985.2012.704874

MacArthur, J. (2013). Sustaining friendships, relationships and rights at school. *International Journal of Inclusive Education, 17*(8), 793–811. doi:10.1080/13603116.2011.602526

MacArthur, J., Kelly, B., & Higgins, N. (2005). Supporting the learning and social experiences of students with disabilities: What does the research say? In D. Fraser, R. Moltzen, & K. Ryba (Eds.), *Learners with special needs in Aotearoa New Zealand* (3rd ed., pp. 49–73). Palmerston North, New Zealand: Dunmore Press.

MacArthur, J., Sharp, S., Kelly, B., & Gaffney, M. (2007). Disabled children negotiating school life: Agency, difference and teaching practice. *International Journal of Children's Rights, 15*(1), 99–120. doi:10.1163/092755607X181720

McCluskey, G., Riddell, S., & Weedon, E. (2015). Children's rights, school exclusion and alternative education provision. *International Journal of Inclusive Education, 19*(6), 595–607. doi:10.1080/13603116.2014.961677

McEvilly, N., Verheul, M., & Atencio, M. (2013). Physical education at preschools: Practioners' and children's engagement with physical activity and health discourses. *British Journal of Sociology of Education, 36,* 832–852. doi:10.1080/01425692.2013.848780

McNaughton, G., & Smith, K. (2009). Children's rights in early childhood. In M. J. Kehily (Ed.), *An introduction to childhood studies* (2nd ed., pp. 161–176). Maidenhead and New York, NY: Open University Press.

Marcus, R. F. (1991). The attachments of children in foster care. *Genetic, Social and General Psychology Monographs, 117*(4), 347–394.

Masson, J. (2009). Child protection. In H. Montgomery & M. Kellett (Eds.), *Children and young people's worlds: Developing frameworks for integrated practice* (pp. 145–164). Bristol, UK: Policy Press/Open University.

Matheson, I. (2015). *Slipping down ladders and climbing up snakes: The educational experiences of young adults who were in foster care.* (Thesis, Doctor of Education). University of Otago. Retrieved from http://hdl.handle.net/10523/5769

Maurás, M. (2011). Public policies and child rights: Entering the third decade of the Convention on the Rights of the Child. *Annals of the American Association of Political and Social Science, 633*(1), 52–65. doi:10.1177/0002716210382993

Mayall, B. (2009). Generational relations at family level. In J. Qvortrup, W. A. Corsaro, & M-S. Honig (Eds.), *The Palgrave handbook of childhood studies* (pp. 175–187). London, UK: Palgrave-McMillan.

Maybin, J., & Woodhead, M. (Eds.). (2003). *Childhoods in context.* Hoboken, NJ: John Wiley & Sons Ltd.

Meade, A., Robinson, L., Smorti, S., Stuart, M., & Williamson, J. (2012). *Early childhood teachers' work in education and care centres.* Wellington, New Zealand: Te Tari Puna Ora or Aotearoa, New Zealand Childcare Association.

Meadows, S. (2010). *The child as a social person.* New York, NY: Psychology Press.

Melton, G. B. (2005a). Treating children like people: A framework for research and advocacy. *Journal of Clinical Child and Adolescent Psychology, 34*(4), 646–657. doi:10.1207/s15374424jccp3404_7

Melton, G. B. (2005b). Mandated reporting: A policy without reason. *Child Abuse and Neglect, 29*(1), 9–18. doi:10.1016/j.chiabu.2004.05.005

Melton, G. B. (2009). Foreword. In B. Lonne, N. Parton, J. Thomson, & M. Harries (Eds.), *Reforming child protection* (pp. xi–xiv). London, UK: Routledge.

Melton, G. B. (2010a). In search of the highest attainable standard of mental health for children. *Child Welfare, 89*(5), 57–72. Retrieved from http://search.proquest.com.ezproxy.otago.ac.nz/docview/866205638?accountid=14700

Melton, G. B. (2010b). Angels (and neighbors) watching over us: Child safety and family support in an age of alienation. *American Journal of Orthopsychiatry, 80*(1), 89–95. doi:10.1111/j.1939-0025.2010.01010.x

Melton, G. B. (2014). Strong communities for children: A community-wide approach to prevention of child maltreatment. In J. Korbin & R. Krugman (Eds.), *Handbook of child maltreatment 2* (pp. 329–339). Dordrecht, Netherlands: Springer Science. doi:10.1007/978-94-007-7208-3_17

Meltzoff, A. N., Kuhl, P. K., Movellan, J., & Sejnowski, T. J. (2009). Foundations for a new science of learning. *Science, 325*(5938), 284–288. doi:10.1126/science.1175626

Miljeteig, P. (2000). Children's democratic rights: Are we ready? What can we learn from young workers. In A. B. Smith, M. Gollop, K. Marshall, & K. Nairn (Eds.), *Advocating for Children: International perspectives on children's rights* (pp. 159–175). Dunedin, New Zealand: Otago University Press.

Miljeteig, P. (2005). Children's democratic rights: What we can learn from young workers organizing themselves. In J. Mason & T. Fattore (Eds.), *Children taken seriously in theory, policy and practice* (pp. 123–135). London: Jessica Kingsley.

Miller-Perrin, C. L., & Perrin, R. D. (2013). *Child maltreatment, an introduction* (3rd ed.). Los Angeles, CA: Sage.

Ministry of Justice. (2011). United Nations Convention on the Rights of the Child. Retrieved March 9, 2015 from http://www.justice.govt.nz/policy/constitutional-law-and-human-rights/human-rights/international-human-rights-instruments/international-human-rights-instruments-1/united-nations-convention-on-the-rights-of-the-child

Ministry of Social Development. (2012). Factsheet on Important Changes to: Domestic Purposes Benefit – Sole Parent. Retrieved March 25, 2015 from http://www.workandincome.govt.nz/documents/dpb-sole-parent-oct-factsheet.pdf

Mizen, P., Pole, C., & Bolton, A. (2001). Why be a school age worker? In P. Mizen, C. Pole, & A. Bolton (Eds.), *Hidden hands: International perspectives on children's work and labour* (pp. 37–54). London, UK: Routledge-Palmer.

Montgomery, H. (2009). Children, young people and poverty. In H. Montgomery & M. Kellett (Eds.), *Children and young people's worlds: Developing frameworks for integrated practice* (pp. 165–180). Bristol, UK: The Policy Press.

Montgomery, H. (2010). The rights of the child: Rightfully mine! In D. Kassam, L. Murphy, & E. Taylor (Eds.), *Key issues in childhood and youth studies* (pp. 49–158). London and New York, NY: Routledge.

Moore, T., & Oberklaid, F. (2014). Health and child well-being. In A. Ben-Arieh, F. Cassas, I. Frønes, & J. Korbin (Eds.), *Handbook of child well-being* (pp. 2259–2279). Dordecht, Netherlands: Springer. doi:10.1007/978-90-481-9063-8_89

Morrow, V. (1994). Responsible children? Aspects of children's work and employment outside school in contemporary UK. In B. Mayall (Ed.), *Children's childhoods: Observed and experienced* (pp. 128–143). London, UK: Falmer Press.

Morrow, V. (2004). Children's 'social capital': Implications for health and well-being. Health Education, *104*(4), 211–225. doi:10.1108/09654280410546718

Morrow, V. (2009). Children, young people and their families in the UK. In H. Montgomery & M. Kellett (Eds.), *Children and young people's worlds: Developing frameworks for integrated practice* (pp. 61–76). Bristol, UK: The Policy Press.

Morrow, V. (2010). Should the world really be free of 'child labour'? Some reflections. Editorial. *Childhood, 17*(4), 435–440. doi:10.1177/0907568210387334

Morrow, V. (2013a). Troubling transitions? Young people's experiences of growing up in poverty in Andhra Pradesh. *Journal of Youth Studies, 16*(1), 86–100. doi:10.1080/13676261.2012.704986

Morrow, V. (2013b). Whose values? Young people's aspirations and experiences of schooling in Andhra Pradesh, India. *Children and Society, 27*(4), 258–269. doi:10.1111/chso.12036

Morrow, V., & Boyden, J. (2010). Social values and child labour. In A. Fassa, D. Parker, & T. Scanlon (Eds.), *Child Labour: A public health perspective* (pp. 69–78). Oxford, UK: Oxford University Press.

Munro, E. (2008). *Effective child protection* (2nd ed.). London, UK: Sage.

Murray, H. (2012). *Is school education breaking the cycle of poverty for children? Factors shaping education inequalities in Ethiopia, India, Peru and Vietnam.* Policy Paper 6, Young Lives, Oxford, UK: Oxford Department of International Development, University of Oxford.

Myers, W. (2001). The right rights? Child labor in a globalizing world. *Annals of the American Academy of Political and Social Science, 575*(1), 38–55. doi:10.1177/0002716201575001003

Neale, B., & Flowerdew, J. (2007). New structures, new agency: The dynamics of child-parent relationships after divorce. *International Journal of Children's Rights, 15*(1), 25–42. doi:10.1163/092755607x185546

Nelson, J., Palonsky, S., & McCarthy, M. (2007). *Critical issues in education: Dialogues and dialectics.* (6th ed.). New York, NY: McGraw-Hill.

Newell, P. (2011). The human rights imperative to eliminate physical punishment. In J. Durrant & A. B. Smith (Eds.), *Global pathways to abolishing physical punishment: Realising children's rights* (pp. 7–26). New York, NY: Routledge.

NICHD Early Child Care Research Network. (2000). Characteristics and quality of child care for toddlers and preschoolers. *Applied Developmental Science, 4*(3), 116–135. doi:10.1207/S1532480XADS0403_2

NICHD Early Child Care Research Network. (2005). *Child care and child development: Results from the NICHD study of early child care and youth development.* New York, NY: The Guildford Press.

Nieuwenhuys, O. (2009). From child labour to children's working movements. In J. Qvortrup, W. A. Corsaro, & M-S. Honig (Eds.), *The Palgrave Handbook of Childhood Studies* (pp. 289–300). London, UK: Palgrave-McMillan.

Nutbrown, C. (1996). Questions for respectful educators. In C. Nutbrown (Ed.), *Children's rights and early education: Respectful educators – capable learners* (p. xvi, pp. 99–108). London, UK: Paul Chapman Ltd.

Oakley, A. (1994). Women and children first and last: Parallels and differences between children's and women's studies. In B. Mayall (Ed.), *Children's childhoods: Observed and experienced* (pp. 13–32). London, UK: The Falmer Press.

O'Brien, M. (2015, May 14). *Prevention: The best way to address poverty.* Briefing Papers. Child Poverty Action Group. Retrieved October 9th, 2015 from http://briefingpapers.co.nz/2015/05/prevention-the-best-way-to-address-child-poverty/

O'Donnell, M., Scott, D., & Stanley, F. (2008). Child abuse and neglect – is it time for a public health approach. *Australian and New Zealand Journal of Public Health, 32*(4), 325–330. doi:10.1111/j.1753-6405.2008.00249.x

O'Donovan, R., Berman, N., & Wierenga, A. (2015). How schools can move beyond exclusion. *International Journal of Inclusive Education, 19*(6), 645–658. doi:10.1080/13063116.2014.961686

OECD. (2011). Infant mortality. *Health at a Glance 2011: OECD Indicators,* OECD Publishing. http://dx.doi.org/10.1787/health_glance-2011-10-en

Olweus, D. (1993). *Bullying at school.* Oxford, UK: Blackwell.

Olweus, D., & Limber, S. (2010). Bullying in school: Evaluation and dissemination of the Olweus bullying prevention program. *American Journal of Orthopsychiatry, 80*(1), 124–134. doi:10.1111/j.1939-0025.2010.01015.x

O'Neill, D. (2010). *Schoolchildren in paid employment: A summary of research findings.* Wellington, New Zealand: Department of Labour.

Ortiz, I., & Cummins, M. (2011). *Global inequality: Beyond the bottom billion.* New York, NY: UNICEF.

Osman, N. (2005). Children's perceptions of school. In J. Mason & T. Fattore (Eds.), *Children taken seriously in theory, policy and practice* (pp. 182–190). London, UK: Jessica Kingsley.

Osvaldsson, K. (2011). Bullying in context: Stories of bullying on an internet discussion board. *Children & Society, 25*(4), 317–327. doi:10.1111/j.1099-0860.2011.00383.x

Owen, S. (2011). The United Kingdom: The ongoing struggle to achieve legal reform. In J. Durrant & A. B. Smith (Eds.), *Global pathways to abolishing physical punishment: Realising children's rights* (pp. 256–274). New York, NY: Routledge.

Parnell, W. (2002). Food for a healthy brain: Critical nutrients in early life. *Childrenz Issues, 6*(2), 35–38. Retrieved October 9, 2015, from http://search. informit.com.au/documentSummary;dn=458407766107402;res=IELFSC> ISSN: 1174-0477.

Pearce, A., Kirk, C., Cummins, S., Collins, M., Elliman, D., Connolly, A. M., & Law, C. (2009). Gaining children's perspectives: A multiple method approach to explore environmental influences on healthy eating and physical activity. *Health and Place, 15*(2), 614–621. doi:10.1016/j.healthplace.2008.10.007

Peters, L., & Lacy, L. (2013). 'You're not listening to us': Explicating children's school experiences to build opportunity for increased participation within school communities in the United States. In B. B. Swadener, L. Lundy, J. Habashi, & N. Blanchet-Cohen (Eds.), *Children's Rights and Education* (pp. 115–133). New York, NY: Peter Lang.

Phillips, D. (1995). Giving voice to young children. *European Early Childhood Education Research Journal, 3*(2), 5–14. doi:10.1080/13502939585207731

Prout, A. (2005). *The future of childhood.* Abingdon, Oxon, UK: Routledge.

Prout, A., & James, A. (1997). A new paradigm for the sociology of childhood? Provenance, promise and problems. In A. James & A. Prout (Eds.),*Constructing and reconstructing childhood: Contemporary issues in the sociological study of childhood* (2nd ed., pp. 7–33). London, UK: The Falmer Press.

Pryor, J., & Emery, R. E. (2004). Children of divorce. In P. B. Pufall & R. P. Unsworth (Eds.), *Rethinking childhood* (pp. 170–190). New Brunswick, NJ: Rutgers University Press.

Public Health Advisory Committee (PHAC). (2010). *The best start in life: Achieving effective action on child health and wellbeing: A report to the Minister of Health.* Wellington, New Zealand: Ministry of Health.

Pufall, P. B., & Unsworth, R. P. (Eds.). (2004). *Rethinking childhood.* New Brunswick, NJ: Rutgers University Press.

Pugh, G., & Selleck, D. (1996). Listening to and communicating with young children. In R. Davie, G. Upton, & V. Varma (Eds.), *The voice of the child: A handbook for professionals* (pp. 120–136). London, UK: The Falmer Press.

Qiu, W., Schvaneveldt, P. L., & Sahin, V. (2013). Children's perceptions and definitions of family in China, Ecuador, Turkey and the United States. *Journal of Comparative Family Studies, 64*(5), 641–547. Retrieved from http://connection.ebscohost.com/c/articles/91978596/childrens-perceptions-definitions-family-china-ecuador-turkey-united-states

Qvortrup, J. (1997). A voice for children in statistical and social accounting: A plea for children's right to be heard. In A. James & A. Prout (Eds.), *Constructing and reconstructing childhood: Contemporary issues in the sociological study of childhood* (2nd ed., pp. 85–102). London, UK: The Falmer Press.

Qvortrup, J. (2001). School-work, paid work and the changing obligations of childhood. In P. Mizen, C. Pole, & A. Bolton (Eds.), *Hidden hands: International perspectives on children's work and labour* (pp. 91–107). London, UK: Routledge-Palmer.

Ramey, S. L. (2005). Human developmental science serving children and families: Contributions of the NICHD study of early child care. In NICHD Early Child Care Research Network (Ed.), *Child care and child development: Results from the NICHD study of early child care and youth development* (pp. 427–436). New York, NY: Guilford Press.

Ransom, M. (2012). Teaching Strategies: The Convention on the Rights of the Child: Suggestions for educator action. *Childhood Education, 88*(6), 394–397. doi:10.1080/00094056.2012.741488

Ravitch, D. (2013). *Reign of error: The hoax of the privatization movement and the danger to America's public schools.* New York, NY: Knopf.

Raynor, M. (1993). *The right of the child to be heard and to participate in legal proceedings: Article 12 of the UN Convention on the Rights of the Child.* Paper presented at the First World Congress on Family Law and Children's Rights, Sydney.

Read, J., Blackburn, C., & Spencer, N. (2012). Disabled children and their families: A decade of policy change. *Children & Society, 26*(3), 223–233. doi:10.1111/j.1099-0860.2012.00435.x

Reeve, S., & Bell, P. (2009). Children's self-documentation and understanding of the concepts 'healthy'and 'unhealthy'. *International Journal of Science Education, 31*(14), 1953–1974. doi:10.1080/09500690802311146

Reinbold, G. W. (2014). Realising young children's right to health under the Convention on the Rights of the Child. *International Journal of Children's Rights, 22*(3), 502–551. doi:10.1163/15718182-55680019

Reynolds, A. J. (1994). Effects of a preschool follow-on intervention for children at risk. *Developmental Psychology, 30*(6), 787–804. doi:10.1037/0012-1649.30.6.787

Reynolds, A. J., Temple, J. A., White, B. A., Ou, S-R., & Robertson, D. L. (2011). Age-26 cost-benefit analysis of the child-parent center early education program. *Child Development, 82*(1), 379–404. doi:10.1111/j.1467-8624.2010.01563.x

Ribbens McCarthy, J., Hooper, C-A., & Gillies, V. (2013). Troubling normalities and normal family troubles: Diversities, experiences and tensions. In J. Ribbens McCarthy, C-A. Hooper, & V. Gillies (Eds.), *Family troubles?*

Exploring change and challenges in the family lives of children and young people (pp. 1–21). Bristol: Policy Press.

Ridge, T. (2003). Listening to children. *Family Matters, 45,* Winter, 4–9. Retrieved October 9, 2015 from https://aifs.gov.au/publications/family-matters/issue-65/listening-children

Ridge, T. (2009). 'It didn't always work': Low-income children's experiences of changes in mothers' working patterns in the UK. *Social Policy and Society, 8*(4), 503–513. doi:10.1017/s147474640999008x

Rietveld, C. (2005, December 7). *Teacher responses to children's spontaneous reactions to differences in their classmates with down syndrome: Implications for teaching and learning.* Paper presented at the New Zealand Association for Research in Education conference, Dunedin, New Zealand.

Rigg, A., & Pryor, J. (2007). Children's perceptions of families: What do they really think? *Children & Society, 21*(1), 17–30. doi:10.1111/j.1099-0860.2006.00028.x

Ritchie, A., Morrison, E., & Paterson, S. (2003). Care to learn? The educational experiences of children and young people who are looked after. *Scottish Journal of Residential Child Care, 2*(2), 51–62. Retrieved from http://www.celcis.org/media/resources/publications/Care_to_Learn.pdf

Ritchie, J., & Rau, C. (2013). Renarrativizing indigenous rights-based provision within "mainstream" early childhood services. In B. Swadener, L. Lundy, J. Habashi, & N. Blanchet-Cohen (Eds.), *Children's Rights and Education* (pp. 134–149). New York, NY: Peter Lang.

Rizzini, I., & Thaplyial, N. (2005). *The role of schools in the protection and promotion of children's rights in Brazil.* Unpublished paper, CIESPI, Rio de Janeiro, Brazil.

Rogoff, B. (1990). *Apprenticeship in thinking: Cognitive development in social context.* New York, NY: Oxford University Press.

Ruck, M. D., Keating, D. P., Saewyc, E. M., Earls, F., & Ben-Arieh, A. (2014). The United Nations Convention on the Rights of the Child: Its relevance for adolescents. *Journal of Research on Adolescence.* doi:10.1111/jora.12172

Rutherford, G. (2012). In, out or somewhere in between? Disabled students' and teacher aides' experiences of school. *International Journal of Inclusive Education, 16*(8), 757–774. doi:10.1080/13603116.2010.509818

Sanderson, L. J. (2011). *I learn stuff: An ethnographic case study of disabled senior secondary students' school experiences.* (Unpublished Masters thesis). Childhood and Youth Studies, University of Otago, Dunedin, New Zealand. Retrieved from http://hdl.handle.net/10523/1983

Saunders, B. J., & Goddard, C. (2010). *Physical punishment in childhood: The rights of the child.* Chichester, UK: Wiley-Blackwell.

Schaffer, H. R. (1992). Joint involvement episodes as context for development. In H. McGurk (Ed.), *Childhood social development: Contemporary perspectives* (pp. 99–129). Hove, UK: Lawrence Erlbaum Associates.

Schoenmaker, C., Juffer, F., van IJzendoorn, M., & Bakermans-Kranenburg, M. (2014). Does family matter? The well-being of children growing up in institutions, foster care and adoption. In A. Ben-Arieh, F. Cassas, I. Frønes, & J. Korbin (Eds.), *Handbook of child well-being* (pp. 2197–2228). Dordecht, Netherlands: Springer. doi:10.1007/978-90-481-9063-8_179

Scott, D. (2006, February). *Sowing the seeds of innovation in child protection.* Keynote address to 10th Australasian Child Abuse and Neglect conference, Wellington, NZ. Retrieved from http://www.cfecfw.asn.au/sites/default/files/Monograph%206%20Sowing%20the%20Seeds%20of%20Innovation%20in%20Child%20Protection%20Web.pdf

Shealy, C. N. (1995). From Boys Town to Oliver Twist: Separating fact from fiction in welfare reform and out-of-home placement of children and youth. *American Psychologist, 50*(8), 565–580. doi:10.1037/0003-066x.50.8.565

Shonkoff, J., & Phillips, D. (2000). *From neurons to neighborhoods: The science of early childhood development.* Washington, DC: National Academy Press.

Smith, A. B. (1997). How do we ensure the 'best interests' of children in out-of-home care? Messages from research. *Childrenz Issues, 1*(1), 23–27. Retrieved October 9, 2015 from http://search.informit.com.au/documentSummary;dn=460047467578123;res=IELFSC> ISSN: 1174-0477.

Smith, A. B. (1999). Quality childcare and joint attention. *International Journal of Early Years Education, 7*(1), 85–98. doi:10.1080/0966976990070107

Smith, A. B. (2002). Interpreting and supporting participation rights: Contributions from sociocultural theory. *International Journal of Children's Rights, 10*(1), 73–88. doi:10.1163/157181802772758137

Smith, A. B. (2005). Effective discipline and supporting change. In A. B. Smith, M. M. Gollop, N. J. Taylor, & K. Marshall (Eds.), *The discipline and guidance of children: Messages from research* (pp. 131–142, Chapter 3). Wellington: Office of the Commissioner for Children. [ISBN 0-909039-15-1] 165 pages.

Smith, A. B. (2007). Children and young people's participation rights in education. *International Journal of Children's Rights, 15*(1), 147–164. doi:10.1163/092755607x181739

Smith, A. B. (2011). Relationships with people, places and things: Te Whāriki. In L. Miller & L. Pound (Eds.), *Critical Issues in the Early Years Series. Theories and approaches to learning in the early years* (pp. 149–162). London, UK: Sage.

Smith, A. B. (2013a). A theoretical framework for childhood. In N. Higgins & C. Freeman (Eds.), *Childhoods: Growing up in Aotearoa New Zealand* (pp. 29–43, Chapter 2). Dunedin, New Zealand. Otago University Press.

Smith, A. B. (2013b). *Understanding children and childhood: A New Zealand perspective* (5th ed.). Wellington, New Zealand: Bridget Williams Books.

Smith, A. B. (2015a). Changing the law on physical punishment in New Zealand. *Enhancing children's rights: Connecting research, policy and practice* (pp. 33–47, Chapter 3). Basingstoke, UK: Palgrave MacMillan.

Smith, A. B. (2015b). Child protection: Policies for vulnerable children in New Zealand. *Enhancing children's rights: Connecting research, policy and practice* (pp. 111–126, Chapter 8). Basingstoke, UK: Palgrave MacMillan.

Smith, A. B. (2015c). Conclusion: Challenges for research on children's rights. *Enhancing children's rights: Connecting research, policy and practice* (pp. 259–273, Chapter 18). Basingstoke, UK: Palgrave MacMillan.

Smith, A. B., & Bjerke, H. (2009). Children's citizenship. In N. J. Taylor & A. B. Smith (Eds.), *Children as citizens? International voices* (pp. 15–34, Chapter 1). Dunedin, New Zealand: Otago University Press.

Smith, A. B., Gollop, M., & Taylor, N. J. (2000). Children in foster and kinship care. In A. B. Smith, N. J. Taylor, & M. M. Gollop (Eds.), *Children's voices: Research, policy and practice* (pp. 72–90). Auckland, New Zealand: Pearson Education.

Smith, A. B., Grima, G., Gaffney, M., & Powell, K. (2000). *Early childhood education: Literature review report to Ministry of education.* Dunedin, New Zealand: Children's Issues Centre, University of Otago.

Smith, A. B., & Gollop M. M. (2001). What children think separating parents should know. *New Zealand Journal of Psychology, 30*(1), 23–31. Retrieved October 9, 2015 from http://search.proquest.com.ezproxy.otago.ac.nz/docview/212440774?accountid=14700

Smith, A. B., Nairn, K., Sligo, J., Gaffney, M., & McCormack, J. (2003). *Case studies of young people's participation in public life: Local Government, boards of trustees and the youth parliament.* Dunedin, New Zealand: Children's Issues Centre

Smith, A. B., & Taylor, N. J. (1996). Panel discussion – family members' perspectives on family changes. In A. B. Smith & N. J. Taylor (Eds.), *Supporting children and parents through family changes* (pp. 61–72). Dunedin, New Zealand: University of Otago Press.

Smith, A. B., Taylor, N. J., & Tapp, P. (2003). Rethinking children's involvement in decision-making after parental separation. *Childhood, 10*(2), 203–218. doi:10.1177/0907568203010002006

Snook, I., & O'Neill, J. (2010). Social class and educational achievement: Beyond ideology. *New Zealand Journal of Educational Studies, 45*(2), 3–18. Retrieved October 9, 2015 from http://search.informit.com.au/documentSummary;dn=6 21745966557638;res=IELHSS> ISSN: 0028-8276.

Sokalski, H. J. (1994). *Strengthening families. International perspectives.* Proceedings of the International Year of the Family Conference, Auckland, New Zealand: International Year of the Family Committee and Office of the Commissioner for Children.

Southall, D. P., Burr, S., Smith, R. D., Bull, D. N., Radford, A., Williams, A., & Nicholson, S. (2000). The child-friendly healthcare initiative (CFHI): Healthcare provision in accordance with the UN convention on the rights of the child. *Pediatrics, 106*(5), 1054–1064. Retrieved October 9, 2015 from http://pediatrics.aappublications.org/content/106/5/1054.short

Stafford, A., Laybourn, A., Hill, M., & Walker, M. (2003). 'Having a say': Children and young people talk about consultation. *Children and Society, 17*(5), 361–373. doi:10.1002/CHI.758

Stainton Rogers, W. (2009). Promoting better childhoods: Constructions of child concern. In M. J. Kehily (Ed.), *An introduction to Childhood Studies* (2nd ed., pp. 141–160). Maidenhead and New York, NY: Open University Press.

Stephens, S. (1995). Introduction: Children and the politics of culture in "Late Capitalism". In S. Stephens (Ed.), *Children and the politics of culture* (pp. 3–48). Princeton, NJ: Princeton University Press.

Straus, M. (1996). Spanking and the making of a violent society. *Pediatrics, 98*(4), 937–841. Retrieved October 9, 2015 from http://pediatrics.aappublications. org/content/98/4/837.short

Sylva, K., Melhuish, E., Sammons, P., Siraj-Blatchford, I., & Taggart, B. (2004). *The final report: Effective preschool education. (Technical Paper 12).* London, UK: DfES/Institute of Education, University of London.

Tapp, P., & Taylor, N. (2002). Protecting the family. In M. Henaghan & B. Atkin (Eds.), *Family law policy in New Zealand* (2nd ed., pp. 75–124, Chapter 3). Wellington, New Zealand: LexisNexis Butterworths.

Taylor, N., Fitzgerald, R., Morag, T., Bajpai, A., & Graham, A. (2012). International models of child participation in family law proceedings following parental separation/divorce. *International Journal of Children's Rights, 20*(4), 645–673. doi:10.1163/15718182-55680006

Taylor, N., & Gollop, M. (2015). Children's views and participation in family dispute resolution in New Zealand. In *Enhancing children's rights: Connecting research, policy and practice* (pp. 242–258, Chapter 17). Basingstoke, UK: Palgrave MacMillan.

Taylor, N. J., Gollop, M., & Smith, A. B. (2000). Children and young people's perspectives on the role of counsel for the child. In A.B. Smith, N.J. Taylor, & M.M. Gollop (Eds.) *Children's voices: Research, policy and practice* (pp. 110–133). Auckland, New Zealand: Longman.

Taylor, N. J., Smith, A. B., & Nairn, K. (2001). Rights important to young people: Secondary student and staff perspectives. *International Journal of Children's Rights, 9*(2), 137–156. doi:10.1163/15718180120494892

Taylor, N., Tapp, P., & Henaghan, M. (2007). Respecting children's participation in family law proceedings. *International Journal of Children's Rights, 15*(1), 61–82. doi:10.1163/092755607x185555

Taylor, N., Wood, B., & Smith, A. B. (2011). New Zealand: The achievements and challenges of prohibition. In A. B. Smith & J. Durrant (Eds.), *Global pathways to abolishing physical punishment: Realising children's rights* (pp. 182–196, Chapter 14). New York, NY: Routledge.

Thomas, N. (2009). Children, young people and politics in the UK. In H. Montgomery & M. Kellett (Eds.), *Children and young people's worlds: Developing frameworks for integrated practice* (pp. 7–22). Bristol, UK: The Policy Press.

Tobin, J. (2011). Understanding a human rights based approach to matters involving children: Conceptual foundations and strategic considerations. In A. Invernizzi & J. Williams (Eds.), *The human rights of children: From vision to implementation* (pp. 61–98). Farnham, UK: Ashgate.

Todres, J. (2010). Children's health in the United States: Assessing the potential impact of the Convention on the Rights of the Child. *Child Welfare, 89*(5),

37–56. Retrieved October 15, 2015 from http://search.proquest.com.ezproxy.
otago.ac.nz/docview/866205747?accountid=14700

Tomasello, M. (1999). *The cultural origins of human cognition.* Cambridge, MA: Harvard University Press.

Tucker, M. J. (1974). The child as beginning and end: Fifteenth and sixteenth century English childhood. In L. De Mause (Ed.), *The history of child-hood: The evolution of parent-child relationships as a factor in history* (pp. 229–259). London, UK: Souvenir Press.

UNICEF. (2011). Equal access to education. Retrieved from http://www.unicef.org/education/index_access.html

UNICEF. (2014). *Committing to child survival: A promise renewed.* Progress Report 2014. New York, NY: UNICEF.

United Nations Children's Fund. (2015). Access to education improves for one million children. Retrieved from http://reliefweb.int/report/world/access-education-1-million-children-improved-through-10-year-unicef-and-ing-partnership

United Nations Committee on the Rights of the Child. (2001). *General Comment No. 1: The aims of education.* UN Doc CRC/GC/2001/1. Geneva. Retrieved from http://www.refworld.org/docid/4538834d2.html

United Nations Committee on the Rights of the Child. (2005). *General Comment No. 7: Implementing child rights in early childhood.* Committee on the Rights of the Child, CRC, Geneva. Retrieved February 20, 2014 from http://www2.ohchr.org/english/bodies/crc/docs/AdvanceVersions/General-Comment7Rev1.pdf

United Nations Committee on the Rights of the Child. (2006). *General Comment No. 8: The right of the child to protection from corporal punishment and other degrading punishment.* Geneva. Retrieved from http://www.refworld.org/docid/460bc7772.html

United Nations Committee on the Rights of the Child. (2009). *General Comment No 12: The right of the child to be heard.* Geneva. Retrieved from http://www.refworld.org/docid/4ae562c52.html

United Nations. (1989). *Convention on the rights of the child.* Geneva: United Nations. Retrieved from www.un.org/documents/ga/res/44/a44r025.htm

United Nations. (2007). *Convention on the rights of persons with disabilities.* Geneva: United Nations. Retrieved from http://www.un.org/disabilities/convention/convention.shtml

United Nations. (2013). *General Comment No. 15 (2013) on the right of the child to the enjoyment of the highest attainable standard of health art 24.* CRC/C/GC/15. Retrieved July 1, 2015 from http://tbinternet.ohchr.org/_layouts/treatybodyexternal/TBSearch.aspx?Lang=en&TreatyID=5&DocTypeID=11

Van Bijleveld, G., Dedding, C., & Bunders-Aelen, J. F. (2015). Children's and young people's participation within child welfare and child protection services: A state-of-the-art review. *Child Welfare, 20,* 129–138. doi:10.1111/cfs.12082

Vandell, D. L., Belsky, J., Burchinal, M., Steinberg, L., Vandergrift, N., & NICHD Early Child Care Research Network. (2010). Do effects of early child care extend to age 15 years? Results from the NICHD study of early child care and youth development. *Child Development, 81*(3), 737–756. doi:10.1111/j.1467-8624.2010.01431.x

Veerman, P. E. (1992). *The rights of the child and the changing image of childhood.* Dordrecht, the Netherlands: Martinus Nijhoff Publishers.

Veerman, P. E. (2010). The ageing of the UN convention on the rights of the child. *The International Journal of Children's Rights, 18*(4), 585–618. doi:10.1163/157181810x522360

Vygotsky, L. S. (1978). *Mind in society: The development of higher mental processes.* Cambridge, MA: Harvard University Press.

Wald, M. (2014). Beyond maltreatment: Developing support for children in multiproblem families. In J. Korbin & R. Krugman (Eds.), *Handbook of child maltreatment 2* (pp. 251–280). Dordrecht: Springer Science. doi:10.1007/978-94-007-7208-3_13

Webb, E., Horrocks, L., Crowley, A., & Lessof, N. (2009). Using the UN convention on the rights of children to improve the health of children. *Paediatrics and Child Health, 19*(9), 430–434. doi:10.1016/j.paed.2009.05.006

Weingarten, L., Kircher, J., Drendel, A. L., Newton, A. S., & Ali, S. (2014). A survey of children's perspectives on pain management in the emergency department. *The Journal of Emergency Medicine, 47*(3), 268–276. doi:10.1016/j.jemermed.2014.01.038

Wilkinson, R., & Pickett, K. (2010). *The spirit level: Why equality is better for everyone.* London, UK: Penguin.

Williams, K. R., & Guerra, N. G. (2007). Prevalence and predictors of internet bullying. *Journal of Adolescent Health, 41*(6), Supplement, S14–S21. doi:10.1016/j.jadohealth.2007.08.018

Williams Shanks, T. R., & Danziger, S. K. (2011). Anti-poverty policies and programs for children and families. In J. M. Jenson & M. W. Fraser (Eds.), *Social policy for children and families: A risk and resilience perspective* (2nd ed., pp. 25–56). Thousand Oaks, CA: Sage.

Willow, C. (2015). Taking account of children: How far have we come in England. In A. B. Smith (Ed.), *Enhancing children's rights: Connecting research, policy and practice* (pp. 183–196). Basingstoke, UK: Palgrave McMillan.

Wood, E. (2004). Developing a pedagogy of play. In A. Anning, J. Cullen, & M. Fleer (Eds.), *Early Childhood Education: Society and Culture* (pp. 19–30). London, UK: Sage Publications.

Woodhead, M. (1997). Psychology and the cultural construction of children's needs. In A. James & A. Prout (Eds.), *Constructing and reconstructing childhood: Contemporary Issues in the Sociological study of childhood* (2nd ed., pp. 63–84). London, UK: The Falmer Press.

Woodhead, M. (1999). Combatting child labour: Listen to what the children say. *Childhood, 6*(1), 27–49. doi:10.1177/0907568299006001003

Woodhead, M. (2004a). Foreword. In M. J. Kehily (Ed.), *An introduction to Childhood Studies* (pp. x–xi). Maidenhead, UK: Open University Press.

Woodhead, M. (2004b). Psychosocial impacts of child work: A framework for research monitoring and intervention. *International Journal of Children's Rights, 12,* 321–377. doi:10.1163/1571818043603607

Woodhead, M., Dornan, P., & Murray, H. (2014). What inequality means for children. *International Journal of Children's Rights, 22,* 467–501. doi:10.1163/15718182-02203006

World Health Organization. (1948). Preamble to the Constitution of the World Health Organization. New York, NY: WHO. Retrieved July 1, 2015 from http://www.who.int/about/en/

Wyse, D. (2001). Felt tip pens and school councils: Children's participation rights in four English schools. *Children and Society, 15,* 209–218. doi:10.1002/chi.651

Zeiher, H. (2009). Institutionalization as a secular trend. In J. Qvortrup, W. A. Corsaro, & M-S. Honig (Eds.), *The Palgrave handbook of childhood studies* (pp. 127–139). London, UK: Palgrave-McMillan.

INDEX

THIS TITLE IS FROM OUR PSYCHOLOGY COLLECTION

FORTHCOMING TITLE FOR THIS COLLECTION

The Elements of Mental Tests, Second Edition
by John D. Mayer

Momentum Press is one of the leading book publishers in the field of engineering, mathematics, health, and applied sciences. Momentum Press offers over 30 collections, including Aerospace, Biomedical, Civil, Environmental, Nanomaterials, Geotechnical, and many others.

Momentum Press is actively seeking collection editors as well as authors. For more information about becoming an MP author or collection editor, please visit http://www.momentumpress.net/contact

---

Announcing Digital Content Crafted by Librarians

Momentum Press offers digital content as authoritative treatments of advanced engineering topics by leaders in their field. Hosted on ebrary, MP provides practitioners, researchers, faculty, and students in engineering, science, and industry with innovative electronic content in sensors and controls engineering, advanced energy engineering, manufacturing, and materials science.

Momentum Press offers library-friendly terms:

- perpetual access for a one-time fee
- no subscriptions or access fees required
- unlimited concurrent usage permitted
- downloadable PDFs provided
- free MARC records included
- free trials

The **Momentum Press** digital library is very affordable, with no obligation to buy in future years.

For more information, please visit **www.momentumpress.net/library** or to set up a trial in the US, please contact **mpsales@globalepress.com.**

CPSIA information can be obtained
at www.ICGtesting.com
Printed in the USA
BVHW071231230520
579937BV00006B/67